From Alienation to Surplus Valu

From Alienation to Surplus Value

Paul Walton
and
Andrew Gamble

SHEED AND WARD

ACKNOWLEDGEMENTS

Marxism, as we indicate in the following essays, is a living theoretical tradition; and we owe any addition this book may make to its understanding to our involvement in that movement.

We are also particularly indebted to the following for their advice, criticism and support at various stages of our work: Charles Butler, Jeff Coulter, Jean Gardiner, Toni Racklin, Hugo Radice, Christine Rodway, Amanda Sebastyen, Martha Sonnenberg, Ian Taylor and Henry Tudor.

Student Now that makes sense! How good, to see one's
          way!
Mephistopheles All theory, my friend, is grey
                  But green is life's glad golden tree.

GOETHE, *Faust*

it couldn't have been more'n a few hours later when i happened to be passing by again—in the spot where the tree
was, a lightbulb factory now stood—'did there used to be
a guy here in a tree?' i yelled up at one of the windows—'are
you looking for work?' was the reply . . . it was then i decided
that Marxism did not have all the answers.

BOB DYLAN, *Tarantula*

CONTENTS

PREFACE TO THE FIRST EDITION

PREFACE TO THE FIRST EDITION

The essays contained in this book are the result of work which was begun three years ago in Durham. In collaboration with Jeff Coulter, now Lecturer in Sociology at Manchester University, we published several articles. These early articles form the basis for the work in this book—indeed two of the articles are re-produced here in a rewritten form—and thus, although our views on Marx have changed since that time, the debt we owe to Jeff Coulter is immense. We are deeply grateful for his contributions and criticisms during that earlier stage in the evolution of this work.

The increasing availability in recent years of previously ob-scure or unobtainable works of Marx has given rise, in Europe and America, to an industry of Marxist interpretation. The bulk of this work has been concerned with 'what Marx really said'.

In this book, our central argument is that a true understand-ing of Marx cannot be confined to a correct exegesis of his work. The discussion of Marx without reference to Marx*ism* and without reference to the application of Marx's theory to the pre-sent, neglects the central questions of theory and practice. We are still living under the social system which Marx describes as capitalism. And Marxism persists as a living tradition—not merely as a developing social theory and as a major influence on other social theory, but also in the form of a political move-ment. Thus, we should not merely ask 'Is this what Marx really said?' but 'Was it true?' and 'Is it still true?' Our position is that, in asking these questions, we can at last see the deluge of refutation that has rained on Marx's work during the last hun-dred years in its true perspective. That is, we believe it to be apparent that the relevance of Marx's work has never been greater.

This collection of essays is firmly anchored in current debates within Marxism. It is not an exercise in substantive analysis, nor indeed a detailed exegesis of the kind provided in many text-books. We want to show how an understanding of how Marx arrived at the premises of his method, and what these premises were, is the only standpoint from which different Marxist tendencies can be assessed and criticised in any meaningful way. Such a critique—if it is successful—cuts through much debate about whether Marxism is ethical philosophy or science, for it emphasises the practical interest that informs Marxism: what kind of knowledge can assist in liberating man.

The collection may appear at first sight to be a rather disparate set of commentaries. Indeed, it is certainly not our intention to suggest that Marxists as diverse as Marcuse, Habermas, Althusser, Engels and Lukacs can be simply lumped together and treated as if they belonged to a similar tendency. But the unity of our work emerges in our critique of these writers' works and positions. That unity we assert to be the clue to a correct understanding of Marx. We want to argue, firstly, that Marx's work has to be understood as continuously evolving and revolving around a concern for the 'dialectics of labour' and that the assessments of the writers mentioned above must proceed in terms of *their* understanding of this central dialectic in Marx. But, secondly, in urging a return to this dialectic with its basis in the very specific ontology contained in Marx's method, we also want to show how such a dialectic contains the promise of a Marxist science. We are concerned, that is, to reject the position that a concern with Marx's ontological premises is simply neo-Hegelian or metaphysical, and to demonstrate that the possibility of Marxist science is implicitly and inextricably bound up with an ontological grasp of the nature of man.

PREFACE TO THE SECOND EDITION

This book was conceived and written between 1969 and 1971, a time of renewed controversy over the meaning of Marx's work. It was intended as an intervention in the debates then in progress over the scientific status of *Capital*, Marx's intellectual relationship to Hegel, and the unity of his early and later writings. Shortly after it was published we were awarded as its authors the Isaac Deutscher Memorial Prize for 1972.

In their enthusiasms, their judgements, and above all their style, these essays reflect the preoccupations of those years. If we were writing the book again now, there is much we would change. Many passages, particularly in chapter one, could be expressed more simply and clearly; some of our criticisms of other Marxists now seem too sweeping (Engels especially gets a raw deal); and the analysis of Marxist economics in chapter six should be read only as a preliminary survey of the field.

Despite these qualifications, however, we remain convinced of the central idea that runs through these essays: understanding and interpreting Marx requires first of all a firm grasp of the premises which he worked out in his early writings through critiques of Hegel and Feuerbach, and which then led him to study political economy—an undertaking which was to occupy him for the rest of his life. Marx's breakthrough in the 1840s was to arrive at materialist premises that allowed human history to be conceived as an object of scientific rather than philosophical study. Although there is clearly an important change between the early critiques of philosophy and the later critiques of political economy we reject any simplistic idea of a decisive 'epistemological' break occurring in the 1840s. The later writings are inconceivable without the former.

One essay was therefore devoted to challenging Louis Althusser's interpretation of Marx, then at the height of its influence. We argued that Althusser and his followers ignored a whole set of questions concerning the status and objectivity of the

'science' they were so keen to proclaim was the essence of
Marxism, and that they misunderstood the nature of the early
philosophical writings. The main influence of Althusser on
Marxism since that time has been the encouragement of a barren
formalism and extreme indifference to historical and economic
analysis of social formations. Instead, in the work of such
important Althusserians as Nicos Poulantzas and Paul Hirst we
are offered endless catalogues of concepts whose ontological and
epistemological status remains mysterious. Hegel's jibe at Kant
is apposite. He complained that Kant's insistence on finding the
right method before beginning analysis was rather like
Scholasticus' advice to learn to swim before entering the water.
Certainly few of the Althusserians have cared to get their feet
wet.

Althusserian Marxism was an important and at times fruitful
reaction to the excesses of Marxist humanism, some versions of
which had elevated alienation to be Marx's central concept and
identified Marx very closely with Hegel as an anti-scientific
thinker. In these essays we rejected this view as strongly as we
rejected the Althusserians' worship of abstract scientific
objectivity, and stressed that Marx's premises should not be
confused with the substantive analysis of capitalist social
formations. Indeed we argued that Marx's method pointed
inexorably to the need to study political economy in order to
understand the conditions for overthrowing the rule of capital.
The ignoring of political economy by several important Marxists,
including Marcuse, Habermas and Lukacs, indicated a
departure from Marx's original premises and therefore from his
method of analysis. We argued that the relative loss of interest in
political economy by Marxists since 1945 had to be overcome if
Marxism was to recover its full strength as a method of analysis
and as social and political theory. In the last two chapters we
discussed Marx's critique of political economy and surveyed
some of the main changes and challenges to Marxist economics
since the nineteenth century.

Our hopes about the direction of Marxist studies has been
abundantly realized. Alongside the growing difficulties of the
capitalist world-economy there has recently been a great surge of
interest in Marxist and radical economics in many countries. The
strength of the Conference of Socialist Economists in Britain is
one indication of this. We ourselves have pursued the questions

and issues which are raised (often sketchily) in the last two chapters, in a new book: *Capitalism in Crisis: Inflation and the State* (London, Macmillan, 1976).

In the last few years Marxism has shown new life and energy and gained many new adherents as a method of understanding and changing social reality. Since finishing this book we have for the moment abandoned the more theoretical questions with which these essays are concerned and plunged into empirical and historical studies, but we hope that the book still provides an introduction to these debates and will encourage readers to read some of the main protagonists and Marx himself.

THE IMAGE OF MAN IN MARX[1]

> What indeed can the nature of a man be, apart from that
> which he concretely is in his present existence? How can a
> Marxist believe in a real human nature, concealed by oppres-
> sive circumstances?
>
> [Sartre, *Literary and Philosophical Essays*, London
> 1968, 228].

In a letter to Ruge in 1843, Marx made it clear that his prime
concern was to 'make man a human being'. He realised this aim
in the *Economic and Philosophical Manuscripts of 1844*. The
premises regarding man laid out in these manuscripts provide the
basis from which he conducted his later research and analysis.
Moving from man in general to man as modified in particular
historical periods, he developed detailed socio-scientific concepts
and theories which allowed him to engage in very specific explanations and predictions. Yet it is only Marx's grasp of the
special characteristics of man in *general* that allow him to avoid
the problem of relativism that are raised by his studies of specific
historical formations.

Marx's conception of man as a teleological being developing
his capacities through labour allows him to demand the liberation of man from any constraints upon such development. Therefore Marx's view of human liberation does not necessitate an
ethical *a priori*. In fact his attack upon utopian socialism is designed to stress the arbitrary nature of any merely ethical im-
perative. Marx always starts from man as such, not some ideal
conception of what man should be. Thus when Marx writes
about what man can become, this is not viewed as just a poten-

[1] A preliminary, rather Hegelian, version of this essay appeared
in: P. Walton, A. Gamble and J. Coulter, *Social Theory and Practice*,
Vol. 1, no. 2 (Fall 1970), 69–84.

tial but rather is a statement about the way in which man's natural powers are constrained by oppressive circumstances.

Man as Social Being

Nothing is more false than the way in which society has been treated both by economists and by socialists in relation to economic conditions.... Society does not consist of individuals; it expresses the sum of connections and relationships in which individuals find themselves

> [D. McLellan (ed.), *Marx's Grundrisse*, London 1971, 77].

The human essence is no abstraction inherent in each single individual. In its reality, it is the ensemble of the social relations

> [Marx, *Theses on Feuerbach* VI, Marx–Engels, *Selected Works* II, London 1950, 366].

For Marx, one feature of the human condition is that man is a social animal. We cannot conceive of him, nor can he exist, apart from society. 'The individual *is the social being*.'[2] From this perspective man is not seen atomistically—men interact and relate to one another as a fact of existence. Already in such a position there is an implied critique of the model of 'economic man' used as a starting point for all bourgeois political economy. Man therefore is understood as man only in the context of social relationships. Unless we grasp that in this way man is a social being, there will be a tendency to reduce our conception of man to the animal. But this is not the only distinction between man and animals. Marx argues that men first distinguish themselves from animals when they engage in production, in labour. What marks out human activity is not the mere fact of consciousness, for animals too have a type of consciousness, but the fact that human activity is rational, is governed and defined by purposes. Man's special capacity lies in the unfolding of his productive powers, in the teleology of labour:

It is as though one were to say: from the standpoint of society

---

[2] K. Marx, *Economic and Philosophical Manuscripts of 1844* (EPM), trans. M. Milligan, ed. D. J. Struik, New York 1961, London 1970, 138.

there are neither slaves nor citizens: both are men. Rather they are so *outside society* [McLellan, *Grundrisse*, 77].

So outside of society man is a special animal because he has powers that distinguish him from other animals. Man's teleological capacity marks him off as a special being. Yet of course man only exists in society, so society cannot be opposed to a determinate individual as though they were two different concrete phenomena. The term used by Marx, *Gemeinwesen*, conveys precisely the unity of man and society and its ambiguity—the term can be translated either as 'man in a social relation' or as 'commune'.[3]

It is because man is both a social animal and the only teleological animal that Marx can see man as both world-producing and world-produced, both autonomous and determined.

> ... just as society itself produces man as man, so is society produced by him. Activity and mind, both in their content and in their mode of existence, are social: social activity and social mind [EPM, ed. Struik, 137].

Human labour *objectifies* (creates products which constitute the human world for man) and therefore objectification of social labour establishes 'even though in an estranged form ... true anthropological nature'. We shall see later why this estrangement occurs and what its consequences are. Labour creates the human world by embodying itself in objects; this objectification is anthropologically necessary. As the human world is social, and man is a social being, labour creates man himself: by acting upon nature to change it, to humanly transform it, man changes his external world and thereby alters the set of relations he has with it (types of responses, exercise of his powers, etc) and in this way he changes himself. Nature ('man's inorganic body') exists as human only for social man[4] and productive activity transforms it into life-engendering use-values. This ongoing humanisation of nature takes place socially:

Man is in the most literal sense of the word a *zoon politikon*,

[3] S. Avineri, 'The Hegelian Origins of Marx's Political Thought' *Review of Metaphysics* 21 (1967–68), 33–56.

[4] EPM, ed. Struik, 137.

not only a social animal, but an animal which can develop into an individual only in society. Production by isolated individuals outside of society—something which might happen as an exception to a civilised man who by accident got into the wilderness and already dynamically possessed within himself the forces of society—is as great an absurdity as the idea of the development of language without individuals living together and talking to one another

> [Marx, *A Contribution to the Critique of Political Economy*, Chicago 1940, 268].

As a sentient being with objective powers, man can only express his being in real, sensuous objects, i.e., by externalising. For Marx, 'a non-objective being is a non-being'.[5] The expression of human intentionality towards external reality is social productive activity. Man is in all stages of his development a social being capable of world- and self-production—his 'anthropogenesis' remains constant.[6]

Man as Species Being

But if man is a determinate being only in society and if it is because man is constantly in society, that he is constantly a social being, how can Marx describe a state of human liberation? For will not any such description be subject to the problems of relativism? One kind of answer is given by Freudian and Christian theorists who postulate a fixed *a priori* nature, as yet unrealised in society. But Marx fiercely attacked any attempt to erect such a static, a-historical ethical standard. For Marx, any talk of the essence of man was metaphysical unless it referred to the essential determining elements which shape a given society. For being in a given society is part of the ontological state of man, and therefore freedom and liberation cannot be anything apart from overcoming the essence of a particular society.

Yet by itself this does not overcome the problem of relativism. For from this viewpoint freedom as a yardstick would only be

[5] Marx, EPM, 181 (otherwise rendered as 'A being which does not have its nature outside itself is not a natural being'—Milligan).

[6] See S. Avineri, 'Homo Faber', *The Social and Political Thought of Karl Marx*, London 1968, esp. p. 85.

measurable against historically specific constraints. But what of freedom in general? For a conception of this Marx returns to his account of man's special character. Marx took up Feuerbach's conception of man as *Gattungswesen*, as species being, and infused this term with a new content. Man as a species is distinct from animals by virtue of his ability to engage in purposive production. Yet this production has occurred under the constraints of particular class societies. Species production should be production in general, not production for a particular part of the species. Full human liberation, then, means the realisation by the whole species of its special nature. The possibility of achieving species being, however, is not for Marx some utopian ideal; rather it is a real possibility emerging out of the historical development of the productive forces:

> Ricardo, rightly for his time, regards the capitalist mode of production as the most advantageous for production in general, as the most advantageous for the creation of wealth. He wants *production for the sake of production*, and this with *good reason*. To assert, as sentimental opponents of Ricardo did, that production as such is not the object, is to forget that production for its own sake means nothing but the development of human productive forces, in other words *the development of the richness of human nature as an end in itself*. To oppose the welfare of the individual to this end, as Sismondi does, is to assert that the development of the species must be *arrested* in order to safeguard the welfare of the individual. . . . Apart from the barrenness of such edifying reflections, they reveal a failure to understand the fact that although, at first, the development of the capacities of the *human* species takes place at the cost of the majority of human individuals and even classes, in the end it breaks through this contradiction, and coincides with the development of the individual; the higher development of individuality is thus only achieved by a historical process
>
> [Marx, *Theories of Surplus Value*, Part 2, Moscow 1962, 117–18].

Freedom for Marx, then, lies in man's achieving his natural species state, in which self-production is realised under conditions of sociality in an unrestrained and reciprocal fashion. Marx gives instance after instance of particular paradigms of this general possibility. For example, he states that:

> The immediate, natural and necessary relation of person to person is the relation of man to woman. In this natural species relationship man's relationship to nature is immediately his relation to man, just as his relation to man is immediately his relation to nature—his own natural destination. In this relationship, therefore, is sensuously manifested, reduced to an observable fact, the extent to which the human essence has become nature to man, or to which nature to him has become the human essence of man. From this relationship one can therefore judge man's whole level of development
>
> [EPM, ed. Struik, 134].

The *humanised* relation of two reproducing animals is precisely its nature as a *reciprocal* activity, entered into freely and consciously, with the aim of satisfying the other as oneself. This constitutes full sociality. It also furnishes a criterion for the assessment of the human condition. The character of contemporary life can be judged according to how far it fulfils man's species-nature, which is defined from the above as a general manifestation between human beings of their voluntary association: '... free, conscious activity is man's species character'.[7] Coerced and asymmetrical relations cannot be regarded as exhibiting this species character.

The activity of the human species, which separates it from the other animal species, is the exteriorisation of its powers in objects—the creation of a specifically 'objective' world of its own. Whereas animals only reproduce themselves within themselves, men reproduce themselves in external objects.

> ... an animal only produces what it immediately needs for itself or its young. It produces one-sidedly, whilst man produces universally. It produces only under the dominion of immediate physical need, whilst man produces even when he is free from physical need *and only truly produces in freedom therefrom* [EPM, 113].

This is a crucial statement of Marx's. If man only truly produces

[7] EPM, 113.

in freedom from material constraints, if he only produces himself in labour when all his human senses and powers are geared to his conscious self-production, when his senses 'have therefore become directly in their practice theoreticians', then man has not yet realised his nature. This is the starting-point of Marx's whole theory of communism as human emancipation.

It should by now be apparent that while Marx does not solve the problem of freedom and what is necessary for a free society with some rigid notion of a human essence, he could nonetheless posit species being as a valid state of freedom. A mistake often made by superficial readers of Marx's 'philosophical anthropology' is to think that such a notion of freedom involves a kind of secular eschatology, a kind of finite or limited end to possible human development. This is untrue. Whilst the attainment of species being will enable man in freedom from need to concentrate upon his self-production, developing through his own voluntary activity, there is no given end to this process. In this sense, whilst species being is the social state fitted to realise this conscious self-production, the actual content of that self-production is decided by emancipated man himself. As Marx states:

> Communism ... is hence the actual phase necessary for the next stage of historical development in the process of human emancipation and rehabilitation ... but communism as such is not the goal of human development—which goal is the structure of human society [EPM, 146].

Feuerbach and Marx

Marx's image of man and freedom has frequently been jettisoned by more sombre Marxists because of their belief that it is fundamentally Hegelian or metaphysical. Much of this occurs because Marx's position appears to resemble that of his Young Hegelian predecessors. For this reason it is necessary to clearly distinguish between Marx's position and that of Feuerbach. We must remember that for Marx man is always a social being. Yet Feuerbach conceptualises man as an 'abstract—*isolated*—human individual'.[8] Marx commented:

[8] Marx, *Theses on Feuerbach* VI.

The human essence, therefore, can with him be comprehended only as 'genus', as an internal, dumb generality which merely naturally unites the many individuals [*Theses on Feuerbach* VI].

Moreover, because Feuerbach's concept of 'species' was unhistorical, a view of human nature based upon a lowest common denominator, it completely overlooked human nature as a product of human activity. By omitting the labour process from his anthropology, Feuerbach neglected the historical conditions for the realisation of the natural powers of man. Marx wrote:

The abstract hostility between sense and spirit is inevitable so long as the human sense for Nature, or the human meaning of Nature, that is, consequently, the natural sense of man, has not yet been produced through man's own labour [EPM].

Marx's position is thus distinguished from Feuerbach's in a number of ways. Yet Feuerbach was an important development in Left Hegelian thought, for he showed that 'the secret of theology is anthropology',[9] and therefore that Hegelian philosophy was a further theological system, a mystification of man's own being. Yet despite this insight, Feuerbach himself could never rise above an abstract, individualised notion of man; and of society as 'I and Thou'. Marx took up this whole question of the advances and limitations of the Young Hegelians in the *German Ideology* and castigated them in the following fashion:

... they extracted pure unfalsified Hegelian categories such as 'substance' and 'self-consciousness'; later, they desecrated these categories with more secular names such as 'species', 'the Unique', 'Man', etc [*German Ideology*, London 1965, 29–30].

Feuerbach's man-in-the-last-resort turns out to be *in* society almost by accident; there is in his scheme a hypostatisation of social relations with respect to the individual. Nothing could be further from Marx's conception. In Marx we find historical development infused into the notion of 'species-being' derived from Feuerbach's anthropology. In Marx's sense, alienated man cannot be termed a 'species-being'. Feuerbach could not see this

[9] L. Feuerbach, 'Vorläufige Thesen', *Werke*, ed. F. Jodl 1904, ii. Whereas Feuerbach anthropologised theology and speculative philosophy, Marx sought to politicise anthropology.

because of his crude materialism which reduced man to a being produced by his material conditions and not a dynamic agent actually *producing the conditions that produce him*. Marx, in his *Theses on Feuerbach*, debunks the scholastic, theoretical one-sidedness of this kind of materialism:

> The materialist doctrine concerning the changing of circumstances and education forgets that circumstances are changed by men and that the educator must himself be educated. This doctrine has therefore to divide society into two parts, one of which is superior to society
>
> [*Theses on Feuerbach* III, MEGA, section 1, vol. 1, 533].

For clearly, if the world is solely a product of material conditions, and not of man's own making, how can man change it? Feuerbach's anthropological premises are fundamentally un-dialectical.

Feuerbach's 'real humanism' had, however, achieved one main conceptual cleavage from Hegel—it had been able to criticise philosophical idealism *transformatively*, that is, by *concretising the abstractions* and by *materialising the human* elements of the schema. Yet whereas Feuerbach's transformative critique led him to wish to unite the 'sanguine principle of French sense-perception and materialism' with 'the phlegm of German meta-physics'[10] in order to establish Man at the centre of his subject-matter, Marx insisted that philosophy could be abolished.

By this he means that the true solution to Feuerbach's theor-etical search for a humanist theory can be resolved by starting with man as such instead of with man as the empirical individual. Hegel's great theoretical achievement was to stress once again the teleological nature of being, yet he had done this theologi-cally, he had not restricted teleology to man as such. Feuerbach's achievement was to grasp that the only source of teleology in the universe was man, but he then turned this into a static individual attribute. Marx combined Hegel's concept of teleology with Feuerbach's humanism, and this enabled him to see man as a teleological being developing through his own labour, yet con-strained by the particular social circumstances that prevented

[10] L. Feuerbach, *Sämtliche Werke* II, 591, cited in D. McLellan, *The Young Hegelians and Karl Marx*, London 1969, 105.

man's full realisation. It is only from this perspective that we can make sense of Marx's insistence that the conflict between the individual and the species could be ended. For as he states, the true solution to Feuerbach's search for humanism is to be found in communism.

> Human emancipation will only be complete when the real, individual man has absorbed himself into the abstract citizen; when, as an individual man, in his everyday life, in his work, in his relationships, he has become a species-being; and when he has recognised and organised his own powers as social powers. . . .
>
> [Marx, *Frühe Schriften* 1, 479, cited in McLellan, *Young Hegelians*, 104].

Alienation

But mankind as yet does not exist in freedom. There are still major conflicts between the individual and the species. Marx, by indicating the kind of constraints which prevent the realisation of man's distinct species-nature, describes historically man's alienation from his own powers. To describe why it is that man cannot act as a species being using the full possibilities inherent in the teleology of labour, Marx demonstrates how the human species develops in alienation. Indeed what Marx has to show historically is why it is that man should be alienated from his natural powers. His historical analysis outlines how from the animality of primitive communism man endeavours to combat scarcity and dominate nature.

The history of this endeavour is human 'pre-history': only when the productive forces which develop 'in the womb of bourgeois society' (the most productive hitherto and also the most universally socialised mode of production) are unleashed, can the 'pre-history of human society' end, and real human history begin.[11]

The fundamental alienation of man, then, is from nature. In the process of overcoming this, mankind necessarily effects a

[11] Citations from Marx, 'Preface to the Contribution to the Critique of Political Economy' (1859), Marx–Engels, *Selected Works* I, 329.

division of labour. As Venable notes, Marx (and Engels) distinguish between two kinds of division of labour: the 'social
division' and the 'manufacturing division'.[12] Marx insists that
these have 'opposite starting-points':

> ... within a tribe, there springs up naturally a division of
> labour, caused by differences of age and sex, a division that is
> consequently based on a purely physiological foundation....[13]

... and is therefore anthropologically necessary. Yet with the development of cities and urban life, there then develops a 'separation between town and country'[14] and class stratification super-

[12] V. Venables, *Human Nature, The Marxian View*, Cleveland
1966. 118 ff—in the EPM p. 159 we find that the division of labour
takes place 'within alienation', whereas in Marx's notes of early 1845
the order is reversed, and alienation is seen as the *resultant* of the
division of labour as in *The German Ideology*. In the EPM Marx
maintains that alienation is prior to private property, whereas in both
The German Ideology and the 1857–8 notes for the *Contribution to
the Critique of Political Economy*, this order is reversed. A. James
Gregor, reviewing both the Bottomore and Struik editions of the MSS
of 1844 (in *Science and Society*, 29 (1965) 357–362) states that this is
evidence for the de-ontologising of the concept and its relativisation.
We deduce differently from Marx's work. Here, we locate three kinds
of alienation, all anthropological, which combine in the conception
of alienation. The whole development of man is based upon his fight
to dominate nature from which, powerless over it, he is alienated.
Marx does not use this term explicitly, but by introducing it we can
make sense here of both an alienation *before* the division of labour,
and a *different type after it.* This would be contingent upon private
property, which gives rise to its own forms of alienated existence
analysed in the text. Marx notes that 'their restricted relation to one
another determines men's restricted relation to nature, *just because
nature is as yet hardly modified historically*' (*German Ideology*, 42, our
italics). The division of labour is an attempt to overcome this primary
alienation which leads to other forms of alienation. This original plight
of the species was predestined for it by virtue of its objectifying and
humanising relation to nature itself.

[13] Marx, *Capital* 1, Moscow 1961, 351. See the whole section on the
'Division of Labour and Manufacture'.

[14] *Capital* 1, 352. 'Exchange does not create the differences between
the spheres of production, but brings what are already different into
relation ... the foundation of every division of labour that is well-

venes. The relations between 'freeman and serf, patrician and plebeian, lord and serf, guide-master and journeyman', capitalist and proletarian, designate the history of all pre-human society as 'the history of class struggles'.[15]

The starting-point for this unnatural 'manufacturing division of labour' is class society. Classes within the species develop with modes of production built up to pacify nature and relieve man from material constraints. These modes of production become increasingly more collective, inter-related and universal as the process of defeating scarcity and humanising nature unfolds. The limits to social development are always in part the limits of material existence. The manufacturing division of labour is historically necessary, but only as a precondition for freedom. It is essential to man that he produces himself in freedom from physical need—it is inessential to him that he be segmented, compartmentalised and assigned specific life-tasks, once abundance has been created. The class that perpetuates the manufacturing division of labour, whilst it may have been historically progressive (in the sense of preparing the material foundation for the realisation of human freedom) becomes historically reactionary once it has laid that foundation yet persists in increasing the productive forces in its own interests, not in the interests of the species.

History is premised upon human objectifications. In other words, human history can only be conceived as the history of human actions. But these objectifications have not brought about species-being. Why not? Because man's self-production and world-production up to now has not been production of himself as a free, conscious being realising universal human needs (physical and cultural), but rather production of himself as an unfree, unselfconscious being realising sectional needs as a priority over those of the whole species:

> ... the natural sense of man has not yet been produced through man's own labour.

---

developed, and brought about by the exchange of commodities, is the separation between town and country.' Thus *exchange* is the bridge between the social and the manufacturing divisions of labour.

[15] Marx and Engels, *The Communist Manifesto*, Moscow 1965, 39.

The manufacturing division of labour subsumes a myriad of activities pursued by particular individuals. The re-integration of the particularised man into the social totality demands the abolition of the division of labour, which cripples 'the capabilities of the species'[16] and separates the interests of the individual from those of the community as a whole. Let us summarise the main effects of the division of labour within class society.

(a) It separates intelligence from labour and makes of each a general and exclusive arena of human action, instead of treating the two as aspects of 'true anthropological nature'.[17] The dichotomy between mental and manual labour removes many of the intellectual potentialities of the labour-process, and incorporates science as an alien power. (This division has other implications which we shall examine shortly.)

(b) Detail labour in manufactures produces no commodities; only the sum total of the detail labours—the common product—is a commodity.

(c) The process of human objectification becomes reduced to a set of differentiated work tasks that realise only this or that aspect of the human powers. Man becomes 'mutilated ... into a fragment of a man, (degraded) to the level of an appendage of a machine' in his direct productive activity.

(d) As long as man is a *total particularity*, an atomised set of specialised functions, as long as there is a 'cleavage between the particular and common interest ... man's own deed becomes an alien power opposed to him, which enslaves him instead of being controlled by him'.[18]

(e) As man is a social being, then, 'to subdivide a man is to execute him, if he deserves the sentence, to assassinate him, if he does not.... The subdivision of labour is the assassination of a people.'[19]

Marx arrives at none of these formulations through an ethical or metaphysical conception of what man should be, but through a concrete consideration of what man essentially is. The division of labour is 'the estranged, alienated positioning of human ac-

16 Marx, *Capital* 1, 329.
17 Cf note 3.
18 Marx and Engels, *The German Ideology*, 45.
19 Marx, *Capital* 1, 399, cited in Venables *Human Nature*, 132.

tivity as a real activity of the species or as activity of man as a
species being'.[20] Again we encounter the concept of 'alienation'.
We must now examine this concept more thoroughly, both in its
theoretical and its social dimensions.

If the object of labour is the objectification of species life,[21] then
the appropriation of the object, the product of labour, by another constitutes a denial of that species life:

> In tearing away from man the object of his production, (this)
> tears from him his species-life, his real objectivity as a member
> of the species and transforms his advantage over animals into
> the disadvantage that his inorganic body, nature, is taken away
> from him.[22]

As the human being becomes a commodity who must sell his
labour-power to live or, before capitalism, part with a portion of
his product to those with power over him, he is alienated from
his own powers. These human powers cease to be his own property—he is alienated from his own body.[23] As labour ceases to be
the vehicle of human purposes, but rather just a means to satisfy
other ends, so is man himself reduced to a means rather than an
end.

Alienation, however, does not refer to simply one structure of
human existence. Rather there are three principal structures of
alienated existence in Marx's theory.

(i) *Alienation of labour from its product*. The institutions of
private property, contingent upon the division of labour, necessitated certain property relations. Dominant groups within the

[20] Marx, EPM, ed. Struik, 159. It must not be deduced from this and
other remonstrances of Marx's that he aimed at a utopian abolition of
the whole division of human activities in any form (a mistake made
by N. Rotenstreich, *Basic Problems of Marx's Philosophy*. Indiana-
polis/New York 1965). It is only the forced division of labour that is
imposed upon man and alien to him that Marx wishes to see abolished.

[21] Marx, EPM, 114.

[22] EPM, 114. In this sense, a man under these conditions may as well
be a mere animal from the way he is treated by his fellows—he receives just enough to satisfy his animal needs (cf Struik's introduction,
p. 47).

[23] EPM, 114, and cf 113.

species possessing a monopoly over productive property reproduce their assets and provide for the subsistence of the species
only by appropriating the products of human labour-power. In
the sphere of political economy (the sum total of human labour
in a given period), objectification thus becomes 'a loss of the
object and bondage to it; appropriation as estrangement, as
alienation'.[24]

(ii) *Human self-alienation.* The producer's activity, his powers,
do not obey his own dictates, but those of another for whom he
is a productive vehicle. 'It is the loss of his self.'[25] In his human
functions, man is reduced to an animal; only in his animal functions (sex, nutrition, etc) can man feel freely active and therefore human. 'But abstractly taken, separated from the sphere of
all other human activity and turned into sole and ultimate ends,
they are animal functions.'[26]

(iii) *Alienation of man from man.* Producers no longer produce use-values assigned to satisfy specific needs for others. He
produces exchange-values which only satisfy needs distantly,
under impersonal market conditions. Money as 'men's estranged,
alienating and self-disposing species nature ... the alienated
ability of mankind' acts as the 'pimp between man's needs and
the object'.[27] Man becomes a means and not an end for other
men. The conflicting interests arising within the productive
system establish competitive relations between them. As stated
earlier, this structure of alienation involves the dehumanisation
of man.

Together then these three structures combine to allow Marx
to state that man is alienated from his species nature.

'Conscious life activity' is man's species-being. 'It is only because he is a species being that he is a conscious being, i.e., that

[24] EPM, 108.
[25] EPM, 111. In *Capital* 3, Zurich ed. 1933, 108, Marx shows that 'the
relations of capital conceal indeed the inner connection (of the facts)
in the complete indifference, exteriorisation and alienation in which
it places the worker in relation to the conditions of the realisation of
his own labour'. (Cited by Struik, EPM, 235.)
[26] EPM, 111.
[27] EPM, 168, 165.

his own life is an object for him. Only because of this is his activity free activity.'[28] Alienated labour *reverses* this, making his life activity 'imposed, forced labour ... the labour of self-sacrifice'.[29]

In *The Holy Family*, Marx states that 'the propertied class and the class of the proletariat present the same self-alienation'.[30] The former class finds in its power a mere semblance of human existence, whereas the latter, powerless, is annihilated in its self-alienation. The two classes are both at the mercy of the caprices of the market, the anarchic, uncontrolled and unconscious regulator of the productive process. But the proletariat finds its self-alienation a greater abasement—a greater 'contradiction between its human nature and its condition of life, which is outright, decisive and comprehensive negation of that nature'.[31]

This statement by Marx is important because it reveals quite clearly that Marx felt that the proletariat was more dehumanised than the bourgeoisie by the structure of society. The young Lukacs was mistaken in suggesting that the reverse was the case and that therefore the proletariat being more human had truth on its side.

Marx did not (like Hegel) investigate the possibility of abolishing alienation only in terms of its dialectical sublation, its *'Aufhebung'* in consciousness alone. Nor did he accept Feuerbach's view that alienation can be overcome by true self-knowledge. A correct grasp of Marx's own statements on alienation reveal that all the talk about this being merely a question of metaphysics fails to distinguish between Marx and his predecessors. In Marx's work, 'thought and being are indeed distinct, but they also form a unity'.[32]

---

[28] EPM, 113.

[29] EPM, 111.

[30] Marx and Engels, *The Holy Family*, Moscow 1956—Marx's section on Proudhon, Chapter VI, p. 51.

[31] Ibid. cf also EPM, 118—'the whole of human servitude is involved in the relation of the worker to production'.

[32] Marx, EPM, 138 (otherwise rendered, 'Thinking and being are thus no doubt distinct, but at the same time they are in unity with each other'—Milligan). Alienation is anthropologically *structural*.

Alienation, Reification and Consciousness

Before we can discuss the peculiar kind of consciousness produced within alienated society, it is necessary to examine the Marxist conception of consciousness in general. For Marx, 'It is not the consciousness of men that determines their being, but on the contrary, their social being that determines their consciousness'.[33] This statement is often interpreted as a causal, or rigidly deterministic one. But Marx was continually concerned to totalise human attributes; just as the distinction between individual and society was obliterated in the concept of man as a social being, so is the distinction between being and consciousness also obliterated. It is not that, for example, being a proletarian involves having a proletarian consciousness; rather, it is that man as world-producing and world-produced being is both determined and autonomous in his consciousness. There is therefore a mutually reconstituting interaction between human ideas and the conditions they confront. Marx is careful never to stress one side of the dialectical process at the expense of the other. Man as world-produced derives his conceptual apparatus from his social matrix: man as world-producing is able to recast, reject, reflect upon his world with his consciousness and as he effects changes in that world, so does he alter the external reality from which he derives further categories of thought.

The process just described may be termed *teleological or purposive* consciousness. Marx gives an illustration:

We pre-suppose labour in a form that stamps it as exclusively human. A spider conducts operations that resemble those of a weaver, and a bee puts to shame many an architect in the construction of her cells. But what distinguishes the worst architect from the best of bees is this, that the architect raises his structure in imagination before he erects it in reality. At the end of every labour-process, we get a result that already existed in the imagination of the labourer at its commencement. He not only affects a change of form in the material on which he

[33] Marx, *Preface to A Contribution to the Critique of Political Economy*, Marx–Engels, *Selected Works*, I, 329.

works, but he also realises a purpose of his own that gives the law to his modus operandi ... [*Capital* 1, Moscow 1961, 178].

But man in class society is not free to realise his own purposes. He only realises the purposes of the ruling group. But many people within class society fail to realise that purposes other than present purposes could be realised. Marx argues that the comprehension of the social world under alienation is reified. For when human products are alien facts independent of the control of most members of society, there arises a corresponding structure of consciousness, reification. Moreover, theoretical consciousness as the province of a few alone is clearly the historical product of human pre-history which fails to realise the human faculties of every member of the species and instead concentrates upon developing only one or two specific faculties in each person—'each man has a particular, exclusive sphere of activity which is forced upon him'.[34] The social determination of the form of consciousness described here as theoretico-reflective is such that the content of that consciousness will be voluntaristic.

The peculiar structural position of the intellectual frees his consciousness from the determinations that pervade the universe for the alienated producer. The intellectual can therefore choose whether to become an abstraction of alienated man establishing himself as a measure of that alienation,[35] or a philosopher of the ruling class, who makes it his 'chief source of livelihood to develop and perfect the illusions of the class itself'.[36] The former will be acting as a *dereifying agent*, the latter as an *ideologist*. Let us examine more closely these two concepts. Reification (*Versachlichung*) is the process of comprehension of the world under alienation. When human products become alien facticities, standing independent of man, there arises a corresponding structure of consciousness which divorces the act of world-production from the agency of human producers. The human world is no longer conceived as social, as man-made. Human relations instead are seen as functions of relations between things. This characteristic of 'thinghood' pervades the consciousness of man, and

[34] Marx and Engels, *The German Ideology*, 45.
[35] *German Ideology*, 61.
[36] Marx, *Capital* I, 72.

impinges upon the reflective consciousness of philosophers, writers, economists, sociologists and politicians (to a greater or lesser extent, depending upon their position in the power structure and their unique socialisation). Reified consciousness, because it cannot conceive of man as social, and reduces human activity to autonomous, law-governed structures, is precisely *false consciousness*. The object of human labour becomes a commodity with attributes other than those invested in it by the producer. It appears therefore to have a life of its own:

> ... the existence of things *qua* commodities, and the value-relation between the products of labour which stamps them as commodities, have absolutely no connection with their physical properties and with the material relations arising therefrom. There it is a definite social relation between men that assumes, in their eyes, the fantastic form of a relation between things

> [Marx, *Capital* I, Moscow 1954, 72].

This revelation whereby Marx deciphers the hieroglyph of social production within alienation is termed by him *The Fetishism of Commodities and the Secret Thereof*. It echoes an earlier analysis of Marx's in an 1842 edition of the *Rheinische Zeitung*, the radical German journal of which he was editor for a brief period. In this analysis Marx showed that the theft of lumber involved penalties which designated a perversion of the relationship between man and thing. Lumber, inanimate matter, is seen as determining the relations of one human being to another insofar as they are both conceived not as human beings but as functions of lumber itself—one an owner, the other a thief. Lumber as an expression of social relations is placed at the centre of the social relation itself—that of owner to thief.[37] This reification of social relations can only occur in conditions where men do not act toward each other as human beings. The market, the present human institution for the satisfaction of animal needs, is looked upon as a fixed, immutable entity to be obeyed; it takes on a

[37] Marx, *Critique of Hegel's Philosophy of Law*, cited in Eduard Urbanek 'Roles, Masks and Characters: A Contribution to Marx's Idea of the Social Role'. *Social Research*, Vol. 34, no. 3 (1967), 529-63.

super-human form. Its laws are not understood as the totality of the social relations which compose it—they are 'natural'. The market is beyond the conscious control of its participants—it therefore appears as self-sustaining.

Historically, pre-capitalist reification occurs within a context where man has not yet dominated nature. Here, as Marx demonstrates in his *Critique of Hegel's Philosophy of Law*, reification appears as the 'biologising' of social relations.

Men are seen not as men but as manifestations of 'blood' (genealogy) or other biological properties, the role of 'birth' in terms of the location within society is seen as determining the character and destiny of human beings.

> The aristocracy's pride in their blood, their descent, in short the genealogy of the body ... has its appropriate science in heraldry. The secret of the aristocracy is zoology
>
> [Marx, *Critique of Hegel's Philosophy of Law* 1, 311].

The place of land in the world of the feudal-manorial system was so central to the domination of nature that men conceived of themselves in terms of the phenomena they were seeking to master; every first-born son in the succession of property-owners becomes for them

> ... the inheritance, the property, of inalienable landed property, the predestined substance of its will and its activity. The subject is the thing and the predicate is the man. The will becomes the property of property.... The owner of entailed landed property becomes the serf of the landed estate.
>
> [Marx, EPM (Bottomore's translation)].

Feudal alienation, as distinct from capitalist alienation, presented only two structures of the alienated condition of the species. First, it comprised alienation of man from himself insofar as feudal man was incapable of controlling the conditions for his self-production. Secondly, it comprised alienation of the producer from his product insofar as anything which he produced over and above his own subsistence was appropriated by his lord, who in turn acted toward the peasant not as a human being in his own right but in his capacity as appropriator.

Bourgeois society presents a concatenation of all forms of human alienation (previously outlined) and the reduction of man to a commodity through the medium of his labour-power (his basic, human, power) announced a more thorough, more deep-rooted alienation of man from man, of producer from product, of man from himself. The market structure (the anatomy of civil society, in Marx's terms) precluded any voluntary, reciprocal relationship between producers, denied any bonds of vassalage between property-owners, and thus established a competitive and dehumanised social order which added a new dimension to all pre-existing forms of alienation from man's species nature.

Dereification, the process whereby social relations between men are revealed as such and therefrom conceived as changeable, commences at the level of reflective consciousness, where it remains *critical theory*. When transmuted to the practical level of the masses, it becomes *revolutionary praxis*, leading to the struggle for authentic being. Just as we have termed reifying consciousness *false consciousness* within alienation, *dereifying consciousness* aims at helping conditions where species being can be realised.

Conclusions

In his early works, and even in his later polemical works, Marx offers a logical solution to the history of class society. For it is obvious by now that Marx's central concern is how alienated class-divided society can be abolished.

> This is our reply. A class must be formed which has radical chains, a class in civil society which is not a class of civil society, a class which is a dissolution of all classes, a sphere of society which has a universal character because its sufferings are universal, and which does not claim a particular redress because the wrong which is done to it is not a particular wrong but wrong in general
>
> [Marx, *Early Writings*, ed. T. B. Bottomore, London and New York 1963, 107].

Productive workers are the social class most active in the process of creation of values, yet the worker becomes all the poorer the more he produces. He becomes an ever cheaper commodity the more he creates commodities. 'With the increasing value of the world of things proceeds in direct proportion the devaluation of the world of men.'[38] So for Marx human emancipation takes place through revolutionary action directed at the overthrow of class society. Although this emancipation takes the 'political form of the emancipation of the workers', nevertheless it is not solely their own emancipation that is concerned 'because (it) includes the emancipation of humanity as a whole'.[39]

This merely logical solution is rendered a good deal more complex in Marx's later substantive analysis of the labour process. As we shall show in later essays, the dialectic of labour can take a savage turn.

But here we are merely concerned to establish the indispensable nature of Marx's anthropological premises. Man's teleological nature is a fundamental ontological given. Much of the debate about the relationship between the 'early' and 'later' (or 'young' and 'mature') Marx overlooks this question. For in 'settling accounts' with his former philosophical outlook, Marx rigorously set to work to analyse concrete conditions within history and society. His political economy constitutes scientific study. But this can only be understood in terms of his specific goal of uniting theory with practice to assist in the achievement of revolution and the total redemption of man's human powers.

To introduce a hiatus between works in which his premises are laid out and the later works of concrete analysis is to consign crucial areas of his thought to some folly of his youth—it is to radically devalue the criterion for liberation and the libertarian basis of scientific socialism to some secondary place in a developmental scheme in which other premises, alien to Marx, could be inserted with impunity. It leaves Marxism open to the charge of relativism and defenceless in the confrontation with revisionism. All social theory implies some conception of the human; for Marx this was not a question of abstract definition, but an extrapolation from men in their actual, perceptible process of development under definite conditions. This does not make of the whole of Marxism an 'anthropology' in which evidence is accrued to

[38] *Early Writings*, 118.
[39] Marx and Engels, *The Holy Family*, Moscow 1956, 53.

substantiate original premises. This has certainly been one tendency in Marxism, which Lukacs in self-criticism describes as:

... the tendency to view Marxism exclusively as a theory of society, as social philosophy, and hence to ignore or repudiate it as a theory of nature

[G. Lukacs, *History and Class Consciousness*, London 1971, Preface to the new edition, xvi].

Rather we portray Marxism as a body of revolutionary theory, breaking from all other social theories on the basis of an explicit rejection of idealism and mechanistic materialism. That rejection was achieved by transforming the (idealistic or mechanistic) *content* of concepts such as 'alienation', 'species', 'universality', 'praxis'. Once refurbished within a dialectical schema as anthropological presuppositions, they could be dropped from the later, concrete analyses.

Of course, it could be argued that Marxism has no assumptions about humanity to defend—that, as some Marxists would claim, it is all a matter of identifying oppression and exploitation within various social structures, locating the oppressed and exploited social forces whoever they may be, and uniting enough of them into a vanguard party to confront the agencies of oppression. But this raises more problems than it settles. In the essays that follow we shall show some of the theoretical consequences of deviating from Marx's premises. For the moment our only contention here is that a return to the presuppositions and assumptions of Marxism, which are anthropological, provides us with the clearest conceptual apparatus with which to understand Marx's work and with which to confront non-Marxist social science and variations within the Marxist orbit.

2

ALIENATION AND THE DIALECTICS OF LABOUR

Every beginning is difficult, holds in all sciences. . . . The value-form, whose fully developed shape is the money-form, is very elementary and simple. Nevertheless, the human mind has for more than 2,000 years sought in vain to get to the bottom of it. . . . *With the exception of the section on value-form, therefore, this volume cannot stand accused on the score of difficulty.* I pre-suppose of course, a reader who is willing to learn something new and therefore think for himself

> [Marx, Preface to the first German edition of *Capital*,
> *Capital* I, Moscow 1954, 7–8].

The laws of political economy express the estrangement of the worker in his object thus: the more the worker produces; the less he has to consume; *the more values he creates, the more valueless, the more unworthy he becomes, the better formed his product, the more deformed becomes the worker; . . . the more powerful labour becomes, the more powerless becomes the worker;* . . . Political economy conceals the estrangement inherent in the nature of labour by not considering the direct relationship between the worker (labour) and production. It is true that labour produces for the rich wonderful things—but for the worker it produces privation. It produces palaces—but for the worker, hovels. It produces beauty—but for the worker, deformity. It replaces labour by machines, but it throws a section of the workers back to a barbarous type of labour, and it turns the other workers into machines

> [Marx, *Economic and Philosophical Manuscripts of
> 1844*, ed. Struik, 109–110].

Our rather unwilling aim here is to indicate the possible emergence of a view of Marx which, although far from resolving the host of theoretical and practical problems he bequeathed to Marxists, goes some way towards elucidating his main assumptions. Moreover, and more ambitiously, it seeks to indicate the way in which his concrete analysis of political economy followed from and is inseparably connected with his view of man. We say unwilling, because as yet nobody has engaged completely successfully in such a task. Rather the most obvious character of Marxism since Marx has been the inability of any individual to deal convincingly and capably with what has been crudely conceived of as the two halves of his work, his philosophical foundations and his economic science.

In part, but in part only, this has had to do with the fact that much material was not available or at least not available in English. But we know the problem is greater than mere availability. In part it is a sheer question of our ability. Whatever the faults of the French and English Althusserian school, they are correct to stress the difficulty of reading *Capital*.[1] It is not simply a question of the quantity and complexity of Marx's work, but that much of it is written in different styles, with a varied audience or, as in the case of the *Grundrisse*,[2] no audience in mind. It is not just that the *Economic and Philosophical Manuscripts* are different from the *Grundrisse*, which in turn is different from *Capital*, but also that, taken individually, none are really complete. David McLellan has argued that the most complete work of Marx is the *Grundrisse*, but that 'Marx's intellectual development is a process of "self clarification", which cannot be split into periods or be treated as a monolith'.[3] He is undoubtedly correct in saying that Marx's work shows variation, moves in different directions, focuses on different problems, yet our firm belief is that from 1844 it forms a unity. Historically, Marxism's task is to unearth, reveal, and apply a theory derived from such a unity. In this respect it follows that the genius of a Marxist such as George Lukacs derives from his struggle and qualified success in doing just this. For Lukacs, reading Marx, saw as *necessary* what was only partially acknowledged with the discovery of the

[1] Louis Althusser and Etienne Balibar, *Reading Capital*, London 1971.

[2] See the English selections: David McLellan, *Marx's Grundrisse*, London 1971. Also K. Marx, *Pre-Capitalist Economic Formations*, edited and with an introduction by Eric Hobsbawm, London 1964.

[3] D. McLellan, 'Marx and the Missing Link', *Encounter*, December 1970.

Economic and Philosophical Manuscripts, namely that a correct grasp of Marx's dialectics of labour is essential if we are to understand the unity of Marx's total work. But Lukacs himself now admits the inadequacy of *History and Class Consciousness* on this score. Indeed in a recent interview, published posthumously, he had this to say about his early as compared with his present work:

> In the West, there is a tendency to erect them into 'classics of heresy', but we have no need for that today. The twenties are a past epoch; it is the philosophical problems of the sixties that should concern us. I am now working on an *Ontology of Social Being* which I hope will solve the problems that were posed quite falsely in my early work, particularly *History and Class Consciousness*. My new work centres on the question of the relationship between necessity and freedom, or, as I express it, teleology and causality. Traditionally, philosophers have always built systems founded on one or the other of these two poles. They have either denied necessity or denied human freedom. My aim is to show the ontological interrelation of the two, and to reject the 'either-or' standpoints with which philosophy has presented man. The concept of labour is the hinge of my analysis. ... The notion of alternatives is basic to the meaning of human labour, which is thus always *teleological*—it sets an aim which is the result of a choice. It thus expresses human freedom
>
> [G. Lukacs, 'Interview on His Life and Work', *New Left Review* 68 (July–Aug. 1971), 51].

To put it bluntly, there are good rather than merely expedient reasons for Lukacs' rejection of much of this work. We shall return to his rejection later, but for the moment let us grasp this cautionary tale, that one of the greatest modern Marxists misunderstood Marx on man.

The difficulties in understanding the unity of Marx's thought are enormous, then, and they only multiply when we consider the distance between the materialist humanism of the EPM and the mathematical transformation problems elaborated in *Capital*. For a host of reasons, the unity in Marx is obscure, indeed the very depth and breadth of his work serve as a constant reminder that most of us are alienated specialists for whom it is a painful struggle to understand, 'a Hegel turned economist, a Ricardo turned socialist'.[4] But, given our aim, we shall attempt to lay out the assumptions which seem to inform Marx's work and relate his central concepts to our conception of his work's unity.

The Dialectics of Labour

We have argued earlier that Marx's image of man, his materialist anthropology, reveals the fundamental premises of his scientific analysis of concrete historical formations. Our first problem here then, is what is Marx's conception of man, and is this conception consistent throughout his work?

Most of the debate over the relationship between 'the early', 'the middle' and 'the mature' Marx, overlooks the centrality of Marx's ontological assumptions. Many of the political and polemical writings on Marx have rooted themselves in issues irrelevant to his ontological concerns. Yet many of the mistakes made by otherwise brilliant scholars start here, in their failure to recapture Marx's ontological position. Lukacs' overwilling but truthful criticism of his own work, correctly grasps its own central mistake, namely that:

> ... the book's most striking feature is that, contrary to the subjective intentions of its author, objectively it falls in with a tendency in the history of Marxism that has taken many different forms. All of them have one thing in common, whether they like it or not and irrespective of their philosophical origins or their political effects: they strike at the very roots of Marxian ontology [*History and Class Consciousness*, xvi].

What is this ontology then? At its simplest the belief that human activity, labour, creation, production, is the mediator between man and society. But more than this, that men only truly produce in freedom. Marx puts it as follows in the *Economic and Philosophical Manuscripts of 1844*:

> An animal only produces what it immediately needs for itself or its young. It produces one-sidedly, whilst man produces uni-

[4] Lassalle to Marx, 12 May 1851, quoted in McLellan, *Marx's Grundrisse*, 41.

versally. It produces only under the dominion of immediate
physical need, whilst man produces even when he is free from
physical need and only truly produces in freedom therefrom
                                          [EPM, ed. Struik, 113].

Marx sees man as the only species capable of purposeful creation.
The human species is different because man is a teleological crea-
ture. Marx argues that man exteriorises himself through the process of his labour, that is through objectification. But as the history of society is a history of class societies, men objectify under
conditions limited by such classes. Thus men cannot truly produce until classless society is achieved. Marx's hatred for all the
pretences of class society follows not from some Victorian
morality but from the limits it imposes on 'man as such'. For
Marx any class society, feudalism, capitalism, whatever, produces
alienation, for real production, the activity of real men, is shaped
and distorted by the social constraints of such societies. The
ability to see the unity of Marx's work lies in seeing it as a developing exercise and an analysis of the dialectics of labour. Any
viewpoint which abandons this beginning collapses into reduc-
tionism or idealism. Indeed this is Marx's special claim. For the
Marxist proposition that labour or man is the only existing form
of teleological being is the only theory which establishes man's
unique character. It thus locates man as *determined yet determining*. It was Lukacs' early inability fully to grasp the significance of this that led him to be able to dismiss an otherwise great
work as idealist in its implications. He criticises himself in the
following fashion:

I must confine myself here to a critique of *History and Class
Consciousness*, but this is not to imply that this deviation from
Marxism was less pronounced in the case of other writers with
a similar outlook. In my book this deviation has immediate
consequences for the view of economics I give there and fundamental confusions result, as in the nature of the case economics
must be crucial. It is true that the attempt is made to explain
all ideological phenomena by reference to their basis in economics but, despite this, the preview of economics is narrowed
down because its basic Marxist category, labour as the mediator of the metabolic interaction between society and nature, is

missing. Given my basic approach, such a consequence is quite natural. It means the most important real pillars of the Marxist view of the world disappear and the attempt to deduce the ulti-mate revolutionary implications of marxism in as radical a fashion as possible is deprived of a genuinely economic founda-tion. It is self evident that this means the disappearance of the ontological objectivity of nature upon which this process of change is based. But it also means the disappearance of the *interaction* between labour as seen from a genuinely materialist standpoint and the evolution of the men who labour

[*History and Class Consciousness*, xvii].

This is not low, expedient self-criticism, it is a genuine confession of his earlier misconstruction of Marx's view of labour. But where does this confusion arise? What is it that is difficult to grasp, if not Marx's startling reliance upon the special character of human as opposed to non-human labour. A careful reading of Lukacs' self-criticism gives us the reason for his earlier con-fusion. It is not that he did not consider that society and nature are mediated by praxis, but rather that praxis as a concept does not concretely grasp the special characteristic of the human species. As he states:

I directed my polemics against the over-extension and over-evaluation of contemplation. Marx's critique of Feuerbach only reinforced my convictions. What I failed to realise how-ever was that in the absence of a basis in real praxis, *in labour as its original form and model*, the over-extension of the con-cept of praxis would lead to its opposite: a relapse into ideal-istic contemplation [*History and Class Consciousness*, xviii].

But what then is the nature of labour, and why is it essential to start there in the study of man? In *Capital* Marx says the follow-ing:

To know what is useful for a dog, one must study dog-nature. This nature itself is not to be deduced from the principle of utility. Applying this to man, he that would criticise all human acts, movements, relations, etc. by the principle of utility, must first deal with human nature in general, and then with human nature as modified in each historical epoch

[*Capital* i, Moscow 1954, 609].

In short, his position is that to know what is useful for mankind, we must first deal with labour in general and then labour as modified and constrained by particular kinds of historical formations. This is of course what Marx attempted; the unity informing his work is his constant insistence on basic premises which reveal the dialectics of labour.

> The labour process, which antedates value, and serves as its starting point, thus again makes its appearance *within capital*, as a process which occurs inside its substance and forms its content. The labour process, because of its abstractness, and its material nature, is equally characteristic of all forms of production [McLellan, *Marx's Grundrisse*, 78].

From a description of man's alienation from labour, in the *Economic and Philosophical Manuscripts*, through his middle works, in the *Grundrisse*, we finally move to the concrete measure of exploitation of man's labour power in *Capital*. Again and again, Marx stresses the general and special nature of the exclusive and unique characteristic of human labour. He states the following in *Capital*:

> We shall, therefore, in the first place, have to consider the labour process *independently of the particular form it assumes* under given social conditions.
>
> Labour is, in the first place, a process in which both man and Nature participate, and in which man of his own accord starts, regulates, and controls the material re-actions between himself and Nature. He opposes himself to Nature as one of her own forces, setting in motion arms and legs, head and hands, the natural forces of his body, in order to appropriate Nature's productions in a form adapted to his own wants. By thus acting on the external world and changing it, he at the same time changes his own nature. He develops his slumbering powers and compels them to act in obedience to his sway. We are not now dealing with those primitive instinctive forms of labour that remind us of the mere animal. An immeasurable amount of time separates the state of things in which a man brings his labour-power to the market for sale as a commodity, from that state in which human labour was still at its first instinctive stage. We pre-suppose labour in a form which stamps it as *exclusively human*. A spider conducts operations which

resemble those of a weaver, and a bee puts to shame many an architect in the construction of her cells. But what distinguishes the worst architect from the best of bees is this, that the architect raises his structure in his imagination before he erects it in reality. At the end of every labour process we get a result that already existed in the imagination of the labourer at its commencement. He not only effects a change of form in the material on which he works, but he also realises a purpose of his own [*Capital* I, Moscow 1954, 178].

It is this revolutionary grasp of and insistence on the way in which man's special teleological nature is held back by class society that drove Marx to spend thirty years demonstrating that the conditions political economists assumed were law-like and permanent were nothing more than the crippling transient forms of bourgeois society. Marx's unity is nothing less than the central ontological category of labour. Understanding this, and reading *Capital*, we are able to see that the *Economic and Philosophical Manuscripts* are not 'metaphysical rubbish' but the general foundation for Marx's continually developing analysis of the conditions constraining labour. For Marx literally meant that the history of class society is pre-history, it is an alien history, a history of the animal in man, for as he notes in the EPM:

In tearing away from man the object of his production, (this) tears from him his species-life, his real objectivity as a member of the species, and transforms his advantage over animals into the disadvantage that his inorganic body, nature, is taken away from him [EPM, ed. Struik, 144].

It goes without saying that this perspective on Marx has its own difficulties, not the least of which is expecting too much from it. For by itself, without detailed analysis, it is no more than a limited exposition of historical materialism, it is not in itself a theory from which predictions or tendencies can be derived. But it does resolve many problems. Lukacs says the following of this approach.

As with every genuinely ontological question, the correct answer immediately appears trivial: it is usually like Columbus's egg. Yet one need only examine more closely the definitions resulting from the Marxian manner of dealing with the teleology of labour in order to appreciate its potential ability to resolve far-reaching and false problems and to create decisive consequences. To anyone familiar with Marx's thought, it is obvious that his position on Darwin clearly reveals Marx's rejection of any teleological existence outside labour, i.e. human praxis. In fact, Marx's recognition of the teleology of labour far surpasses even the solutions of his great predecessors such as Aristotle and Hegel since he sees labour not as one of the many manifestations of teleology in general, but as the only point at which a teleological project can be ontologically demonstrated as an actual instance of material reality. This correct cognition of reality illuminates ontologically a number of problems. First, it gives a simple and obvious basis to the decisive and real characteristic of teleology, i.e. that it can only be realised through a project. We need not repeat the Marxian definition in order to comprehend the impossibility of all labour unless preceded by such a project which determines the labour-process in all its stages. Of course, this essential characteristic of labour has been clearly recognised by Aristotle and Hegel. However, since they also attempted to teleologically comprehend the organic world and the course of history, in each case they were forced to invent a subject for the required project, e.g. Hegel's world spirit, which inevitably transformed reality into a myth. But Marx's rigorous and exactly defined relegation of teleology to labour (to social praxis) eliminating it from all other spheres of being, does not limit its scope. On the contrary, its significance grows through the insight that social being, the highest level of being known to us, is originally constituted through this actual teleological force activity within it. It emerges from organic life, the level upon which it is based, by developing into a new and independent form of being. We can rationally speak of social being only if we comprehend that its genesis, its becoming distinct from its basis and the emergence of its reliance on labour is a function of the continuous realization of teleological projects.[5]

[5] G. Lukacs, 'The Dialectic of Labour: Beyond Causality and Teleology' *Telos* 6 (Fall 1970), 162–174. (This seems to be an extract from the earlier mentioned work by Lukacs on the 'Ontology of Social Being' at 165–166.)

Yet even when we accept the dialectic of labour our problems are not resolved, for the next question is how do we analyse concrete reality from these assumptions. In the same context Lukacs says:

> Therefore, the problem which emerges here is not whether or not labour is teleological. Rather the real problem lies in giving a truly critical and ontological analysis of the almost unlimited generalization of the elemental fact—from everyday life to myths, religion and philosophy
>
> ['The Dialectic of Labour', 162].

Lukacs goes on to point out how one can begin to analyse the 'dialectic of labour'. What is important about this later position of Lukacs is that it resolves the question which many non-Marxist philosophers have asked of Marxism, namely how can something be determined and determining:

> The history of philosophy indicates the intellectual struggle between causality and teleology as the categorial foundation of reality and its movement. In order to spiritually harmonize their God with the cosmos and with the world of man, every theologically-oriented philosophy was forced to announce the superiority of teleology over causality. Such an hierarchy of creator and creation, and thus the priority of the teleological project, is unavoidable, even if God merely winds the universal clock to set the system of causality into motion. On the other hand, every pre-Marxian materialism that denied the transcendental constitution of the world was also forced to reject the possibility of a truly active teleology. We have already seen how even Kant, in his epistemological terminology, is forced to speak of the irreconcilability of causality and teleology. Yet, if along with Marx, we recognise teleology as an exclusive active category in labour, it necessarily follows a real as well as a necessary co-existence of causality and teleology. Of course, the opposition remains, but only within a real and uniform process whose movement is a result of the reciprocal action caused by the opposition. In order to realise the reciprocal action, this opposition transforms even causality into projected reality without changing its essence
>
> [Lukacs, 'The Dialectic of Labour', 166].

Marx was the first thinker to overcome the philosophical opposition between causality and teleology, by grounding his analysis in the dialectics of labour. He then went on to derive operational concepts from his dialectics of labour that were intended both to account for and to help reveal the dynamics and direction of social change. What we have to show is how alienation is linked to the labour theory of value in Marx's work and in so doing highlight their dependence upon his view of man.

For an apparent but often unstated assumption of much so-called 'critical theory'[6] is that Marx lacked concepts which (even if correctly applied) could adequately account for a radical change in social reality. Indeed what much of this theorising comes down to, is the search for concepts usable within a Marxist framework but allowing one to deal more ably with the mediations between subject and object. This would be unobjectionable if these conceptual 'developments' were consistent with Marx's dialectics of labour, but all too frequently such developments depend upon unacknowledged breaks. At its worst and most open it can lead Marxists of the calibre of Herbert Marcuse to openly attempt his ludicrous synthesis of Freud and Marx in a manner that does an injustice to both. It is precisely because Marx's categories are dependent upon his special ontological view of man that they cannot be properly assimilated into alternative theories which have contrary ontological assumptions. It is for this reason, despite its many weaknesses, that we develop briefly an earlier collaborative study that sought to show the limitations of Berger and Pullberg's anthropology as against that of Marx.[7] For a moment's consideration of their ontological position demonstrates their own refusal to see *social analysis as a real possibility*.[8] Whereas Marx's analysis of alienation is not only consistent with his ontological position but allows of operational developments which account for the way in which the various structural forms of class rule form the basis for alienation and extend its scope.

[6] Especially true of the old and new Frankfurt school of Marxism: Adorno, Horkheimer, Habermas, etc.

[7] P. Walton, J. Coulter and A. Gamble, 'Philosophical Anthropology in Marxism', *Social Research* 37, 2 (1970), 259–274.

[8] P. Berger and S. Pullberg, 'Reification and the Sociological Critique of Consciousness', *History and Theory* IV (2) and *New Left Review* 35.

Ontology and Alienation: Marx, Berger, Pullberg and Luckmann

Given our previous discussion, Marx's conception of alienation can be briefly restated: namely that the distinction between animal being and human beings lies in man's utilisation of his teleological power, of the realisation of this power through *objectification*. But, argues Marx, in a class society man labours not for the species but for dominant groups within that species. It follows that, within this system of alien-labour, it is not the interests and purposes of mankind that are realised but the particularistic purposes of the ruling class. So any analysis of the ways in which various forms of class rule come into being and are maintained is really an analysis of different forms of alienation which prevail within such societies. Marx's historical analysis of the shift from feudalism to capitalism is an analysis revealing developments in alienated existence. We have argued earlier that for Marx capitalism announced human mastery over nature. Previous epochs had prepared the ground for this mastery, each with their own configurations of alienated existence. The market grew from capitalist accumulation, undertaken by the bourgeoisie against the prevailing feudal relations, and became the new limiting area for the satisfaction of human needs; even the former subsistence-orientation and direct appropriation of surplus product which characterised feudalism was transformed by the development of market relationships. With this transformation, production assumed a new dimension of alienation. Under feudalism, the *use-value* of human labour-power to the human species had been a matter for calculation by the feudal ruling-class on the basis of personal greed, limited by the walls of their stomachs. That is, the feudal lord could choose to be more or less philanthropic in terms of the amount of *surplus-product* appropriated from his peasants. Marx analysed that under the capitalist *exchange*-relationships, use-value is reduced to the exchange value of commodities; and alienation takes on a new feature, for capitalism transformed human labour-power itself into an exchange-value over which neither bourgeois nor proletarian had control. Not surplus-*product* but surplus-*value* is appropriated, as alienated *labour-power* reduced to a quantifiable unit of productive exchange-value.

The historical tracing of different forms of alienation does not involve Marx, as the followers of Althusser suggest, in some 'epistemological rupture' from the concept of alienation; rather it is the revelation of the basis for different kinds of alienation.

In part, this confusion has arisen because alienation from labour is specific to capitalism. In previous societies labour-power was not bought and sold like a commodity. What confronted man as an alien power was land and nature.

All modes of production are different ways of extracting labour. But in pre-capitalist societies this extraction is determined by the personal relations of dependence that are established between those who labour and the class that has monopolised the means of labour, the land or the person of the labourer. Labour is not alienated from itself, it is still the producer of *use-values*, a portion of which are appropriated by the landowning class. Only under capitalism does production become primarily production for *exchange-value*. This means that labour for the first time becomes a commodity; its consumption by the capitalists is the creation and reproduction of capital. For the first time private property depends on the *continual alienation of labour*, on the sale by the worker of his labour power. This sale is the means by which the productivity of labour is developed, and the domination of labour over nature finally established. But at the same time it is the universal alienation of man because it is the life activity of man that is alienated and not merely the means of labour. The mode of extracting surplus labour becomes economic in character, because it is rooted in the conditions of the labour process itself and not in the personal bondage that the feudal lords exercise over the labourers.

But let us leave this debate for the moment to indicate how social analysis from a different ontological standpoint is forced time and again into uncertainty and contradiction.

Berger and Pullberg examine and utilise alienation and its associated consciousness, reification, in the following manner. *They* suggest that alienation stands in the same relation to reification as does *objectivation* to *objectification*. *Objectivation* is the process whereby man externalises himself—*objectification* involves the moment in the process of objectivation when man establishes distance from the producing and the product to 'take cognisance of it and to make it an object of consciousness'. So reification is understood as 'objectification in an alienated mode'. Reification for Berger and Pullberg exists when man sees his own creations as external things, as alien creations, when man as a world-producing being sees his world as an alien world of things in which he cannot recognise his self-exteriorised humanity, his own teleological labour. Berger and Pullberg state that, whilst objectivation and objectification are anthropologically necessary components of social life, alienation and reification are not anthropologically necessary components of the human condition.[9] Yet, given this ontological view of man's labour, in the course of their work they jettison this position as too radical. For when it comes to an analysis of social institutions in coercive societies such an anthropology would demand a critique. What they do in their work is to abandon the attempt to explain reification in terms of alienation and fall back on an alternative ontological position which suggests that hierarchy and reification are inevitable.

> Nor can we enter the question of the ultimate root of these processes, which we strongly suspect to lie in some *fundamental* terrors of human existence, notably the terror of chaos—which is then assuaged by the fabrication of the sort of firm order that only reifications can constitute
>
> [Berger and Pullberg, 'Reification', *New Left Review* 35, 68 (italics added)].

This switching of ontological positions at crucial theoretical moments highlights the superiority of Marx's own ontological consistency. Marx would suggest that 'class terror'—not 'fundamental terrors of human existence'—is the ultimate root of reification—the virtue of such a position being that since classes are social, they are open to study. Berger and Pullberg's, and Berger and Luckmann's publications,[10] are interesting works to compare

[9] Of course, for Marxists, objectification is the only term which will be used and which therefore could be viewed as anthropologically necessary—and alienation is only a specific mode of objectification. By distinguishing between objectification and objectivation, Berger and the writers of this tendency are dangerously near psychologism.

[10] P. Berger and T. Luckmann, *The Social Construction of Reality*, New York 1966; and Berger and Pullberg, 'Reification'.

with Marx's, for not only do they accept many of Marx's premises but they also frequently and mistakenly are taken to be 'critical' or 'radical' exercises. Their basic ontological position, however, is diametrically opposed to Marx's insistence on the teleological nature of man. As one perceptive critic has suggested, Berger and Luckmann's *Social Construction of Reality* is little more than the 'Social Construction of Unreality'.[11] One can go further and suggest that any break with Marx's ontological position does not really allow of social analysis except on the basis of reifications. Ivan Light comments, in his review of *The Social Construction of Reality* that:

> Berger and Luckmann are obsessed with a demonic vision of social uncertainty—a state of mind which seems to them basically unpalatable to social actors. Hence they postulate a kind of drive-reduction mechanism which, when uncertainty rears its head in society, causes actors to reduce or eliminate the source of their discomfort by re-establishing certainty
>
> [Light, 'Social Construction', 193].

He then elucidates their ontology with the following quotation from their book:

> The primacy of the social objectivations of everyday life can retain its subjective plausibility only if it is constantly protected against terror. On the level of meaning, the institutional order represents a shield against terror. To be anomic, therefore, means to be deprived of this shield and to be exposed, alone, to the onslaught of nightmare
>
> [Berger and Luckmann, *The Social Construction of Reality*, 102].

He goes on to demonstrate the contradictory reliance in Berger and Luckmann upon a reified view of knowledge by suggesting:

> *The logic of their own dialectic similarly requires Berger and Luckmann to transcend their own premises.* Their argument requires them to conclude that the drive for epistemological certainty will itself someday be transcended by those who have

[11] Ivan Light, 'The Social Construction of Unreality' (review article) *Berkeley Journal of Sociology* XIV (1969), 189–199.

raised themselves to the level of comprehending theoretically the historical movement as a whole. Since Berger and Luckmann have already raised themselves to this level, we might have expected that *institutionalized* uncertainty would emerge as their vision of the future.

The basic emotion of existential anxiety is, moreover, only a subjective meaning which some people attach to a universe bereft of objectively constituted meanings. This emotion is not a mirror of the objective universe expressing itself in human consciousness. Berger and Luckmann should understand this since it is based on their own repeatedly stated premise. Nonetheless, they exempt existential anxiety from the treatment they accord *all other* objectified meanings. Hence, their treatment is self-contradictory at the root. Their stated premises leave them no alternative but to conclude that the search for objectively constituted meanings is itself the basic illusion of the historical drama

[Light, 'Social Construction', 197–8].

By engaging in this comparative exercise, what we are claiming for Marx is the correctness and *consistency* of his ontological conception of the dialectics of labour. If we now turn to Marx's own writings, we can attempt to demonstrate such a *consistency*, and thereby reveal the developing unity of his works.

Value and Political Economy

In the *Economic and Philosophical Manuscripts of 1844* Marx said the following:

As we have discussed the concept of private property by an analysis of alienated labour, so with the aid of these two factors we can evolve all the categories of political economy, and in every category, e.g. trade, competition. capital, money, we shall discover only a particular and developed expression of these fundamental elements

[quoted in Erich Fromm, *Marx's Concept of Man*, New York 1961, 107].

But of course there are limitations, for although in a general sense Marx's assertions here can be upheld, it is also the case that Marx's dialectic or historical materialism is not a theory which, by itself, can lead to prediction and assessment of given social formations. Marx says the following, in a letter to L. Kugelmann, highlighting his concern to apply and operationalise his own assumptions:

> All that palaver about the necessity of proving the concept of value comes from complete ignorance both of the subject dealt with and the scientific method. Every child knows that a nation which ceased to work, I will not say for a year, but even for a few weeks, would perish. Every child knows, too, that the masses of products corresponding to the different needs require different and quantitatively determined masses of the total labour of society. That this *necessity* of the *distribution* of social labour in definite proportions cannot possibly be done away with by a *particular form* of social production but can only change the *form* in which it *appears*, is self-evident. No natural laws can be done away with. What can change, in historically different circumstances, is only the *form* in which these laws operate. And the form in which this proportional distribution of labour operates, in a state of society where the inter-connection of social labour is manifested in the *private exchange* of the individual products of labour, is precisely the *exchange value* of these products. Science consists precisely in demonstrating *how* the law of value operates
>
> [Letter of 11 July 1868, Marx–Engels *Selected Works* II, London 1950, 418–19].

But this 'science' is not a break from his early work: rather it can only be meaningfully understood as an application of his dialectics of labour. David McLellan comes *near* to this position when he suggests that: 'Marx's thought is best viewed as a continuing meditation on central themes broached in 1844'. McLellan is, in this respect doing valuable work in refuting those theorists who insist on claiming a break in Marx's work. His selections from the *Grundrisse* reveal that:

> The most striking passage of the *Grundrisse* in this respect is the draft plan for Marx's *Economics* which is couched in ... language that might have come straight out of Hegel's *Logic*. Since these sections are typical of large parts of the *Grundrisse*, several of the accounts of Marx's thought produced by scholars

of the older generation—Daniel Bell, Sidney Hook, Lewis Feuer—must now be judged to have been mistaken. It was the thesis of these writers that there was a radical break between the young and the old Marx; and that the major proof of this was held to be the absence, in the later writings, of the concept of alienation so central to the earlier writings

[*Marx's Grundrisse*, 13].

However, he also suggests:

The *Grundrisse*, while containing the themes central to the *Paris Manuscripts*, treats them in a much 'maturer' way than was possible before Marx had achieved a synthesis of his ideas on philosophy and economics [*Marx's Grundrisse*, 14].

I am not at all sure what this could mean—for Marx's theoretical genius, his 'synthesis', is his starting-point in the dialectics of labour. Of course he develops new concepts and rejects old ones. But this exercise is only meaningful if we start from the teleology of labour laid out in the *Economic and Philosophical Manuscripts*. What McLellan seems to be getting at is what Martin Nicolaus has referred to as

. . . an amusing tendency, at least in the academic circles known to me, to repeat an experiment Marx ventured when he was twenty-six, namely to try to squeeze the concept of alienated labour hard enough to make all the categories of sociology, politics and economics come dripping out of it, as if this philosopher's touchstone were a lemon. The drippings are flavorful but somewhat lacking in substance

[M. Nicolaus, 'Proletariat and Middle Class in Marx: Hegelian Choreography and the Capitalist Dialectic', *Studies on the Left* (Jan.–Feb. 1967), 40–41].

Now of course it is true that substance is derived by Marx not by rejecting his foundations but rather in developing his accounts and explanations in a detailed fashion.

Certainly it is also true that there are sharp changes in Marx's work, which it is important to understand. McLellan, for example, has argued:

From the point of view of economics, the *Grundrisse* contains the first elaboration of Marx's mature theory. There are two key changes of emphasis. Firstly, instead of analysing the market mechanisms of *exchange*, as he had done earlier, Marx now starts from a consideration of *production*. Secondly, he now says that what the worker sells is not his *labour*, but his *labour power*. It is a combination of these two views that gives rise to the doctrine of surplus value. For, according to Marx, surplus value is not created by exchange but by the fact that the development of the means of production under capitalism enables the capitalist to enjoy the use-value of the worker's labour-power and with it to produce values that far exceed the mere exchange value of this labour-power—which amounts only to food for the worker's subsistence. In fact, virtually all the elements of Marx's economic theory are elaborated in the *Grundrisse* ['Marx and the Missing Link', 42].

If there is a break in Marx, it is here—a conceptual break, not an epistemological, philosophical or ontological break. Briefly, the break is Marx's shift from merely viewing capitalism as extracting surplus from labour to his scientific demonstration of how this is based on the extraction of surplus-value, and in demonstrating that this distinguishes it from feudalism. It is not merely the existence of a market, but the way in which the market utilises and extracts value, that Marx sees as a defining feature of political economy. In Nicolaus' words:

... the shift from the market concept to the surplus concept marks in my opinion the central difference between 'Young' and 'Mature' Marxist thought ['Hegelian Choreography', 49].

Again, we repeat, this is a conceptual rather than a philosophical shift. Paul Mattick has recently argued in his excellent book on Marx and Keynes that:

Despite Hilferding's assertion, the materialist conception of history is not identical with the labor theory of value. It discusses social development in general, of which capitalism is only a special case. The labor theory of value refers to the specific social relations which operate under capital production. Capital production transforms the laboring process into a value-producing process and the social relations into economic categories. The labor theory of value does refer to the inescapable need—common to all societies—to work and to distribute the social labor in definite proportions. But this general necessity is manifested in a law of value only in capitalism, and only because the market economy cannot divorce the value-producing process from the production process itself. The law of value does not operate apart from market relations and is not a necessary requirement for the social organization of labor. But the social organization of labor is necessary for social production, and capitalism finds its answer to this need in the law of value

> [P. Mattick, *Marx and Keynes: the Limits of the Mixed Economy*, Boston 1969, 34–35].

There is, then, a unity in Marx but not a unity which explains all situations: merely a unity which provides the premises from which such explanations must begin.

Habermas' Critique of Marx's Premises

There are of course a number of critiques which attack any attempt to derive a radical social theory from premises about man. These do not concern us here. Within the Marxist tradition, however, there have been critiques of Marx which have asserted either that Marx's view of man is incomplete or that Marx's early conception of the dialectic of labour is inadequate for the task he sets himself, with the result that he lapses into positivism. Indeed if Habermas is correct, Marx's search throughout his early writings for a truly critical outlook on reality was a failure. Whatever he achieved in his later works in the way of a radical social theory was despite rather than because of his philosophical premises:

> The philosophical foundation of this materialism proves itself insufficient to establish an unconditional phenomenological self reflection of knowledge and thus prevent the positivistic atrophy of epistemology.... I see the reason for this in the *reduction of the self-generative act of the human species* to labour

> [J. Habermas, *Knowledge and Human Interests*, Boston 1971, London 1972, 42].

Habermas goes on to add:

> In his empirical analyses Marx comprehends the history of the

species under categories of material activity *and* the critical abolition of ideologies, of instrumental action *and* revolutionary practice, of labour *and* reflection at once. But Marx interprets what he does in the more restricted conception of the species' self reflection through work alone. The materialist concept of synthesis is not conceived broadly enough in order to explicate the way in which Marx contributes to realising the intention of a really radicalised critique of knowledge. In fact, it even prevented Marx from understanding his own mode of procedure from this point of view [*ibid*].

Habermas is suggesting two things at once. Firstly, that the dialectics of labour is too narrow a method for a truly radical social theory; and yet at the same time he suggests that in his empirical work, Marx frequently used other approaches, most importantly for Habermas, that of symbolic interaction:

For the analysis of the development of economic formations of society he adopts a concept of the system of social labour that contains more elements than are admitted to in the idea of a species that produces itself through social labour. Self-constitution through social labour is conceived *at the categorial level* as a process of production, and instrumental action, labour in the sense of material activity, or work designates the dimension in which natural history moves. *At the level of his material investigations*, on the other hand, Marx always takes account of social practice that encompasses both work and interaction

[Habermas, *Knowledge and Human Interests*, 52–3].

Habermas' critique of Marx depends on distinguishing between instrumental action, the control over technical and natural forces, and communicative action, the development of reflective interaction. It is a modern version of an old critique. For Habermas is suggesting that the development of the productive forces under capitalism has occurred at such a rate that they are not restrained by the class nature of these societies. By making a sharp distinction between the way the objective world is created and the way men see that world (instrumental action and communicative action) he comes to believe that work and interaction are separate categories. He is then led into the position that liberation depends on criticising ideology, the existing legitimations of distribution, inequality and power.

But Marx had already struggled with this question. In developing the dialectics of labour he showed that there was an important distinction to be drawn between the forces of production and the relations of production. Habermas accuses Marx of lapsing into a kind of scientific positivism by believing that one phenomenon can be explained in terms of another. He points out that the passive development of the productive forces towards automation in capitalism has not led to an increased freedom from ideological delusions:

> The two developments do not converge. Yet they are interdependent; Marx tried in vain to capture this in the dialectic of forces of production and relations of production. In vain— for the meaning of this 'dialectic' must remain unclarified as long as the materialist concept of the synthesis of man and nature is restricted to the categorial framework of production
> [Habermas, *Knowledge*, 55].

But Marx showed that these two developments do converge. The massive development of the productivity of labour only produced new problems for capitalism. Marx does not reduce consciousness to material conditions. What he suggests is that consciousness must be understood in terms of its potential being limited by and situated within such material conditions: Habermas is driven to revise Marxism, for he suggests that Marx reduces everything to production. But in fact it is Habermas who is reducing the propositions of Marxism to propositions about production. In Marx, the contradiction that will lead to a revolutionary consciousness is between the forces of production and the relations of production. Habermas feels that because he can show that the forces of production have developed within capitalism but without the development towards a revolutionary selfconsciousness, that Marx's premises must be too narrow. What Habermas has forgotten are the relations *of production*. In fact, Habermas' distinction between work and interaction is dialectically inferior to Marx's distinctions, which are threefold. For Marx, the relations of production are the mediation between the forces of production and consciousness. Habermas by contrast draws a distinction only between the forces of production and consciousness. The relations of production are reduced to communicative action, and included within consciousness. There is no necessary relation between instrumental and communicative action. For the time that Marx was writing, Habermas concedes that the subsystem of work was 'embedded' in the institutional framework. But he argues that in modern capitalism the two have become autonomous. There no longer exist any restrictions on the development of the productive forces, because modern industry has discovered a new source of surplus value that is independent of the labour time of workers. This is the 'scientisation of technology'. This is the *reductio ad absurdum* of Habermas' argument, for as we shall show, it removes production from man as such. It suggests that the process of production can be understood without the system of distribution. Marx of course thought otherwise:

> The mode of production of material life conditions the social, political and intellectual life process in general. It is not the consciousness of men that determines their being, but their social being that determines their consciousness. At a certain stage of their development, the material productive forces of society come into conflict with the existing relations of production.... From forms of development of the productive forces these relations turn into their fetters. Then begins an epoch of social revolution. With the change of the economic foundation the entire immense superstructure is more or less rapidly transformed. *In considering such transformations a distinction should always be made between the material transformation* of the economic conditions of production, which can be determined with the *precision of natural science,* and the legal, political, religious, esthetic or philosophic—in short, ideological forms in which *men become conscious* of this conflict and fight it out
>
> [Preface to *A Contribution to the Critique of Political Economy,* Marx–Engels, *Selected Works* I, London 1950, 329 (italics added)].

Another reason why Habermas criticises Marx's premises is that he wishes to show that the labour theory of value is no longer operative in modern capitalism, and that as a result the productive system will produce no contradictions that could give rise to a revolutionary movement. Hence all future revolutions will depend on the critique of ideologies. To show that this is not the case, and that Marx was right both in the premises he adopted and in his concentration on the political economy of capitalism, there has to be an examination of contemporary conditions, the same conditions that have led Habermas to declare Marxism outmoded in the struggle to liberate man. Habermas gives the following reasons for abandoning the labour theory of value:

> Since the end of the nineteenth century the other develop-mental tendency characteristic of advanced capitalism has become increasingly momentous: the scientization of tech-nology. The institutional pressure to augment the productivity of labour through the innovation of new technology has always existed under capitalism. But innovations depended on sporadic inventions which, while economically motivated, were still fortuitous in character. This changed as technical development entered into a feedback relation with the progress of the modern sciences. With the advent of large-scale industrial research, science, technology, and industrial utilization were fused into a system. Since then, industrial research has been linked up with research under government contract, which primarily promotes scientific and technical progress in the military sector. From there information flows back into the sectors of civilian production. *Thus technology and science become a leading productive force, rendering inoperative the conditions for Marx's labour theory of value.* It is no longer meaningful to calculate the amount of capital investment in research and development on the basis of unskilled (simple) labour power, when scientific-technical progress has become an independent source of surplus value, in relation to which the only source of surplus value considered by Marx, namely the labour power of the immediate producers, plays an ever smaller role
>
> [J. Habermas, *Towards a Rational Society*, London and Boston, Mass., 1971, 104 (italics added)].

Habermas misunderstands Marx here, for, as the description of Marx's position was intended to reveal, it is not that the labour theory of value is inoperative but rather that there is no deter-

mined prediction of proletarian revolution which can be drawn
from the theory by itself. Furthermore, as the theory anthro-
pologises the production process it cannot be that 'science' is an
independent source of value—for how could it be independent
of 'socially necessary labour' (even the most highly skilled)?
What is fascinating about this perspective on Marx is that even
if proletarian revolution is not inevitable it is nevertheless the
case (according to Marx in the *Grundrisse*) that some kind of
breakdown in capitalism (as it moves towards full automation)
is likely, since the contradiction between the *forces* and *relations*
of production, far from being overcome, are just beginning to
manifest themselves. As Marx puts it:

> To the degree that large-scale industry develops, the creation
> of real wealth comes to depend less on labour-time ... and more
> on the power of the instruments which are set in motion dur-
> ing labour-time, and whose powerful effectiveness itself is not
> related to the labour-time immediately expended in their pro-
> duction, but depends rather on the general state of science
> and the progress of technology.... Large industry reveals that
> real wealth manifests itself rather in the monstrous dispropor-
> tion between expended labour-time and its product, as well
> as in the qualitative disproportion between labour, reduced to
> a pure abstraction, and the power of the productive process
> which it supervises. Labour no longer appears as an integral
> element of the productive process; rather, man acts as super-
> visor and regulator of the productive process itself.... He
> stands at the side of the productive process, instead of being
> its chief actor. With this transformation, the cornerstone of
> production and wealth is neither the labour which man directly
> expends, nor the time he spends at work, but rather the appro-
> priation of his own collective productive power, his under-
> standing of nature ... exercised by him as a social body—in
> short, it is the development of the social individual. The theft of
> other people's labour-time, on which contemporary wealth rests,
> appears as a miserable basis compared to this new one created
> by large-scale industry itself. As soon as labour in its direct
> form has ceased to be the great well-spring of wealth, labour-
> time ceases and must cease to be its measure, and therefore
> exchange-value the measure of use-values .... With that, the

system of production based on exchange-value collapses....
Capital is its own contradiction-in-process, for its urge is to
reduce labour-time to a minimum, while at the same time it
maintains that labour-time is the only measure and source of
wealth. Thus it reduces labour-time in its necessary form in
order to augment it in its superfluous form; thus superfluous
labour increasingly becomes a precondition—a question of life
or death—for necessary labour. So on the one side it animates
all the powers of science and nature, of social co-ordination
and intercourse, in order to make the creation of wealth (relatively) independent of the labour-time expended on it. On the
other side it wants to use labour-time as a measure for the
gigantic social powers created in this way, and to restrain them
within the limits necessary to maintain already-created values
as values. Productive forces and social relations—both of
which are different sides of the development of the social
individual—appear to capital only as means, and only means
to produce on its limited basis. In fact, however, these are the
material conditions to blow this basis sky-high

> [*Grundrisse*, quoted by M. Nicolaus, 'The Unknown
> Marx', *New Left Review* 48, (Mar.-Apr. 1968), 58–59].

The contradiction in modern capitalism, then, is its measure of
labour-time and its use of labour-time. As David McLellan has so
succinctly stated, 'there are other alienations than those based
on sweated labour', and anarchy of class accumulation is one.
From its beginning in 1844, to the last volumes of *Capital*, Marxism is an exercise in applying dialectics to labour. Capitalist
science and innovation, the application of machinery, will not
save such a society—nor will it overcome alienated labour. As
Marx sarcastically noted in *Theories of Surplus Value*, the entire
bourgeois faith in science and machinery does not deny the

> ... wonderful prospect: the labouring class has to bear all the
> 'temporary inconveniences'—unemployment, displacement of
> labour and capital—*but wage-labour is nevertheless not to be
> abolished, on the contrary it will be reproduced on an ever
> growing scale, growing absolutely, even though decreasing
> relatively to the total capital which employs it*
>
> [Marx, *Theories of Surplus Value* II, London and New
> York, 1969, 572].

These all too topical developments in the dialectics of labour cry out for the free development of mankind unhindered by all the rubbish of class society. The most remarkable feature of Marxism is its ability to become more revelant each time social theorists proclaim its demise. The demise of pauperisation does not necessarily imply the death of proletarian revolution, for what we are beginning to witness is the *realisation* within society that under capitalism there can be no 'just exchange' for labour. That *any* given payment for labour time is arbitrary. It is in the wake of such consciousness that there could be not just one or two but many revolutions. In such a situation there is still the possibility that all power will pass to the people.

3

ENGELS AND SCIENTIFIC MARXISM

> It is all very well for you to talk. You can lie warm in bed and study ground rent in general and Russian agrarian conditions in particular with nothing to disturb you—but I am to sit on the hard bench, swill cold wine, suddenly interrupt everything again and get after the blood of the boring Dühring
>
> [Letter from Engels to Marx, Marx–Engels, *Correspondence*, London 1934, 342–43].

The intellectual relationship of Engels and Marx has created a great deal of discussion and controversy, which helps to raise important questions about Marxist method. On the one hand, there is the official Soviet picture of the two men as two comrades-in-arms who thought alike on all major issues, were close friends for over forty years and wrote several books together. This view means that all Engels' works, including those he published after Marx's death, are correct restatements or developments of Marx's own thoughts. This indeed is how they were treated by the socialist parties of the Second International. This is not surprising since Marx's own work was never completed and many socialists drew their understanding of it from Engels. His pamphlet, *Socialism, Utopian and Scientific*, sold 10,000 copies in Germany as soon as it was published. Engels was the first to set out clearly and concisely the basic principles of Marxism. His interpretation of Marx has therefore had enormous importance, for it is through him that many have learnt how to read Marx.

In the last fifty years he has had numerous critics. Some have blamed on Engels those elements in Marxism they wish to purge, while at the same time wishing to remain orthodox Marxists. The academic critics have generally been of two kinds. There are those who, following the publication of the 1844 manuscripts, have split Marxism into two halves. The result according to Donald Hodges is that:

Because of the association of the one Marxism with liberal values and of the other with the philosophy and scientific outlook of dialectical materialism, the young Marx has become the hero of Marx scholarship and the late Engels its villain

[D. Hodges, 'Engels' Contribution to Marxism', R. Milibrand and J. Saville (eds), *Socialist Register 1965*, 297].

Another brand of Marx scholars has reasserted the unity of Marx's work,[1] and claims that Engels' version of Marxism was a departure from the method that Marx used in both his early and his later works, and helped to create the common view of Marxism as a form of *mechanistic materialism* which stresses the inevitability of both the collapse of capitalism and the establishment of socialism.

Among Marxists who have criticised Engels, two in particular, Lukacs and Althusser, deserve study, for the light they throw on general problems of historical materialism. Lukacs' attack was delivered in *History and Class Consciousness*. Writing about the dialectical method he said:

Engels' arguments in the 'Anti-Dühring' decisively influenced the later life of the theory. However we regard them, whether we grant them classical status or whether we criticize them, deem them to be incomplete or even flawed, we must still agree that this aspect is nowhere treated in them. That is to say, he contrasts the ways in which concepts are formed in dialectics as opposed to 'metaphysics'; he stresses the fact that in dialectics the definite contours of concepts (and the objects they represent) are dissolved. Dialectics, he argues, is a continuous process of transition from one definition into the other. In consequence a one-sided and rigid causality must be replaced by interaction. But he does not even mention the most vital interaction, namely the *dialectical relation between subject and object in the historical process*, let alone give it the prominence it deserves. Yet without this factor dialectics

[1] In particular, S. Avineri, *The Social and Political Thought of Karl Marx*, Cambridge 1968.

ceases to be revolutionary . . . for it implies a failure to recognise that in all metaphysics the object remains untouched and unanalysed so that thought remains contemplative and fails to become practical: while for the dialectical method the central problem is *to change reality*

[*History and Class Consciousness*, London 1971, 3].

Lukacs therefore criticises Engels on epistemological grounds. He argues that unless science and theory are conceived as practical-critical activity, then thought is separated from being and must become either voluntaristic or fatalistic.[2] By this he means that society will be analysed as a system governed by inexorable laws in the same way as the natural world is. Socialism as a practical goal then becomes either a matter of ethics, of conscious choice (voluntarism), or an inevitability, the only possible outcome of the historical process, which will take place whatever men do (fatalism). Lukacs believes, however, that Marx's epistemology, derived from Hegel, involves neither fatalism nor voluntarism. Instead it conceives theorising as an aspect of practical-critical activity. The unique fact of social action for Lukacs is that men constitute the world through their own activity; hence the social world is not a fixed, natural system external to the individual. The individual is the social world. 'To posit oneself, to produce and reproduce oneself—that is *reality*.'[3]

But men do not experience the world as though it was their own creation, but as an external, controlling power. They appear to be confronted not by social relations but by natural relations. The task of practical-critical activity becomes to unmask the reified character of the social world, so that man can 'become conscious of himself as a social being, as simultaneously the subject and object of the socio-historical process'.[4] This possibility has been created by capitalism, which has socialised society by making all men interdependent through the division of labour, the ever-widening market, and the co-operative nature of the production process.

[2] See Lucien Goldmann, 'Is there a Marxist sociology?', *International Socialism* 34 (Autumn 1968), 13–21, for an exposition of Lukacs' position and its transcendence of voluntarism and fatalism.

[3] Lukacs, *History and Class Consciousness*, 15.

[4] Lukacs, 19.

At the same time capitalism also creates the class that alone can fully understand the great revolution in social life which the bourgeoisie has brought about:

> It was necessary for the proletariat to be born for social reality to become fully conscious. The reason for this is that the discovery of the class-outlook of the proletariat provided a vantage point from which to survey the whole of society ... the unity of theory and practice is only the reverse side of the social and historical position of the proletariat. From its own point of view self-knowledge coincides with knowledge of the whole so that the proletariat is at one and the same time the subject and object of its own knowledge [Lukacs, 19–20].

Thus Lukacs' understanding of the dialectical method and his criticism of Engels rests on his conception of theory and practice, on their fusion in practical-critical activity, which for him involves no subjective ethical choices, but is based on identification with the class situation of the proletariat, the class in society that alone can understand society and thereby transform it.

> The essence of the method of historical materialism is inseparable from the 'practical and critical' activity of the proletariat ... the dialectical materialist knowledge of reality can arise only from the point of view of a class, from the point of view of the struggle of the proletariat. To abandon this point of view is to move away from historical materialism, just as to adopt it leads directly into the thick of the struggle of the proletariat [Lukacs, 20–21].

The task that theory has in this view, is to dereify the world, that is, to unmask the 'fetishism' and the reifications which abound in society. These are created because of the rationalising character of capitalism, which standardises and homogenises social relations, thus providing the given material 'facts' of orthodox social science. But *when* these facts are seen from the standpoint of the historical process as a totality (which can only be from the standpoint of the proletariat, the first 'universal' class in history) they take on a new meaning. Thus Lukacs is proposing that the interest behind the search for knowledge of society has to be to advance the aims of the proletariat, which, because it is the 'solution to the riddle of history', supplies the criterion for deciding which ideas are true and which are false; and the proletariat as an actual group in society is deemed to be represented by the party.

Lukacs' main aim in advancing this conception of Marxism, as he himself has said, was to combat the 'purely contemplative nature of bourgeois thought' and hence 'the bourgeois and opportunistic currents in the workers' movement that glorified a conception of knowledge which was ostensibly objective but was in fact isolated from any sort of praxis'.[5] There is no doubt that he was right to see Engel's interpretation of Marx as an important reason for the rise of a positivistic Marxist science of society and nature.

Lukacs wrote of Marx's method:

> It is of the first importance to realize that the method is limited here to the realms of history and society. The misunderstandings that arise from Engels' account of dialectics can in the main be put down to the fact that Engels—following Hegel's mistaken lead—extended the method to apply also to nature. However, the crucial determinants of dialectics—the interaction of subject and object, the unity of theory and practice, the historical changes in the reality underlying the categories as the root cause of changes in thought etc.—are absent from our knowledge of nature
>
> [*History and Class Consciousness*, 24 n.].

Engels certainly believed that dialectics was a method that could be applied to society and nature equally, and that it offered laws or principles such as the transformation of quantity into quality and the negation of the negation as valid for the study of all phenomena. Dialectics he says is:

> a method of arriving at new results . . . it forces its way beyond the horizon of formal logic, it contains the germ of a more comprehensive view of the world
>
> [Engels, *Anti-Dühring*, Moscow 1954, 186].

In abstract form, this is not so different from Lukacs' view of dialectics as the instrument of dereification. What it omits, of course, from Lukacs' point of view, is to make dialectical or

[5] Lukacs, xviii. (Preface to the new edition, 1967.)

critical analysis at the same time practical activity. Engels presents dialectics always as a general scientific method, which would be true whether it was used to change society or not. He opposes dialectics to metaphysics, but both are treated as methods of enquiry, both presuppose an external world, entirely separate from consciousness:

> In nature amid the welter of innumerable changes the same dialectical laws of motion force their way through as those which in history govern the apparent fortuitousness of events
>
> [Engels, *Anti-Dühring*, 17].

Since he believes in the objective scientific status of historical materialism it comes as no surprise that he splits judgements of fact from judgements of value:

> Marx rejected the 'political, social and economic ideal' you attribute to him. A man of science has no ideals, he elaborates scientific results, and if he is also politically committed, he struggles for them to be put into practice. But if he has ideals, he cannot be a man of science, since he would then be biased from the start
>
> [Letter from Engels to Paul Lafargue, 1884: quoted by M. Godelier, *Socialist Register 1967*, 116 n.].

The weakness of this position, as Lukacs correctly saw, is that it offers no good reason why a Marxist scientist should also be politically committed. Only two positions follow logically, voluntarism and fatalism. Either socialism must be striven for because there are compelling ethical and subjective reasons which provide the ends while science provides the means of action, or socialism is inevitable, and therefore it is stupid to oppose it or to want anything else.

Lukacs tries to overcome this dilemma of applying an objective science in practice, by arguing that historical materialism as a form of knowledge can only be carried on when it is combined with practical commitment to the struggle of the proletariat, because it has no meaning and no validity outside it, and so cannot gain a true understanding of the social totality. Hence its very objectivity and truth do not belong to it as a *method* of enquiry: they do not arise from applying certain rules and following certain procedures. They only emerge when Marxist social theory is linked to the praxis of the proletariat. Since there is no objectivity outside the praxis of social groups, it follows that all social theories are class ideologies, and are relative to the class situation of the groups that propound them. But Lukacs argues that Marxism transcends the partiality and the bias of other social theories, because it is the consciousness of the proletariat, the class on whose conditions of life (wage labour), the whole social totality rests. Thus for the proletariat to become conscious of itself means that the social totality can for the first time be known, changed. Objectivity and truth depend on knowledge of the whole, and any real knowledge of society is only possible if it is linked to the praxis of a social group. The proletariat is the first class in history whose situation and praxis permit a complete knowledge of the social whole, which for Lukacs means also the historical process.

By advancing this idea of theory and praxis, however, Lukacs transforms Marxism into a social philosophy, taking as his central concept the concept of totality. The totality is the whole social world, in which praxis and theory or criticism are merely different aspects. Lukacs holds that knowledge of the totality requires that society be first dereified through criticism, in order to expose the mystifications of what appears as reality and to reveal the social world as an actual totality, all the aspects of which are organically interrelated, instead of being relatively autonomous and disconnected, as they appear in the mirror that conventional thinking holds up to society.

Such a project, however, tends to see in social relationships only relationships of 'intersubjectivity', and therefore in the end, whatever its intentions, reduces changes in reality to changes in the consciousness of reality. Once reality has been dereified by practical-critical activity, the proletariat will perceive their true interests, and understand that their historical role is to overthrow capitalism. But this is to return to the idea of *praxis* held by the Young Hegelians and Feuerbach. The result is that despite the goal and the intention of changing reality with the help of criticism, such criticism never gets beyond contemplating reality. Lukacs himself sums this up as follows:

What I failed to realize, however, was that in the absence of a basis in real praxis, in labour as its original form and model, the overextension of the concept of praxis would lead to its opposite; a relapse into idealistic contemplation

[*History and Class Consciousness*, xviii (1967 Preface)].

The reason is that there can only be one real starting point for 'practical-critical activity'. If the premises are wrong, then the attempt to link theory and practice, so that theory becomes more than just the reflection of practice, will fail. The result will be similar to what Marx criticised in Feuerbach:

the thing, reality, sensuousness, is conceived only in the form of the object or of contemplation, but not as human sensuous activity, practice, not subjectively [*Theses on Feuerbach* I].

The implication is that Feuerbach, despite his desire to change the world through criticism, was debarred from doing so by his false notion of the 'thing, reality, sensuousness'. He therefore only succeeded in restoring the barrier between contemplation and practice, and provided a theory that did not deal with human liberation at all, because it was fixed at the level of the isolated individual.

The highest point attained by contemplative materialism, that is materialism which does not comprehend sensuousness as practical activity, is the contemplation of single individuals in 'civil society'.
The standpoint of the old materialism is 'civil' society: the standpoint of the new is *human* society, or socialised humanity

[*Theses on Feuerbach* IX and X].

We should be clear what this means: Marx suggests that the premises for a materialist analysis of society determine the practical value of the results, determine, that is, not the 'objective' truth of these results in a void, but what kind of emancipating knowledge they provide. At its most basic level the choice of standpoints is between single individuals in civil society or human society, ideas that were elaborated in the 1844 manuscripts. This choice is not simply an ethical decision confined to the beginning of the research, the selection of a value in a vacuum. Many thinkers, Lukacs and Habermas among them, do actually think that they are choosing 'human society' as their standpoint, but in their actual studies they never get beyond the standpoint of the 'isolated individual', because without a grasp of the real premises of human history it is not possible to develop the concepts and the theory that will allow one to get beyond this standpoint.

What this means is that liberation cannot be discussed independently of the social and natural necessities that underlie all forms of society. It cannot be discussed in the context of capitalism without analysing the particular organisation of labour which capitalism introduces. Marx developed his labour theory of value and his analysis of the laws of motion of capital for this purpose. This is why any attempt to revise Marx's analysis of capitalism as a mode of production must seek either implicitly or explicitly to reject the labour theory of value or claim that it is no longer applicable. For any science in Marx is *dependent upon his critique of political economy*, which establishes the true 'law of value' for the capitalist mode of production.

Althusser also criticises Engels for treating dialectics as a *general* scientific method, but he is completely opposed to Lukacs' solution, which is to fuse theory with practice. For Althusser, theory is a distinct form of practice which is carried on according to its own intrinsic criteria and which produces knowledge. Like Engels, therefore, he believes that Marxism is science, and that it rigorously separates fact and value (the level of ideology). But although there is a general sense in which the social and natural sciences are one, he believes that each science is distinguished by the nature of its object, and therefore by the concepts and methods it fashions to gain knowledge of it. Thus he would agree with Marx's statement that Lukacs quotes:

In the study of economic categories, as in the case of every historical and social science, it must be borne in mind that ... the categories are ... but forms of being, conditions of existence [Lukacs, *History and Class Consciousness*, 4].

What Marxism studies are the structures of a specific social formation. What is more, its knowledge is synchronic; it is abstracted from the time dimension of practice, past, present and future. It is based on the interrelation of structures, not on the linear sequence of structures as they evolve.

But like Engels', Althusser's objective science has difficulties when it comes to establishing its criteria of validity, in particular its most central thesis, namely the determining role of the economy in society in the last instance. The easiest solution is to reduce the economic level to technology. Engels, however, always resisted this. He understood that technology, however much it might appear to embody the principle of 'matter', was itself determined by social relationships. In *Anti-Dühring* he wrote that once feudal relations had been overthrown by the new capitalist class:

> the capitalist mode of production could develop in freedom . . . since steam machinery transformed the older manufacture into modern industry, the productive forces evolved under the guidance of the bourgeoisie, developed with a rapidity and in a degree unheard of before [Moscow 1954, 370].

But he was later to become embarrassed by the widespread interpretation of Marxism as a doctrine that everything could be reduced to the economic base. The fading of his belief in an imminent revolution after the failure of 1848 led him naturally to stress the autonomy and independent development of the superstructures. This shows most clearly in his letters. He complained to Mehring about 'the fatuous notion of the ideologists that because we deny an independent historical development to the various ideological spheres which play a part in history we also deny them any effect upon history'.[6]

In similar style he wrote to Schmidt:

> If therefore Barth supposes that we deny any and every reaction of the political, etc., reflexes of the economic movement itself, he is simply tilting at windmills . . . why do we fight for the political dictatorship of the proletariat if political power is economically impotent. . . . What all these gentlemen lack is dialectic . . . the whole vast process proceeds in the form of interaction (though of very unequal forces, the economic movement being by far the strongest, most elemental and most decisive). . . . Hegel has never existed for them
>
> [Marx–Engels, *Correspondence*, 484].

[6] Marx–Engels, *Correspondence*, 512.

Thus Engels fights the critics of historical materialism by accusing them of holding a very mechanical notion of cause and effect, and not realising that causation need not be always one way. Yet in his stress on the principle of interaction, of the mutual impact of different parts of the whole, he still wishes to hold that the economic movement is the decisive one. The classic text in which he tried to solve this problem is the letter to Bloch: Engels begins by setting out the problem:

> According to the materialist conception of history the determining element in history is *ultimately* the production and reproduction of real life. More than this neither Marx nor I have ever asserted. If therefore somebody twists this into the statement that the economic element is the only determining one, he transforms it into a meaningless, abstract and absurd phrase [*Correspondence*, 475].

Engels then describes how the various superstructures influence the course of history and states:

> There is an interaction of all these elements, in which amid the endless host of accidents ... the economic movement finally asserts itself as necessary [*Correspondence*, 475].

He then gives two reasons for believing that this is the case. In the first place,

> We make our own history, but ... under very definite presuppositions and conditions. Among these the economic ones are finally decisive [*Correspondence*, 475–76].

In the second place,

> history makes itself in such a way that the final result always arises from conflicts between many individual wills, of which each again has been made what it is by a host of particular conditions of life. Thus there are innumerable, intersecting forces, an infinite series of parallelograms of forces which give rise to one resultant—the historical event
>
> [*Correspondence*, 476].

Thus, according to Engels, history is a natural process and is subject to the same laws of movement as nature. The economic movement is ultimately dominant because for each individual, economic circumstances are finally decisive, and therefore the collective 'mean' of all the actions of individuals add up to determination of history by the economy.

Althusser considers that in this second reason that he gives, Engels slips back into a pre-Marxist ideology, the ideology of Hobbes, Locke, Helvetius, Smith and Ricardo, whose starting point is 'the confrontation of these famous *individual wills* which are by no means the starting-point for reality, but for a *representation* of reality, for a *myth* intended to provide a basis...in nature ... for *the objectives* of the bourgeoisie'.[7]

Engels embraces a new version of the notion of a 'General Will' by believing that

the resultant of all the individual wills, and the resultant of these resultants, actually has a *general content*, really embodies determination *by the economy in the last* instance

[Althusser, *For Marx*, 125].

This is an excellent critique of Engels' solution to his problem of finding a basis for historical materialism. But Althusser himself fails to grasp the significance of his own critique. His solution to the problem is to deny that the problem exists at all, so long as the analyst remains at the level of science and does not seek a basis for his science at any other theoretical level, for example philosophy, in which he includes philosophical anthropology. But this sidesteps the whole problem of what is to count as science and how its concepts can be validated. Althusser writes:

every scientific discipline is based at a *certain level*, precisely that level at which *its concepts find a content*.... Such is the level of Marx's *historical theory*; the level of the concepts of *structure, superstructure and all their specifications*. But if the same scientific discipline should set out from *another level than its own*, from a level in which is not the object of *any scientific knowledge* ... then it will fall into an epistemological void, or ... into a *philosophical fullness* [*For Marx*, 127].

The validation of the theory is to be sought instead in the 'effectivity of the structure in its effects'. But as we argue at length elsewhere in this book, this principle offers no clear working

[7] L. Althusser, *For Marx*, London 1969, 125.

solution to the problem of verification. Hence it cannot establish Marxism as an objective science. It is Althusser's science that is floating in an epistemological void (though hardly in a philosophical fullness). He accepts Engels' principle that the economic movement is ultimately dominant but likewise he cannot establish it, since he believes that any anthropological premises are ideological because they are always atomistic, they rest on the isolated individual and his experience.

He therefore fails to grasp one of Marx's most fundamental achievements, the fact that Marx's conception of man is not atomistic.

> Man is a *zoon politikon* in the most literal sense; he is not only a social animal, but an animal that can be individualised only within society. Production by a solitary individual outside society ... is just as preposterous as the development of speech without individuals who live *together* and talk to one another
>
> [Marx, *Contribution to the Critique of Political Economy*, London 1971, 189].

Furthermore, a conception of man and nature and their interaction is indispensable for a study of the various modes of production that have existed in history:

> All periods of production ... have certain features in common: they have certain common categories. ... It is necessary to distinguish those definitions which apply to production in general, in order not to overlook the essential differences existing despite the unity that follows from the very fact that the subject, mankind, and the object, nature, are the same
>
> [Marx, *Contribution*, 190].

Yet this is not to reduce all history to the unfolding of the essence of a subject as Althusser fears. It is not teleological in that sense. Marx states that 'it is ... wrong to consider society as a single subject, for this a speculative approach'.[8] It is merely to understand the 'dialectics of labour', the characteristics of man in general, and production in general, the general form of all history.

Engels himself approached the solution to his problem when

---

[8] Marx, *Contribution*, 199.

he told Bloch that 'we make our own history but under very definite presuppositions and conditions'. But he seems to favour establishing the dominance of the economic elements empirically, in actual historical analysis, without realising that this by itself, however important, is not sufficient.[9] He seems debarred from understanding the real premises of Marx's method because he seeks to make Marxism an objective science on the model of the natural sciences. It is characteristic that, in the passage quoted above, he tries to establish the truth of historical materialism by treating human interaction as analogous to the interaction of chemical particles.

Such a view of science leads naturally to a social technology. Marxism gives men knowledge to control both social and natural law. Thus Engels conceives socialism as man's exercise of technical control over society, just as he already exercises technical control over nature:

> Active social forces work exactly like natural forces: blindly, forcibly, destructively, so long as we do not understand, and reckon with them. But when once we understand them, when once we grasp their action, their direction, their effects, it depends only upon ourselves to subject them more and more to our own will, and by means of them to reach our own ends [Engels, *Anti-Dühring*, 387].

Socialism becomes primarily liberation from the anarchy and waste of capitalist production. Engels understandably had great enthusiasm for modern science and technology, and the opportunities they gave for the elimination of poverty, and this is why he sometimes makes the freeing of the productive forces and their scientific and rational organisation (free from the capitalist trade cycle) the main feature of the future socialist society. The other side, the liberation of man, the overcoming of the alienation imposed by wage labour, can also be found in Engels' writings, but generally as a subsidiary theme. The productive forces came first, and in his mind socialism was obviously one with the developing revolution in science and technology. He was par-

[9] This is the view that predominates in his letters to Schmidt, August 5 1890, October 27 1890; to Bloch, September 21–22 1890; to Mehring, July 14 1893; and to Starkenburg, January 25 1894.

ticularly sour, therefore, about revolutionaries who perceived a certain tension between the ways in which modern technology is organised in factories and human liberation:

> If man, by dint of his knowledge and inventive genius, has subdued the forces of nature, the latter avenge themselves upon him by subjecting him, in so far as he employs them, to a veritable despotism independent of all social organization. Wanting to abolish authority in large scale industry is tantamount to wanting to abolish industry itself, to destroy the power loom in order to return to the spinning wheel
>
> [Engels, 'On Authority', Marx–Engels, *Selected Works* I, London 1950, 576].

He also believed that social harmony and the elimination of conflict depended in a very direct way on changing material conditions:

> In a society in which all motives for stealing have been done away with, in which therefore at the most only lunatics would ever steal, how the preachers of morals would be laughed at who tried solemnly to proclaim the eternal truth: Thou shalt not steal [Engels, *Anti-Dühring*, 387].

In such passages Engels tends to express himself in the manner of the old materialists who believed that man was simply a product of material conditions and that to change them was also to change man. It is no surprise then to find that, the more he appreciated the difficulty and complexity of the productive forces (the material conditions), the more cautious he grew about the arrival of socialism, which at the end of his life he pictured as a long slow process, and contrasted it with his earlier belief that it was imminent.

In 1895 in a new preface to Marx's *Class Struggles in France* we find Engels writing about the 1848 revolution:

> History has proved us, and all who thought like us, wrong. It has made it clear that the state of economic development on the Continent at that time was not by a long way ripe for the removal of capitalist production; it has proved this by the economic revolution which, since 1848, has seized the whole of the Continent, has really caused big industry for the first time to take root. . . .

At that time the masses, sundered and differing according to locality and nationality, linked only by the feeling of common suffering, undeveloped, tossed to and fro in their perplexity from enthusiasm to despair; today the *one* great international army of Socialists, marching irresistibly on and growing daily in number, organization, discipline, insight and certainty of victory. If even this mighty army of the proletariat has still not reached its goal, if, a long way from winning victory with one mighty stroke, it has slowly to press forward from position to position in a hard, tenacious struggle, this only proves, once and for all, how impossible it was in 1848 to win social transformation by a simple surprise attack

[Marx–Engels, *Selected Works* I, 115–16].

To some extent the same change in political outlook can be seen in Marx also. But there is an important difference. Engels' attitude followed naturally from his view of historical materialism as the almost physical science of society which discovered the social laws that once known gave man control over his society and his organisation of production:

Only conscious organisation of social production, in which production and distribution are carried on in a planned way, can elevate mankind above the rest of the animal world socially in the same way that production in general has done this for men specifically

[Engels, 'Introduction to the Dialectics of Nature', in Marx–Engels, *Selected Works* II, 75–76].

The change in Engels' writings and in his political judgements is very much the change that Althusser and his followers claim to find in Marx—namely a sharp break between a philosophical and a scientific problematic. It is interesting to look at Engels' early writings in this connection, in particular the two works that Marx mentions in his Preface to the *Contribution to the Critique of Political Economy*:

Frederick Engels, with whom I maintained a constant exchange of ideas by correspondence since the publication of his brilliant essay on the critique of economic categories ... arrived by another road at the same result as I (compare his Lage der Arbeitenden Klasse in England ...) [London 1971, 22].

The essay on the critique of economic categories is the 'Outlines of a Critique of Political Economy', published in 1844. In this article, Engels subjects the categories of political economy, such as land, labour, capital, value and so forth, to a thoroughgoing critique; only it is a critique undertaken from an explicit moral position, namely the fundamental immorality of the economic system which political economy describes. The basic point of his critique is that an economy based on private property necessarily involves the robbery of the weak by the strong, and the means by which this is achieved is competition. In former societies, the role of force and power in determining both the exchange and the distribution of wealth had been no secret. Even mercantilism, which believed that national wealth depended on the size of a country's balance of payments surplus, 'had a certain Catholic candour and did not in the least conceal the immoral nature of trade. We have seen how it openly paraded its mean avarice'.[10] But with the advent of the 'Luther' of political economy, Adam Smith, and his followers, trade was eulogised as both humane and beneficial to all parties, because it expands production, breaks down local monopolies, makes men interdependent and helps to stop wars. But all this is done, says Engels, only so that 'the one great basic monopoly, property, may function the more freely and unrestrictedly'.[11]

Engels then analyses the result of making the institution of private property the unconcealed premise of political economy. Its immediate consequence is that production is split into two opposing sides—the natural and the human, or land and labour. Human activity is then split into labour and capital (stored-up labour). 'Thus already we had the struggle of these three elements against one another, instead of their mutual support.'[12] To these three elements in production correspond three classes. Two of the elements, land and capital, have been monopolised by particular social groups and so turned into private property. Instead of the productive process being controlled by all the producers,

[10] Engels, 'Outlines of a Critique of Political Economy', K. Marx *Economic and Philosophical Manuscripts of 1844*, Moscow 1959, 161–191, 166.

[11] 'Outlines of a Critique', 167.

[12] 'Outlines of a Critique', 177.

we have competition between the three classes for control of the social product:

> The functions of these three elements are completely different, and are not to be measured by a fourth common standard. Therefore, when it comes to dividing the proceeds among the three elements under existing conditions, there is no inherent standard; it is an entirely alien and fortuitous standard that decides—competition, the slick right of the stronger
>
> ['Outlines of a Critique,' 176].

The landlords and capitalists win in the struggle, because their accumulated rents and profits allow them to survive for much longer than the labourers who have only a subsistence wage.

Thus, for Engels, it is competition that is the source of immorality, for it means that social wealth is distributed according to social power and not according to the value which each class contributes to production:

> Because private property isolates everyone in his own crude solitariness, and because, nevertheless, everyone has the same interests as his neighbour, one landowner stands antagonistically confronted by another, one capitalist by another, one worker by another. In this discord of identical interests resulting precisely from this identity is consummated the immorality of mankind's condition hitherto; and this consummation is competition ['Outlines of a Critique', 177].

The nature of competition means that there is a continual disjunction betwen demand and supply, and so continual trade crises. In this whirlpool of fluctuating prices, says Engels, everyone is forced to become a speculator, whether it is his labour or some other commodity that he is selling, and must try to sell at the most favourable opportunity. The result is that there is no longer any possibility of exchange and distribution based on a moral foundation, i.e., exchange on the basis of 'real' value as opposed to exchange value. By 'real' value Engels means costs of production plus the utility of a good.

But it is in Malthus's theory of population, declares Engels, that 'we have the immorality of the economist brought to its highest pitch'.[13] For, because he takes the existing class structure

[13] 'Outlines of a Critique' 184.

of society based on private property as unalterable, Malthus blames the periodic 'overpopulation' of the country, which is created by the unemployment during slumps in trade, on the poor. He therefore proposes to make poverty a crime, to put a compulsory limit on workers' families and so forth. Engels comments:

> It is just this theory which is the keystone of the liberal system of free trade, whose fall entails the downfall of the entire edifice. For if here competition is proved to be the root cause of misery, poverty, and crime, who then will still dare to speak up for it? ['Outlines of a Critique', 184].

We are not here concerned with the concept of competition, which, as Martin Nicolaus shows,[14] was discarded by both Marx and Engels as the key concept in explaining capitalism when Marx developed the theory of surplus value, but rather with the methods and the assumptions that Engels employs in this article. He criticises political economy from an ethical position, from the standpoint of the human species as a whole, and from this standpoint what appears so immoral about the new exchange economy is that it divides men into distinct social groups who struggle with one another for their own advantage. It makes egoism the basic and necessary principle of human conduct. But at the same time, the economist 'does not know that by his dissolution of all sectional interests he merely paves the way for the great transformation to which the century is moving—the reconciliation of mankind with nature and itself'.[15]

Now in language and conclusions this article finds many echoes in Marx's early work. But we must also note the crucial difference. Whilst Marx uses the problematic and the method of the young Hegelians, what emerges are the concrete premises that direct all his later work. Engels' use of Feuerbach's 'transformative method' does not move in such a direction. It remains merely an intelligent application of this method. He criticises political economy because it is abstract—it does not start from

---

[14] M. Nicolaus, 'The Hegelian Choreography and the Capitalist dialectic', *Studies on the Left* 7 (Jan.–Feb. 1967).

[15] Engels, 'Outlines of a Critique', 168.

real, concrete premises. For example, it starts from private property instead of from labour, and this means that competition is treated as a natural law instead of as the product of a social institution.

But Engels' 'materialist' premises remain very opaque. They amount to a recognition that man has to be the starting-point for an investigation into the nature of social reality, and that man cannot be explained without reference to his material conditions of existence. But Engels is not led on, as Marx was, to inquire into the general, distinguishing characteristics of human activity as such, which alone can form the basis and define the area for the study of human history. Instead these material conditions, which form his starting-point, are those that actually exist and have been mystified by political economy. His next work, *The Condition of the Working Class in England*, therefore, continues the demystification through an empirical study of the material conditions of the English workers that have been created by competitive capitalism. As he himself admitted in a later preface to a new edition, the book 'exhibits everywhere the traces of the descent of socialism from one of its ancestors, German philosophy'.[16]

The book reads as a polemic against unjust conditions, and a call to revolution. It combines moral criticisms of existing reality with a belief in the imminent uprising of the oppressed because of their destitution.

Communism rises above the enmity of classes, for it is a movement that embraces all humanity and not merely the working classes.

The war of poor against rich in England... will (before long) be openly waged by the whole of the proletariat. It is too late for the parties concerned to reach a peaceful solution. The gulf between the two classes is becoming wider and wider. The workers are becoming more and more imbued with the spirit of resistance. The feelings of the proletariat against their oppressors are becoming more and more bitter ... soon it will

[16] Engels, 1892 preface to *The Condition of the Working Class in England*, Marx–Engels, *Selected Works* II, 372.

only be necessary to dislodge a stone and the whole avalanche will be set in motion.

[Engels, *The Condition of the Working Class in England*, ed. W. O. Henderson and W. H. Chaloner, Oxford 1958, 335–36].

What is significant in this is not so much the prediction of revolution, as the kind of analysis that underlies it, when it is compared with Engels' later writings. His intellectual progress contains much more of a sharp break than does that of Marx. From philosophical criticism—the measuring of existing reality against ethical principles—he transferred to the scientific analysis of capitalism as a natural process, following his collaboration with Marx on the *German Ideology*. From understanding materialism as an ethical doctrine which proclaimed that all analysis must start from man, and that freedom lay in how the material conditions of social life were organised, Engels came to see materialism as the general science of nature and history which uncovered the laws that governed the operation of both. The link between the two is that Engels ultimately understood the materialist conception of history as resting directly on an empirical foundation; in his early writings, the actual material conditions of the workers; in his later work, the dialectical laws that could be observed working in history and nature alike.

What we see in his later work are constant attempts to apply the materialist conception of history to actual history and to current political situations. His work in formalising Marx's theories into a doctrine that could interpret the whole of political reality was very important for the survival of Marxism. But at the same time he both extended and altered Marx's own method. Marx himself after the early 1850s wrote no full-length historical studies. Instead he discovered and elaborated the concept that gave him a general model of the capitalist mode of production, its laws of motion and its limits. Engels very much saw his task as showing to socialists the importance of Marx's discoveries, by revealing how they could be used to analyse existing societies.

But he attempted this in part by trying to show that Marxism was a science of such scope that it provided a new world outlook, because it could make sense of all phenomena, whether natural or social. It replaced philosophy as the new key to reality and the new source of knowledge.[17] This explains the importance that he placed on Darwin. Whereas for Marx Darwin finally laid to rest the theological notion that there could be any teleology in nature outside man, Engels interpreted Darwin in a much broader way as showing that the same dialectical laws that control human society also controlled all other forms of life.

But like many other scientists who try to assimilate social to natural science, Engels had much difficulty in deriving the dialectical laws of society with the same ease that natural scientists appear to derive laws of nature. Marx's own theory has two levels —his discussion of the real premises of human history, of what distinguishes man from animals, and his analysis of the specific forms which actual human history has taken, which becomes an analysis of different modes of production. There are no dialectical laws as such, only particular laws or tendencies that belong to particular modes of production. Hence it is misleading to refer to Marx's theory as a philosophy of history,[18] since this is often taken to mean that Marx identifies dialectical laws that are at work in history pushing society towards communism. All that Marx does indicate is that in terms of realising the abstract potentialities of man (as contained in the definition of human action), the development of the forces of production under capitalism offer greater opportunities than ever before. This means that the 'objective meaning' he discerns in history is not a determined sequence of stages, nor the temporal unfolding of some ahistorical essence. Rather it is an understanding of the limits and possibilities that are inherent in human activity itself, i.e., it is a particular conception of what constitutes human rationality. It is not possible to write any history without such conception,

[17] Engels, 'Ludwig Feuerbach and the end of classical German Philosophy', in Marx–Engels, *Selected Works* II, 324–64.

[18] This is the main failing in an otherwise excellent account of historical method in Marx and Engels in three articles by Leonard Krieger: 'The uses of Marx for History', *Political Science Quarterly*, vol. LXXV, no. 3 (1960); 'Marx and Engels as Historians', *Journal of the History of Ideas*, vol. 14, no. 381 (June 1953); 'Editor's Introduction' to F. Engels *The German Revolution*, Chicago 1967, ix–xlvi.

though so blinkered is the practice of historians that they are often not aware of the conception they are applying.

So the question is not whether to discern an objective meaning in history, a meaning that is not available to the makers of that history, *but which to choose*. Only confusion results, however, if this objective meaning is then turned into a series of dialectical laws of motion. This is the mistake that Engels frequently makes. What he then finds of course is that relating 'actual' history to these dialectical laws is a Herculean task. Interpreting history in terms of a dialectical scheme is much easier than substantive analysis and explanation:

> Our conception of history is above all a guide to study, not a lever for construction *à la* Hegelianism. All history must be studied afresh, the conditions of existence of the different formations of society must be examined in detail before the attempt is made to deduce from them the political, civil-legal, aesthetic, philosophic, religious, etc., notions corresponding to them. Up to now but little has been done here because only a few people have got down to it seriously. In this field we can utilise heaps of help, it is immensely big . . .
>
> [Engels to Schmidt, in *Selected Works* II, 442].

Yet he still contrasts the 'historical' and 'logical' methods:

> The logical method of treatment . . . is nothing else than the historical method, only divested of its historical form and disturbing fortuities . . . (it) will be nothing else than the mirror image of the historical course in abstract and theoretically consistent form [Marx–Engels, *Selected Works* I, 339].

Historical analysis then has to account for the accidents, that is, for everything that does not fit in with the dialectical laws. But these accidents also happen to comprise most of history:

> History has its own course, and as dialectically as it may finally turn out, still dialectic must often enough wait long enough upon history
>
> > [Engels, 'Dialectics of Nature', quoted by L. Krieger in his introduction to Engels, *The German Revolution*, xxii].

But this is to admit that dialectics isn't of much help in analysing historical situations. And it was precisely this inadequacy that led Engels to start abandoning dialectical laws altogether in his historical studies. Instead he tried to show how all the various kinds of human activity, subsumed under the labels base and superstructure, were empirically related in the historical movement. This meant acknowledging the independent role of the superstructures, though Engels naturally still wished to assert that the economic base had greater importance. The phrase 'as dialectically as it may finally turn out' has the same role as 'the economic movement finally asserts itself as necessary'. Engels comes to see the materialist conception of history as a heuristic principle.[19] As a result he wrote some valuable history, but at the cost of not being able to establish this method as really distinctive from that of orthodox historians. Since he believed in the unity of science, he believed that there was one correct method of verification of theoretical principles, experiment:

> The empiricism of observation can never suffice to prove necessity. Post hoc, but not propter hoc.... But the proof of necessity lies in human activity, in experiment, in labour. If I can produce the post hoc, it becomes identical with the propter hoc
>
> [Engels, 'Dialectics of Nature', quoted by Krieger, *The German Revolution*, xxviii].

But once again, facts in the past cannot be established as correct by experiment in the present, and the problem of using actual practice as a test for the present and future is to know what a particular outcome means for a theory, whether it invalidates it or not. The belief that a scientific politics can be created by applying an objective science to practice is thus even at this level a chimera.

[19] Cf Engels to Starkenburg, *Correspondence*, 517–518. 'Men make their history themselves, only in given surroundings that condition it and on the basis of actual relations already existing, among which the economic relations, however much they may be influenced by the other political and ideological ones, are still ultimately the decisive ones, forming the red thread which runs through them and alone leads to understanding.'

Marx himself never juxtaposed historical and logical analysis in the ways that Engels did. His dialectical laws of movement are not actual historical laws working behind historical events. They are tendencies drawn from a particular model of the economic system, which rests on particular assumptions. Marx states frequently that the working of these tendencies in reality is modified by many factors that do not however concern him in his present analysis. This suggests a quite distinct approach when making concrete historical, sociological or economic analyses. It is not a question of making the 'facts' fit the logic of a dialectical scheme; or finding explanations when they don't. Instead it provides a framework, a means of stating problems and of developing the necessary concepts and theory that will allow concrete analysis.

Engels' idea of the materialist conception of history, though he partly avoided its consequences in his own historical writing, did great damage to the development of Marxism as a tool for investigating and understanding social reality, and aided its transformation into a doctrine that merely sees in reality the reflection of its own dialectical laws. Lukacs and Althusser correctly criticise him, Lukacs because he left out the practical interest of the theory, and Althusser because he failed to see the difference in the objects of knowledge of social and natural science, and because he failed to establish the principle of economic determination in the last instance. But in another sense they share with Engels a common misunderstanding of Marx's method and Marx's premises. They recreate the unnecessary dilemma between Marxism as an objective science and Marxism as a social philosophy. The excesses of the Lukacs tradition in Marxism are well known. The implications of Althusser's theory are already becoming apparent with its transformation into a doctrine that provides a set of rigorous categories with which reality can be boxed and labelled, rather than understood.

Engels himself was worried about the use to which 'scientific' Marxism was being put. He complained to Schmidt:

> In general the word 'materialistic' serves many of the younger writers in Germany as a mere phrase with which anything and everything is labelled without further study; they stick on this label and then think the question disposed of ... too many of the younger Germans simply make use of the phrase, his-

torical materialism ... in order to get their own relatively scanty historical knowledge ... fitted together into a neat system as quickly as possible, and they then think themselves something very tremendous [Marx–Engels, *Correspondence*, 473].

4

HERBERT MARCUSE

Thus simultaneously with the publication of *One-Dimensional Man* (1964), Marcuse found in the Movement both an emerging practical refutation of some of his claims regarding the closed, oppositionless character of the ruling society and an emerging realization of some of the utopian 'political-erotic' concepts formulated in *Eros and Civilisation* (1955) and he began to direct his own energies increasingly toward the New Left

> [Paul Breines, 'From Guru to Spectre: Marcuse and the Implosion of the New Left', in Paul Breines (ed.), *Critical Interruptions: New Left Perspectives on Herbert Marcuse*, New York 1970, 8].

Only Marcuse has tried to speak the unspeakable in an increasingly urgent effort to reintroduce a utopian cast to socialist theory. *Eros and Civilisation* was his first attempt to outline the contours of the society beyond repressive domination. The *Essay on Liberation* goes even further in explicitly stating the need for a new philosophical anthropology, a frankly 'biological foundation' for socialism

> [Martin Jay, 'Marx's Utopia', *Radical America* vol. 4, no. 3 (April 1970), 21].

Thoroughly objectionable is 'elementary state education' ... it would be much better to preclude the government and the church equally from any influence on the schools ... and there is no help to be got from the rotten evasion that this is a question of a 'State of the future'—the state has need on the contrary of a very rude education by the people

> [Karl Marx, *Critique of the Gotha Programme*, London 1933, 48].

Herbert Marcuse is one of the few Marxist theorists to have been pushed by the media into the consciousness of the public at large. From the esoteric reaches of the Frankfurt school of critical theory he was suddenly and incorrectly flung at the masses as the prophet of the student revolt. Incorrectly, for it was not until his *Essay on Liberation* was published in 1969 that Marcuse clearly identified student militants as a catalytic force of any consequence. In fact from one perspective Marcuse's work is largely an exercise in the dialectics of pessimism. For whilst Marcuse regards the future as the 'link between philosophy and the real history of mankind' for him it is clear that the future is a demand, not an inevitability. A large part of his work is really a corrective to the unthinking optimism which characterises much that passes for Marxism.

Marcuse seems to regard his work as an exercise in 'critical theory'. We examine Marcuse in this essay precisely because his is the most readily available and developed form of 'critical theory' at present influencing Marxists. Moreover, we hope to show that Marcuse's failings as a critical theorist raise a number of the problems that serious theoretical Marxists must now face. How else do we explain student revolts, the rise of a 'middle class'; is Marxism more than metaphysics, is it a science? The answers to these questions are hinted at, and confronted, in various essays in this book, and it is therefore fitting that our first exercise in criticising existing Marxism should assess the leading 'critical theorist' of our time.

Now what is this 'critical theory'? Marcuse suggests what he means by it in an early and magnificent book on *Reason and Revolution*. This work is a thorough polemic against 'positivism', the view that sociology or social theorising is a question of describing the 'facts out there'. Critical theory, argues Marcuse, points to the possibilities inherent in reality which these so-called 'facts' deny. Thus critical theory associates itself with the people in our society who are denied a radically different future. Critical theory is seen as the consciousness of ways in which the world is changing and could be changed.

Yet despite the radical implications of such a position many

of the Frankfurt school[1] were and are still orientated to developing theories of society which can explain in almost social-psycho-
logical terms why it is that the proletariat remains 'falsely conscious'. The lacuna in Marx's work is thus seen as residing in his
account of repression. The work of critical theory is, following
this view, limited to looking for theoretical accounts of the
reasons why men remain deprived yet happy in advanced industrial societies. Marcuse, along with many of his generation of
German Marxists, turned to psychoanalytic theories to bolster up
what they derived from Marx. It is no surprise, therefore, that
much of this work should be an unhappy amalgam of pessimism
and optimism, pessimistic because the agency of revolution, the
proletariat, is abandoned, optimistic in that it concentrates upon
the potential wonders which true liberation will bring forth.
Russell Jacoby, commenting upon this feature of Marcuse's work,
writes that

> *Eros and Civilisation* by Marcuse's own admission is an opti-
> mistic book, sketching the possibilities of a liberated society;
> but it is also his most pessimistic book, not in tone, but in the
> analysis of the 'dialectic of civilisation' that has condemned all
> progress, all revolutions, to betray their promise. Counter-
> revolution is defined by more than external might. Marcuse
> follows the earlier Reich; it is biologically anchored in the re-
> volutionaries themselves.... Marcuse's formulations of pos-
> sible forms of Eros in *Eros and Civilisation* are as optimistic
> as his analysis is pessimistic. The same *Eros and Civilisation*
> contains a defence of Freud's pessimism against the confi-
> dence and the good cheer of the neo-Freudians
>
> [Russell Jacoby, 'Reversals and Lost Meanings',
> Breines, *Critical Interruptions*, 71–72].

The dangers in this position are apparent, namely that one can
easily slip from social analysis into psychologism or even biologism. Indeed this is partly the road that Marcuse has travelled.
This outcome is related to a general fault of this type of theorising, namely its tendency to avoid detailed Marxist economic

---

[1] We refer here to that German tradition starting in Frankfurt which,
with the help of Marcuse, Adorno, Horkheimer and others, developed
into what is referred to as the 'Frankfurt School of Critical Theory'.

assessments of changes in reality. Such theory abandons Marx's scientific work on the labour theory of value and seeks to resolve the problem of the 'happy proletariat' by incorporating the work of theorists such as Freud, whose image of man and society is not only foreign to but largely incompatible with that of Marx.

This attempted marriage by Marcuse of Marx and Freud will be examined and rejected here, for it treats concepts integral to each thinker's project with disdain. Ripping terms out of both theories, as he does, Marcuse makes them come to mean exactly what he wants them to mean; indeed this manner of theorising gives no guarantee as to the authenticity of such concepts, either in the works of Marx and Freud or their applicability to society at large. It can lead to little and is merely a justification for whatever position Marcuse wishes to adopt.

Central to Marcuse's 'Marxism' is the manner in which he recasts Freud. In fact what Marcuse does to Freud governs his whole conception of the nature of industrial society. If one were to be unpleasant it could be argued that the reverse is also the case. Now for Freud civilisation was founded upon repression. It is therefore apparent that if Marcuse wishes to utilise Freud within a Marxist framework he must show the possibility of a non-repressive civilised society. As Alasdair MacIntyre suggests, to do this he must alter Freud in two crucial ways:

> For Freud himself therefore, the theory of society is founded upon two contrasts, that between freedom and happiness and that between sexuality and civilisation. The contrast between freedom and happiness is founded on the fact that for Freud liberation is essentially liberation from the hold that the instinctual desires of infancy and the fixations resulting from the encounter of those desires with the external world still combine to impose upon us. But such liberation depends upon the ego with its grasp of the reality principle having displaced from its sovereignty the instinctual id with its commitment to the pleasure principle. Where the id was, there ego shall be. So the pleasure principle cannot govern the life of the free individual [Alasdair MacIntyre, *Marcuse*, London 1970, 44].

Now Marcuse must obviously reject this view, for, as MacIntyre correctly states, his concern is to link freedom and happiness. As

we shall see, what Marcuse does is to invent the concept of 'repressive desublimation'. In *Eros and Civilisation*, he characterises society as dependent upon *surplus repression* but in *One-
Dimensional Man* the notion that repression is unnecessary seems
in need of more theoretical justification and he takes Freud on
his own ground and comes up with the alternative of 'repressive
desublimation'. We may remember that, for Freud, sublimation
is a deflection of sexual energy which cannot be released in its
own sphere into another sphere (usually higher, since mere deflection is displacement). Desublimation is therefore, and logically, the return of sexuality to its native environment where it
achieves satisfaction. The drive is fulfilled. Now because Marcuse wants to argue that industrial capitalism is repressive, he
alters the concept of desublimation by talking about repressive
desublimation. From this viewpoint sexuality is released as sexuality but·in modes and forms which reduce and weaken erotic
energy in a channelled, all-pervasive, permissive, trivial sexist
fashion. Thus although the drives seem fulfilled they are in reality
confined. Marcuse also, and more mystically, argues that in this
kind of society libidinal gratification becomes subordinate to the
death instinct; all of this in short means that it is not civilisation
which leads to discontents but capitalism which promotes and
allows of only limited expression of our basic instincts and drives.
In *Eros and Civilisation* Marcuse indicates his grounds for
rejecting Freud's equation of civilisation and repression as
follows:

But Freud's own theory provides reasons for rejecting his identification of civilisation with repression. On the ground of his
own theoretical achievements, the discussion of the problem
must be reopened. Does the interrelation between freedom and
repression, productivity and destruction, domination and progress, really constitute the principle of civilisation? Or does
this interrelation result only from a specific historical organisation of human existence? In Freudian terms, is the conflict
between pleasure principle and reality principle irreconcilable
to such a degree that it necessitates the repressive transformation of man's instinctual structure? Or does it allow
the concept of a non-repressive civilisation, based on a fundamentally different experience of being, a fundamentally dif-

ferent relation between man and nature, and fundamentally different existential relations?

The notion of a non-repressive civilisation will be discussed not as an abstract and utopian speculation. We believe that the discussion is justified on two concrete and realistic grounds; first, Freud's theoretical conception itself seems to refute his consistent denial of the historical possibility of a non-repressive civilisation, and second, the very achievements of repressive civilisation seem to create the preconditions for the gradual abolition of repression

[Herbert Marcuse, *Eros and Civilisation*, London 1969, 24].

Following his discussion of repression and its effects on culture and work in *Eros and Civilisation*, Marcuse moves pessimistically onward in *One-Dimensional Man* to discuss the ideology and nature of advanced capitalism. He himself states that the book is ambiguous:

One-Dimensional Man will vacillate throughout between two contradictory hypotheses: (1) that advanced industrial society is capable of containing qualitative change for the foreseeable future; (2) that forces and tendencies exist which may break this containment and explode the society. . . . The first tendency is dominant, and whatever preconditions for a reversal may exist are being used to prevent it

[Herbert Marcuse, *One-Dimensional Man; The Ideology of Industrial Society*, London 1969, 13].

Yet its conclusions are not ambiguous. They are clear and tragic even at the theoretical level. For Marcuse states that

The critical theory of society possesses no concepts which could bridge the gap between the present and its future; holding no promise and showing no success, it remains negative

[*One-Dimensional Man*, 201].

We shall examine in this essay the tortuous route by which Marcuse arrives at such a position and its partial rejection in his *Essay on Liberation*. But we may state part of our assessment in advance; the reason for his peculiar brand of Marxist pessimism follows not so much from his analysis of modern society as it

does from his conception of critical theory and the misunderstanding of Marx's dialectics of labour which are involved in his
conception of such a theory. For Marcuse presents us with a
model of late capitalism which sees social processes as determined by almost supra-social technological or biological forces.
As a result Marcuse has no analysis of the contradictions built
into a society founded on class relationships. His model of society
removes the human agency as such and revises Marx's theory of
human activity and consciousness.

Critical Theory

At the end of *One-Dimensional Man*, Marcuse saw only one
chance of revolutionary protest and that was 'nothing but a
chance'. The chance was that 'the substratum of the outcasts
and outsiders, the exploited and persecuted of other races and
other colours, the unemployed and the unemployable', might
turn to radical action. This would involve a meeting of 'the
most advanced consciousness of humanity and its most exploited force'. But the critical theory of society can give us no
grounds for predicting that this will happen; indeed it is of the
essence of critical theory that it cannot predict

[Alasdair MacIntyre, *Marcuse*, 87].

MacIntyre is overstating his case here, yet there is some truth
behind his position. Critical theory as understood and expounded
by Marcuse seems to have little legitimate reason for making or
justifying predictions. We argue elsewhere in this book that
Marx was aware of this problem and provided in his ontological
premises the basis for a science of labour, of man; but Marcuse
seems to wish to reduce this science to little more than a notion
of potential alternatives which lie in the present. But to justify
one's grasp of tendencies inherent in the present which could
form future outcomes, one must start from *clear non-relativistic
premises*. We argue that Marx overcomes the tension between
present causality and future indeterminacy by rooting his science
in mankind's special characteristic teleology. Marx showed that
men's purposefulness is constrained within class society. Yet he
also demonstrated that the creation and reproduction of such
societies depend upon men's activity, the mode of production

and the way in which such modes were limited and shaped by
the relations of production. Now Marcuse, like Habermas, whom
we examined in Chapter 2, misunderstands this necessary starting-
point. As a result there is no real foundation for Marcuse's critical analysis except the rather vague disparity between the present
and potentiality.

Tackling this question in an essay entitled 'The Concept of
Essence', Marcuse writes that dialectical or 'critical' theory employs two sets of concepts. One describes phenomena as they
appear and determine men's thoughts and actions. The second
grasps the true content—the essence of these appearances.[2] Dialectics is liberation—it frees man from the first level, the level
of the 'mere understanding', the level of empirical social science,
by exposing the real meaning of the facts treated at this level.
The first level of critical theory, however, remains crucial. Marx
makes the distinction clear:

> When reality is depicted, philosophy as an independent branch
> of knowledge loses its medium of existence. At the best its
> place can only be taken by a summing up of the most general
> results, abstractions which arise from the observation of the
> historical development of men. Viewed apart from real his-
> tory, these abstractions have in themselves no value whatso-
> ever
>
> [Karl Marx and Frederick Engels, *The German
> Ideology*, London 1965, 38].

These abstractions 'facilitate the arrangement of historical
material'. This distinction is similar to MacIntyre's between substantive theories and explanatory schemes.[3] Marx's ontological
premises, however, form a special type of explanatory scheme.
But, Marcuse argues, the concept of essence in critical theory is
oriented to the essence of man. The relation of man's essence to
his appearances is conceived as a 'historical disproportion'.

Marcuse writes that the image of man in critical theory 'represents not only what can already be made of man today, what
"in itself" can already be today, but also ... the real fulfilment

[2] Herbert Marcuse, 'The Concept of Essence' in *Negations*, London
1969, 85 ff.

[3] MacIntyre, *Marxism and Christianity*, London 1969, 80.

of everything that man desires to be when he understands himself in terms of his potentialities'.[4]

This criterion is an abstraction from history that enables history to be considered as the history of one species and provides an immanent standard of assessment. Marcuse's criterion is the *'pacification of existence'*. The pacification of existence refers to the option of a planned organisation of the productive forces, the development of 'man's struggle with man and nature, under conditions where the competing needs, desires and aspirations are no longer organised by vested interests in domination and scarcity'.[5] But if this is all that Marcuse's critical theory offers, then it differs little from a left pragmatism: we examine the present structural arrangements of human institutions, see how far they measure up to the option of a pacification of human existence, and work out from this basis what is possible in human achievement, indicating the options with an emphasis upon our extrapolated criterion. What is left unclear, with this starting-point, is exactly what *is possible*. What is vague in such a conception is the nature of the social conditions which allow of free productive activity. It allows of a different institutional context for struggle and competition, not on the basis of a break from alienated pre-history, but on the basis of material abundance. Yet, for Marxism, the historical form of human liberation is grounded in the overcoming of alienation. It is because Marcuse does not use a Marxist conception of alienation with its firm basis in the dialectics of labour—that he is led to justify 'critical theory' via an almost metaphysical conception of man's essence, as having more potential than society allows him to fulfil. For Marx, the division between mental and manual labour is an unnecessary division and a limiting constraint upon the development of the human species. This can be shown to be the case via the kind of historical analysis undertaken by Marx. Marcuse, on the other hand, has no clear starting-point from which to engage in historical analysis. One plank in the Marxist critique of Marcuse must therefore be the weakness of his historical criterion. For the 'pacification of existence' refers not directly to *social re-*

---

[4] Marcuse, 'The Concept of Essence', 72–73.
[5] Marcuse, *One-Dimensional Man*, 30.

lationships between men, but to the potential material conditions of life made possible by industrialism. Hence the proletariat ceases to be the bearer of negativity once it appears to be integrated by the material conditions of late capitalism. Marx's identification of the proletariat as the determinate negation, the universal class, was founded upon a different premise—that of man's role in value creation. Because the proletariat is located in the capitalist mode of production as the principal victim of asymmetrical social relations, its alienations cannot be overcome without the abolition of *class society* and the emergence of *human* society.

Now despite counter tendencies in capitalism which 'integrate' the proletariat, certain structural contradictions continue. For Marx, alienation is a structural rather than a metaphysical concept: the reference is not to alienation from some ahistorical essence but to alienation from labour-power. If critical theory loses sight of Marx's premises it has no alternative but to relapse into idealism and confusions. Indeed, Marcuse seems scarcely to deny this when he writes:

> On the basis of this theory the essence of man is understood in connection with those tendencies which have as their goal a new form of social life as the 'idea' of that which practice must realise.
>
> Considered this way, the image of man represents not only what can already be made of man today, what in itself can already be today, but also—and this is the polemical demand theory raises by means of this concept of essence—the real fulfilment of everything that man desires to be when he understands himself in terms of his potentialities
>
> ['The Concept of Essence', 72–73].

But he is incorrect here—for, as our earlier discussion of the differences between Marx and the Left Hegelians was intended to reveal, Marxism stands in no need of a concept of essence used in this fashion. Marxism is not polemical in the sense implied by Marcuse, in that the ontological givens of men are repressed by the objective features of class societies. The forced division between mental and manual labour, for instance, stands condemned by Marx not because it thwarts the essence of man but rather as one of the miserable yardsticks by which we can demonstrate that capitalism is maintained on a permanent contradiction between the forces of production and the oppressive social relations of production. Let us turn to Marcuse's analysis or model of man and society and examine his rejection or refusal to situate his theory in Marx's premises.

Marcuse's Model

Marcuse's view of human society is a revision of Marxist theory during which he develops his own radicalised version of Freudian metapsychological categories. Both Marx and Freud present the history of civilisation as the history of man's repression. Both assume an external world within which man makes himself; a determinate reality which can be a source of human misconception and 'false consciousness'. Both theories can be termed 'critical' in the sense that the concepts employed by both transcend the mere *description* of phenomena.

Now a large part of the justification for Marcuse's idiosyncratic marriage of Marxist and Freudian schemas is derived from his assertion that political and psychological theory in the present era have become one. He states:

This essay [*Eros and Civilisation*] employs psychological categories because they have become political categories. The traditional borderlines between psychology on the one hand and political and social philosophy on the other have been made obsolete by the condition of man in the present era: formerly autonomous and identifiable psychical processes are being absorbed by the function of the individual in the State—by his public existence.... Psychology could be elaborated and practised as a special discipline as long as the psyche could sustain itself against the public power, as long as privacy was real, really desired and self-shaped [*Eros and Civilisation*, 21].

Without a separate private realm where the individual can be himself, i.e., is self-determining, men are unable to develop a critical consciousness. This motivational explanation is the basis of Marcuse's analysis of modern industrialism and the possibilities of transforming it. Formerly, he alleges, men were able to dissociate themselves from the prevailing social order because a private as well as a political dimension existed, in which 'dissociation could develop into effective opposition'. The eclipse of the private by the public sphere of life has been necessitated in Marcuse's view by the current stage of capitalist development. The reproduction of the 'affluent society' is contingent upon the manipulation of the needs and desires of individuals through new agencies of social control, in particular the media of mass communication. It comes as no surprise, therefore, that Marcuse can push his analysis to suggesting that:

> The mere absence of all advertising and of all indoctrination media of information and entertainment would plunge the individual into a traumatic void where he would have the chance to wonder and to think, to know himself (or rather the negation of himself) and his society.... The non-functioning of television and allied media might thus begin to achieve what the inherent contradictions of capitalism did not achieve—the disintegration of the system [*One-Dimensional Man*, 192–93].

This revolutionary variant of 'Television makes Tories' theme is best considered light-heartedly. But it illuminates a problem which constantly arises in the examination of Marcuse, namely the way in which his metaphors, similes and illustrations take on a reality of their own. It becomes difficult at times to disentangle the romantic from the real. Underlying Marcuse's suggestion here is the argument that the closing of the private dimension by modern society transforms it into a 'closed society'—in short, the available images, descriptions and language usage do not allow qualitatively different forms of action to emerge.

The reason Marcuse advances for this closure is that one-dimensional society provides sufficient satisfaction so that no disjunction appears between 'is' and 'ought' for the majority of the population. 'The products indoctrinate and manipulate; they promote a false consciousness which is immune against its falsehood.'[6] Thus Marcuse believes that false consciousness in the majority of the members of late capitalist societies has reached a new stage in that the possibility of breaking through into true consciousness has become inconceivable.

What Marcuse does here is to split consciousness and struc-

6 *One-Dimensional Man*, 26.

ture. For Marxists, false consciousness can never become 'immune against its own falsehood', for it is false only in the sense that its perception of that society is a perception derived from the ruling ideas of that society. If Marx is correct to suggest that the ruling ideas of an age are the ideas of the ruling class, then any permanent objective contradiction within that society can lead to the possibility of the ruling class ideas being rejected as particularistic and false. Yet Marcuse does not deny these contradictions; rather he divides consciousness out from the structure of society. Yet whilst these *are* in one sense distinct elements, they are also in a more crucial sense a unity. Marcuse, in other terms, seems to want to suggest that there are social contradictions without ideological contradictions; but in fact there are both.

Such contradictory unity finds expression in the most basic contradiction between forces of production and relation of production. For class struggle is the expression in consciousness and action, in praxis, of this dialectical unity. Marcuse's position here is doubly difficult to understand, for in recognising the central contradiction of capitalist society, and yet not fully understanding the dialectics of labour, he stops short of an outright rejection of Marx, in forcing a division between structure and consciousness specifically denied in Marx. Jürgen Habermas, who (as we showed above) wishes to abandon Marx's premises, clearly recognises this tension in Marcuse's work, when he notes that 'for Marcuse, technology and science themselves become ideological'.[7] They act as new ideological legitimations for the ruling class. Now whilst this may be correct as a description of the way in which a ruling class can make an appeal to technocracy as *additional* legitimation of its position, i.e., in attempting to universalise their false claim to rule in the general interest, it is not the case that this ideology is immune from falsification. For its falsehood will be rapidly revealed as an ideological claim when any structural conflict takes effect.

Marcuse is, of course, aware of this problem and throughout his work he points pessimistically to the unlikelihood of such an

[7] Jürgen Habermas *Towards a Rational Society: Student Protest, Science, and Politics*, Boston, Mass., 1968, London 1971, 115.

effective conflict. For example, considering the decline of direct manual labour, he supposes that:

> ... the declining proportion of human labour power in the productive process means a decline in political power of the opposition. In view of the increasing weight of the white-collar element in this process, political radicalisation would have to be accompanied by the emergence of an independent political consciousness and action among the white-collar groups—a rather unlikely development in advanced industrial society
>
> [*One-Dimensional Man*, 45].

As a structural statement, this reveals a profound ignorance of Marx's labour theory of value and its radical implications for advanced capitalism but, that aside, a peculiar characteristic of Marcuse's work remains his insistence on separating structure from consciousness, treating them as a separate yet asserting a unity (with neither offering any hope); they are synthesised in tendentious pessimism.

At times, Marcuse's critique and revision of Marx's approach is more direct and indeed contradictory. Using concepts and Marxist terminology in an *ad hoc* fashion, he reinterprets its scope for his own purposes. For instance, in marrying Marx to Freud, he interprets the Marxist designations of the *modes of production* as *different forms of the reality principle*. Of course, this reduces Marx's characterisation of the modes of production merely to the question of scarcity; which allows Marcuse to go on to assert that, as advanced capitalism has overcome scarcity, the reality principle has been abandoned along with the possibility of revolution. For there are no good reasons to suppose ideology will be challenged as consciousness is no longer subject to reality checks. This horrifying usage of Marxist and Freudian concepts does as much injustice to Freud as to Marx. Marcuse revises both by reducing his assessment of their theories to the question of scarcity.

Scarcity, in Marcuse's scheme, is the original condition of the environmental state in which the human species had to develop and this established the reality principle:

For [Freud's] metapsychology, it is not decisive whether the inhibitions are imposed by scarcity or by the hierarchical *distribution* of scarcity [Marcuse, *Eros and Civilisation*, 114].

Marcuse questions Freud's assumptions and conceives of a non-repressive culture in terms of the liberation from both the biological and the sociological factors (giving rise to the reality principle) as rooted in the termination of scarcity. Marcuse sees the instinctual structure as immune to modification by society on the one hand, yet claims that the socially-generated adaptations of the human organism can 'sink down' to the instinctual level.[8] In this sense, the immediate consumer gratification provided by late capitalism removes the sociological dimension of the reality principle, leaving the liberation from the instinctual constraints to some further stage of human civilisation. He criticises the neo-Freudians for ignoring this further dimension of liberation.[9] It becomes clear that, for Marcuse, the massive provision of immediate gratification has removed the lever by which the masses conceive of any qualitative transformation of society, wherein the biological liberation can be achieved.

At times Marcuse goes even further with his biologism than Freud; he even suggests a biological foundation for socialism. 'The revolution will throw up new men with new needs even at the biological and instinctual level.' For instance in *An Essay on Liberation*, which professes to develop further the ideas of *Eros and Civilisation* and of *One-Dimensional Man*, he argues that critical theorists can no longer take as their political maxim 'to each according to his needs' because these needs are exactly what stand in the way of the present possibilities for revolution in industrial societies. Marcuse states that:

Once a specific morality is firmly established as a norm of social behaviour, it is not only introjected, it also operates as a norm of 'organic' behaviour; the organism receives and reacts to certain stimuli and 'ignores' and repels others in accord with the introjected morality, which is thus promoting or impeding the function of the organism as a living cell in the respective society [*Essay on Liberation*, 11].

[8] *Eros and Civilisation*, 113; cf also his 'Biological Foundation for Socialism' in *An Essay on Liberation*, London 1969, 10.

[9] Marcuse, *Eros and Civilisation*, 213–214.

But if it were the case that introjected morality or ideology oper-
ated in this way, then no change at all would be possible. Alasdair MacIntyre examined this aspect of Marcuse's work and
argued that this unsubstantiated piece of biologism was used as
a 'basis for a political theory' in which the implied elitism of
One-Dimensional Man is made fully explicit.

He suggests that the implication of such a position is that
'human nature is indefinitely malleable'. MacIntyre thus asserts
that Marcuse can erect a political theory which is elitist, based
upon this position, namely that 'the majority cannot voice their
true needs, for they cannot perceive or feel them. The minority
must rescue the necessarily passive majority'.[10] While MacIntyre
is correct in suggesting that Marcuse's all too 'fashionable radical
minority' of blacks, students, etc, is elitist by implication, he is
incorrect in suggesting that it is *necessarily elitist* and moreover
he is gravely wrong in suggesting that Marcuse's statements concerning biology provide the basis for this elitism.

Rather they could lead to defeatism, for the implication of
Marcuse's position is that human nature is indefinitely malleable
only for the ruling class. For once ideology is introjected the possibility of change is remote. Thus revolutionary critical theory
and agitation by class conscious radicals is a waste of time. They
would remain outside this ideology, unable to alter it. But of
course Marcuse stops well short of these implications and in fact
moves from pessimism to optimism in his latest work. What is
really central to a critique of Marcuse is not the careful logic
chopping at which MacIntyre excels but rather the exposure of
his failure to confront sophisticated Marxism. In fact, the basis
of any elitism in Marcuse stems from problems which have characterised all his work since his loss of faith in the possibility of
a proletarian revolution initiated without any radical catalyst
from either a revolutionary group or a 'breakdown in society'.
Logically the situation is simple: if one wants a revolution but
does not believe that the proletariat is about to engage in self-
emancipation, then one has to assume (*a*) a catalyst from outside, or (*b*) an imminent collapse of society because of some in-

[10] MacIntyre, *Marcuse*, 88.

dependent factor which will transform the proletariat into a revolutionary force or (c) a combination of (a) and (b).

The catalyst usually implied under (a) is a revolutionary party or, as at present, students. The usual factor suggested under (b) is a collapse in the economy. Since *Eros and Civilisation* Marcuse has been pessimistic about revolutionary self-emancipation by the proletariat, because of his quasi-Freudian notion of *repressive desublimation*, which inevitably leads to one-dimensional man. His recent temperamental conversion to optimism is only a function of his genuine belief that students, etc, will create the conditions which will awaken the proletariat. Thus MacIntyre's various remarks about changes in Marcuse's assumptions fail to take account of the fact that Marcuse is perfectly consistent within a quasi-Freudian Marxist framework of analysis.

In short Marcuse is driven not to a necessary elitism because of his later biologism but to a neo-elitism because of his attempts to shore up Marxism, not with considered statements about the possibility of social crisis, but rather by explaining the absence of social crisis in terms of a Freudian image of man.

What Marcuse assumes is that there are no good explanations in Marx as to why and how the proletariat can be partially integrated. But Marcuse does not—as Marx would have been driven to—give us a detailed analysis of the changing structure of industrial societies. Rather, Marcuse incorporated Freud, who sees *everybody* as inevitably oppressed. A real criticism of the weaknesses of Marcuse's arguments must start with this position and then go on to explain why it is that a critical theorist chooses position (a) to the exclusion of (b) and (c) in seeking to predict a revolutionary transformation of advanced industrial society.

The immediate answer to this question is that, unlike Marx, Marcuse 'reifies' technology. He seems to see the system as continuing to deliver the goods whatever the circumstances. But as we know, the limitations to the advance of technology and science are in large part dependent upon the nature of investment and expenditure which occurs in the economy. When Marcuse fails to question this process he makes two errors: (a) he fails to see it as giving rise to social conflicts over needs, therefore he is forced to suggest that all 'needs' are false and manipulated (thus his quasi-Freudianism); (b) he avoids analysing why the conflicts on which Marx *predicated* his own optimism have failed to materialise. For if it is the case that the failure of these conflicts to emerge cannot be explained within a Marxian framework, then MacIntyre is correct is suggesting that 'to be faithful to Marxism we have to cease to be Marxists'.[11]

In short, to criticise Marcuse intelligently we have to re-examine the assumptions of Marxism and understand (*a*) any faults in Marx and (*b*) how industrial societies have changed since he presented his analysis.

First, let us turn to the crucial question of Marx's own confidence in the revolutionary nature of the proletariat and whether this was grounded in a scientific understanding of the dialectics of labour or merely Marx's state of mind. We would suggest that Marx's own form of optimism was based upon his belief that he could demonstrate through concrete analysis, first, that capitalism had created the material pre-conditions for socialism, secondly, that capitalist society was founded upon a fundamental structural contradiction between 'the social productive forces and the relations of production'[12] and third, that the probability existed of the development of revolutionary consciousness in a class that formed a majority of the population, the last exploited class in history. As the sole productive class under capitalism, and at the same time the class which benefits least from the productive process, the proletariat is the negation of the capitalist mode of production; by acting to overthrow the existing social order, its members become aware of their own nature and of the true nature of social reality. They are thus liberated.

Marcuse does not dispute the first two factors. Indeed he argues that the enormous growth of productive forces has made socialism a still more concrete historical alternative. Nor does he dispute that capitalism still manifests the basic contradiction between the forces and relations of production. He argues, however, that in the transition from 'free-market capitalism' to 'organised' capitalism a decisive change occurred. The *capitalist class has gained a consciousness of the 'laws' governing their*

[11] *Marcuse*, 61.
[12] Karl Marx, Preface to *A Contribution to the Critique of Political Economy* in Marx–Engels, *Selected Works* I, 329.

own system and the individuals that compose it. He writes that 'Nothing justifies the assumption that the new form of the classic contradiction can be manipulated permanently'.[13] But for the moment it is manipulated, with the result that the third factor in Marx's theory of revolution, the historic agent of change, has disappeared. But if Marcuse truly believes this, he cannot claim to be giving a Marxist analysis, because for Marx manipulation and consciousness of the laws of this contradictory system would not alter the possibility of social crisis. The heart of Marxian social conflict theory lies in its labour theory of value. Simply put, Marcuse's analysis of the contradictions in industrial society differs from Marx's in the following important respect.

Marcuse's whole social analysis is based upon the assumption of a stable relation between the needs of the controlling agents of the system and the needs of those subordinate to those agents. Thus, if the capitalists within the system continue to accumulate capital and the rest of the population within the system gain more in terms of consumer durables, then the system is seen as continuing to run smoothly and consciousness is seen as automatically unquestioning and adjusted. The notion of any real, objective contradiction disappears from Marcuse's analysis; instead, we are left with a *metaphysical* contradiction between what is *present* and what is potentially *possible*. Marcuse's analysis presents us with a picture of social order in which there could be an eternal satisfaction of all classes within that order. He does not understand that the fact that there are classes at all within society for Marx posed a conflicting limitation upon such satisfaction. He fails to see that there can exist objective and uncontrolled contradictions within the system that affect both controllers and controlled alike: that is, if we consider the needs of the controlling agents of the system and the needs of the controlled to be similar, we could perhaps entertain the kind of equilibrium analysis that Marcuse entertains. *But what if the system creates its own needs and generates its own contradictions which are beyond the conscious control of the ruling class or any other group within the system?* Let us assume a society which cannot meet the demands of the productive system as such,

[13] Marcuse, *Negations*, xx.

the demands both of the controlling agents or the ruling class and of the rest of society.

If capitalist society is like this then much of Marcuse's analysis would collapse. The capitalism that Marx was analysing in large part appeared to be such a society and therefore Marx's optimism was not entirely misplaced. What Marcuse does not indicate is in what important respects society does not resemble this description. Indeed his own discussion of the changes in capitalism's structure is based upon limited discussions of the role of automation. But do high incomes, the rise of the middle class and automation in fact abolish the central contradiction of capitalism?

The question we have posed turns upon understanding the utility of what Marx himself expressed as his 'major contribution to the understanding of capitalism—the *labour theory of value*'. In this book we deal with these questions in a number of essays. Suffice it for now to suggest that the labour theory of value is not a reductionist economic analysis, but an analysis designed to show how social contradictions emerge which tend to force the workers to abolish the bourgeois economy. What we have to do if we are to depart from Marx is to show in what way his reasoning is incorrect—which does not seem to be the case.

We may remember that for Marx capitalism meant human mastery over nature. Previous epochs had prepared the ground for this mastery, each with its own configuration of alienated existence. The market grew as a result of capitalist accumulation undertaken by the bourgeoisie, surmounting the prevailing feudal conditions, and became the arena for the satisfaction of human needs; even the former subsistence orientation and direct appropriation of surplus product, which characterised feudalism, was transformed by the development of market relationships. With this transformation, production took on a new dimension of alienation. Under feudalism, the use value of human labour to the human species had been a matter for calculation by the feudal ruling class on the basis of personal greed. That is, the feudal lord could choose to be more or less philanthropic in terms of the amount of surplus product appropriated from his peasants. But under a capitalist exchange relationship, Marx held, the *market dictates the degree of appropriation*. Thus capitalism transformed human labour itself into an *exchange value* over which neither bourgeois nor proletarian had control. Not surplus *product* but surplus *value* is appropriated, as human labour-power is reduced to quantifiable units of productive exchange value. That is, labour produces exchange value. The surplus which accrues to the bourgeoisie is a part of the value created by labour-power which is not *equivalently returned* in *exchange values* (*wages and salaries*). Until this surplus value, in the form of commodities, is used in exchange relationships in the market, commodities cannot become available for human gratification. Marx's humanisation of capitalist economics revealed its dynamics as social, as man-made, and therefore as subject in a class society to a constant contradiction between the forces of production and the social relations of production. Indeed, as we show in the last essay in this book, these contradictions are heightened in the economy of late capitalism. For rising incomes and automation, far from being reasons for pessimism, are conditions which Marx's model of capitalism accounts for, predicts and which form the basis for his revolutionary hopes.

Rejecting the dialectics of labour, Marcuse proceeds with a model based on abundance, repression and his own version of Freud. Bound up in the self-contradictions of wanting revolution yet erecting a model which allows very little hope he is rightly described as pessimistic. For whilst he recognises that 'the precondition for the efficacy of a serious opposition remains the political revitalisation of the working-class movement on an international scale',[14] he sees no possibility of this revitalisation.

> We are no mass movement, I do not believe that in the near future we will see such a mass movement.
>
> [Marcuse, 'Liberation from the Affluent Society', in D. Cooper (ed.), *The Dialectics of Liberation*, London 1968, 191].

Marcuse claims that this kind of assertion is grounded in an analysis of modern society. The proletariat has been *integrated* into the system and for the moment is not a force of opposition. Marcuse might appear to be propounding a type of conspiracy

14 *New Left Review* 45 (Sept.–Oct. 1967), 4.

theory, and his style often seems to suggest this. In fact, however, he is arguing that the manipulation is not cynically plotted by the powerful, but is both logical and rational within the framework of capitalist norms of action. It is the capitalist system as a whole that is irrational, a point which is not recognised as such by the vast majority of manipulators and manipulated precisely because they take as reality the alienated social world they create. Marcuse's pessimism should not be confused with defeatism. He never advocates resignation. His pessimism refers not to his attitude towards action, but to his estimates of the chances of a revolutionary transformation of society in the near future.

> The fact that today we cannot identify any specific class or any specific group as a revolutionary force, this fact is no excuse for not using any and every possibility and method to arrest the engines of repression in the individual.
>
> [Marcuse, 'Liberation from the Affluent Society', 187].

This estimate is based upon his analysis of modern society; his theory is not concerned to invalidate action to change society, but to indicate the context in which such action must take place and so to guide it in as effective a direction as possible.

Yet despite his desire for revolution his own model of industrial society offers little hope. Affluent society, for Marcuse, has terminated the division between public and private spheres of existence. As total objects of administration, most men are no longer able to transcend the immediate forms of their lives either in thought or in action. The opportunity for an *Aufhebung* of late capitalist society has passed; it is now consigned to utopian speculation. For Marcuse, the conditions for mass critical consciousness no longer exist. Capitalism's abundance of commodities has led to a breakdown of the need to maintain a rigid reality principle. Immediate gratification in an enormously wide and varied field has become possible for more individuals than ever before. But such gratification does not produce free individuals— as Marcuse is committed to arguing; the desires and needs that are gratified are not freely chosen but imposed artificially by the productive system through its advertising networks. Measured against Marcuse's notion of human potentials, affluent man is unfree. However great the gratifications in terms of the abundance of commodities, humanity under capitalism is still repressed. Yet a process of desublimation can take place under this repression—a satiation of life instincts is tolerated by, indeed is a consequence of, affluence. But it is a controlled and repressive desublimation. This form of desublimation is termed by Marcuse 'the happy consciousness'—it announces the impossibility of the critical consciousness. Men no longer feel that their conditions of life require transforming; thus, the generation of critical consciousness and the receptivity of men to critical ideas is vastly minimised. The critical ideas once harboured in a sublimated state no longer exist as the process of repressive desublimation unfolds. For Marcuse, false consciousness becomes 'immune against its falsehood'.

We have criticised this conception of false consciousness above, but underlying it is an aspect of Marcuse's Freudianism we have not discussed, namely its dependence upon a fixed energy model of human action. Marx of course, has an open-ended model. It is important for Marcuse to use a fixed energy model because he can then show that modern societies are immune to change because of the organisation and manipulation of needs, all the libidinal energy at the disposal of the masses is used up in those activities sanctioned by the system and so poses no threat to its perpetuation.

> The people recognise themselves in their commodities; they find their soul in their automobile, hi-fi set, split-level home, kitchen equipment [*One-Dimensional Man*, 24].

The immediate gratifications (like these consumer durables) which the affluent society provides for its members exhaust the individual's libido and emasculates him as a revolutionary agent.[15] Such a notion of human needs, however, and such conclusions about revolutionary activity are quite foreign to Marxist analysis. Marx uses what today can be called an open-ended conception of man, in which men's needs develop in interaction with the structure and culture of society. On occasions class society cannot satisfy these perceived needs and is challenged. The difference

[15] Cf Peter Sedgwick 'Natural Science and Human Theory—a Critique of Herbert Marcuse' in R. Miliband and J. Saville (eds), *The Socialist Register 1966* London and New York 1966.

between these conceptions of man is subtle but decisive, if scarcity is overcome. For Marcuse, this will signify the release of libidinal energies into hitherto unavailable channels and thus the absence of the necessary energy for the construction of alternative life schemas. False consciousness will hence 'sink down' to the instinctual level.

But for Marx, scarcity or rather the absence of scarcity is not a factor which interferes with the development of revolutionary struggle. Men's needs cannot be spent, satiated or realised in a once and for all fashion. This relatively abstract question of how we view man and scarcity takes concrete shape in Marcuse's abandonment of Marx's conception of revolution.

Conclusion: Marcuse on Revolution

In this essay we have attempted to show that Marcuse reifies men's social relationships through his amalgamation of Marx and Freud, and so fails to justify his revision of Marx's theory of revolution. Although he is aware of the dangers of elitism, he has to adopt a quasi-elitist position with regard to the strategy of revolution on account of his understanding and rendering of the nature of one-dimensional society. Dialectical theory, he says, is not refuted by the facts of the present era, but in the absence of a practice that can respond to it, it cannot be positive. It defines the historical possibilities of a given social system but 'in the absence of demonstrable agents and agencies of social change, the critique is thrown back to a high level of abstraction. There is no ground on which theory and practice, thought and action, meet.'[16] In this situation, the task of Marcuse's critical theory is to preserve historical alternatives that have become utopian possibilities. It becomes the collective conscience of mankind and appears to occupy much the same role as the 'transcendental subjectivity' of the German idealists who carved out a realm of rationality and freedom in thought alone.

Marcuse arrives at this conclusion through his argument that the proletariat has been integrated into the capitalist system, and on his peculiar conception of the relationship between theory

[16] Marcuse, *One-Dimensional Man*, 11–12.

and practice. Yet, in his latest work, *An Essay on Liberation*, he proclaims:

> The First International was the last attempt to realise the solidarity of the species by grounding it in that social class in which the subjective and objective interest, the particular and the universal coincided [p. 14].

The implication is that the particular and the universal no longer coincide in the proletariat. For this to be true in Marxist terms, Marcuse would have to demonstrate that the class character of capitalism, the nature of the exchange relationships, had altered. Instead, he relies upon his concept of impoverishment. He argues that Marx thought revolutionary consciousness would develop because the proletariat would become aware of their impoverishment relative to the growing social productivity under capitalism. In this sense, the impoverishment of the proletarians has grown relative to other classes in the affluent society, since the only part of the social product that belongs to them is their wages.

But Marcuse sees the development of capitalist productivity as halting the growth of revolutionary consciousness, because it makes possible the scientific manipulation of men's instincts by organising their needs. The proletariat can no longer become aware of its impoverishment in the face of the new social controls that permit immediate gratification—the realm of freedom in the realm of necessity. Only when the proletariat is alienated from civil society in its very existence, so that qualitative change is a matter of *life and death*, will a revolutionary consciousness develop.

Thus, consciousness of *impoverishment* in Marcuse's model leads to a consciousness that is revolutionary. In the period of free, competitive capitalism, *pauperism* was not essential for the development of a consciousness of impoverishment. However, in late capitalism

> We ought to ask ourselves whether we should so readily jettison or re-interpret the Marxist concept of pauperisation. I know that Marx ... insisted that pauperisation should not be seen as the necessary precondition for a revolutionary development and that the most advanced and best-off sectors of the working class could certainly become subjects of the revolution. But

today we should re-examine this view. In other words, we must ask whether it is possible to conceive of revolution when there is no vital need for it

> [Marcuse, 'Socialism in the Developed Countries', *International Socialist Journal*, Year 2, No. 8 (April 1965)].

Modern man, Marcuse argues, is no longer 'alienated in his very existence'. Instead alienation now permeates the individual psyche, so that 'the alienated subject is swallowed up by his alienated existence'.[17] The individual finds himself in the artificial needs of consumer society. Because he accepts them as his needs, he can no longer criticise the social system which produces them. But it is clear that to arrive at this conclusion Marcuse must separate the state from society, must postulate a one-way relationship between socialisation and social control, must turn concrete contradiction into metaphysics, must divorce consciousness from being.

In *Repressive Tolerance*, the criterion he uses for deciding whether a given movement or policy is reactionary or progressive is whether it promotes or blocks the 'pacification of existence'. But who is to interpret the criterion? Marcuse recognises the problem of elitism, but since he denies the possibility of a mass revolutionary movement his conception of revolutionary strategy necessarily becomes elitist.[18]

Following his earlier notion of the conditions under which critical consciousness can arise, he states that the first problem of the new radical forces is to re-create 'the mental space for denial and reflection'. Given the integration of the proletariat, the only group within the system which can create this mental space for itself are the intellectuals. Any intellectual who can achieve this mental solitude is capable of interpreting the pacification-of-existence criterion. Thus the bearers of universality become all those that have 'learnt to think rationally and autonomously'. These are then entitled to 'withdraw tolerance' from reactionary policies and movements, to act undemocratically, to

[17] *One-Dimensional Man*, 26.
[18] Cf the confused account by Maurice Cranston in *Encounter* (March 1969).

use extra-legal means, all in the interests of clearing the way for a subversive majority to develop.

Marcuse fails to notice that by treating the majority as an undifferentiated, indoctrinated, manipulated mass, he moves over to a Jacobin conception of revolution, in which the people for whom the revolutionaries claim to be acting are at the same time regarded as a hostile force. Revolutionary activity involves working against them. The elite defines itself—Marcuse's criterion of admittance is tautological. He evidently hopes that the activity of these radical groups will one day rejoin the activity of an awakened proletariat. But the nature of such political elites is that they increasingly tend to represent only themselves.

Marcuse becomes elitist because he presents the capitalist economy as a closed system. By *reifying contemporary* social relations, he fails to see the contradiction of capitalism in its concrete form and falsifies the concepts of alienation and impoverishment. The problems he raises, however, are undoubtedly important ones for a modern Marxist theory, indeed most of the problems discussed by Marcuse are taken up as central themes elsewhere in this book. He has asked all the right questions. Our objection in this essay has been to his outright rejection of Marx's dialectics of labour—a rejection which has led him into mystification and psychic ambiguity.

5

LOUIS ALTHUSSER AND
STRUCTURALIST MARXISM

... the ... *Theses on Feuerbach*, these few lightning flashes
which break the night of philosophical anthropology with the
fleeting snap of a new world glimpsed through the retinal image
of the old [Louis Althusser, *Reading Capital*, London 1970, 30].

Part 1: Introduction

The followers of Althusser describe his work as an 'intervention'
in the present 'ideological and political conjuncture', which includes de-Stalinisation, the rise of Marxist humanism, and the
Sino-Soviet split.

His response has been to engage in a critique of humanism and
a demonstration of the difference between humanism and
Marxist theory, a task which has demanded a new elaboration
of the distinction between ideological formations and science
[M. Gane, 'Althusser in English', *Theoretical Practice*
No. 1 (Jan. 1971, 4)].

According to another exponent, Andrew Levine,[1] Althusser's
work provides the first real break with the terms of the debate
between the Stalinists and the anti-Stalinists, because it rejects
dogmatism and returns to the principles of Leninism, by restoring theory to its proper place in the revolutionary movement.
He achieves all this by a 'philosophical' reading of Marx
which aims to uncover the assumptions of Marx's method of
analysis and the concepts Marx employed to analyse society. His
main conclusions are familiar enough. *Capital*, he finds, is the
result of the application of a radically new kind of scientific

[1] A. Levine, 'A Reading of Marx', *Radical America*, vol. 3, no. 5
(Sept. 1969), 3–18.

theory, a science of history called historical materialism. There is an epistemological break, both in terms of method and concepts, between Marx's early and later works. In particular, the early works are said to be dominated by a problematic inherited from Hegel and Feuerbach.

This problematic is historicist and humanist. Its historicism is derived from Hegel, whose solution to the traditional problems of philosophy was to understand the world as a unified historical process. Its successive stages were constituted by a single developing subject which created itself and the world by externalising itself in objects (objectification). But in objectifying itself the subject also alienates itself, for it creates objects that take on an independent existence. The subject must therefore repossess the object in order to restore unity and harmony to the world. The development of the subject is this process of alienating and then recovering itself, and it is in these terms that present reality can be grasped in thought, if only retrospectively.

Its humanism is derived from Feuerbach, who opposed 'concrete' premises to Hegel's 'speculative' ones. This meant he began from man rather than from the Idea, and treated thought as a product of man's actual 'sensuous' existence. His aim was to provide a guide for practical action. In his analysis of religion man was alienated from himself because he projected all his best qualities on to a supernatural being, calling it God, which he then experienced as a constraining power. Feuerbach's transformative method of inverting Hegel, which Marx later applied to the state and to 'civil society', supplied him with a criterion—the human essence—by which to judge and criticise existing institutions.

What is common to both is that reality is interpreted in terms of a notion of essence. In Hegel's case this is the historical interaction of subject and object, the unfolding of the potentialities of the Absolute Idea (History is the March of God in the world). For Feuerbach the essence is a conception of human nature. Thus for Hegel the basic question is how we can understand present reality as the culmination of a process of historical development, and for Feuerbach it is how we can criticise existing reality in terms of man's potentialities. Althusser maintains that Marx remained within the circle of these questions in his early writings. Thus Marx's work, far from being a unity, contains two methodologies that are radically opposed. Althusser indeed warns us that such was the magnitude of Marx's theoretical revolution that he himself was not always aware of what his new methodology required. Even in *Capital*, for example, he sometimes uses 'inappropriate' Hegelian language and modes of analysis. This has led to great confusion and many contradictory interpretations. The meaning of Marx's work has therefore to be rescued through philosophical reflection on it. This philosophy is dialectical materialism, whose aim is to reveal Marx's new method as a theoretical system, and to fill in the gaps or 'absences', where Marx is inconsistent, wrong, or has not fully developed the implications of his theory. Althusser scorns attempts to prove that Marx's work is a unity, suggesting they stay at the surface level of the texts and rely on quoting passages that have only apparently similar content from the early and later works.[2]

Thus the distinction between historical materialism and dialectical materialism is crucial to his work. As in the famous 'underlabourer' conception of philosophy,[3] which has produced the contemporary distinction between analytic and synthetic statements, Althusser sees philosophy as theoretical reflection on scientific enquiry. It is thus a secondary activity, in the sense that the knowledge it produces depends on the prior existence of a science. Only science produces *new* knowledge; philosophy then works to transform and articulate this knowledge. Althusser claims that major philosophical revolutions always follow in the wake of the establishment of a new science. According to him,[4] there have been three major scientific revolutions: Mathematics (Thales), which subsequently inspired Plato; Physics (Galileo), which gave rise to the philosophy of Descartes; and History

[2] The writings of Althusser that we shall look at in this chapter are: *For Marx*, London 1969; 'The Politics of Philosophy', *New Left Review* 64 (Nov.–Dec. 1970), 3–12; 'Freud and Lacan', *New Left Review* 55 (May–June 1969), 48–65; *Lénine et la philosophie*, Paris 1970; L. Althusser and E. Balibar, *Reading Capital*, London 1970.

[3] The underlabourer conception of philosophy was put forward by Locke. See P. Winch, *The Idea of a Social Science*, London 1958, chapter 1.

[4] Althusser, 'The Politics of Philosophy', 6.

(Marx), which still awaits its philosophical sequel—although his followers believe that Althusser himself has now provided that.

Althusser, however, has now moved beyond the position he expressed in *For Marx*,[5] according to which philosophy was nothing more than the theoretical reflection of scientific practices. Now he argues that philosophy is also political, because it is the crucial tool in determining whether a given Marxist analysis, programme or strategy is correct, i.e., is in accord with the theoretical principles of Marxism-Leninism. Thus dialectical materialism is the weapon with which deviation is fought.[6]

Much of Althusser's own work has been to turn this beacon on what is very loosely described as Hegelian Marxism, which includes Lukacs, the Frankfurt School, Gramsci (in part), Lefebvre and Sartre. He alleges that their Marxism is based on the problematic and the concepts (especially alienation) of the early works, and that they fail to see that this problematic is incompatible with the science of history that Marx later elaborated. This is because it is based on a philosophical anthropology, which, Althusser says, means that men as concrete individuals come to be seen as the subjects, the makers of history. As a result history is reduced to the consciousness of these individuals.

> History then becomes the transformation of a human nature, which remains the real subject of the history which transforms it. As a result, history has been introduced into human nature. making men the contemporaries of the historical effects whose subjects they are, but—and this is absolutely decisive—the relations of production, political and ideological social relations, have been reduced to historicized '*human relations*', i.e., to inter-human, inter-subjective relations. This is the favourite terrain of historicist humanism
>
> [Althusser, *Reading Capital*, 140].

The methodology is the same even if the 'individuals' are not single human beings, but social classes. In this case the class becomes the creator of history, and this history can therefore only

[5] *Far Marx*, chapter 6, 'On the Materialist Dialectic'. See introduction 'To my English Readers', also the Glossary, and the Introduction to *Reading Capital*.

[6] This is the position developed in *Lénine et la philosophie*.

be understood through the consciousness that the class has of it. This leads to society being viewed as an organic totality, all the different parts receiving their meaning from the class-subject that both creates and unifies the totality. This kind of theory Althusser labels historicist, subjectivist, empiricist, idealist and ideological, by which he means that it doesn't have much to do with science.

It is in contrast to this position that Althusser unfolds his own vision of scientific Marxism. His views and those he attacks can be explored under three main headings: his distinction between ideology and science, his account of the relation between theory and practice, and his conception of the social formation, the basic concept in Marx's theory.

Part 2: Ideology and Science

One of the favourite logic chops of the Althusserian is to show how seemingly dissimilar theories are in fact at best only inversions of one another, because they share the same problematic, i.e., the same theoretical structure and methods. Thus Hegel, the early Marx, the Frankfurt School, the classical political economists, Weber, not to mention all the varieties of positivist social theory, are all dumped in the same pit—empiricism. Althusser manages this remarkable feat by claiming that the only alternative to science in theory is ideology, and ideology is always invincibly empiricist. The reason is that ideology fails to distinguish clearly between the object of analysis and the concepts used to explain it. Hegel falsely imagines that knowledge arises when the concepts of philosophy adequately reflect the movement of reality. For Althusser, the object of knowledge is never the real, the concrete:

> ... concrete-in-thought is produced through work on abstractions-in-thought, both of which are appropriations, but in different forms, of the real-concrete, which lies outside thought
>
> [Gane, 'Althusser in English', 6].

Thus theoretical *knowledge* only results when a conceptual scheme is employed that identifies correctly the structures of the object under study. Empiricism, by contrast, opposes

> ... a given subject to a given object and calls knowledge the

abstraction by the subject of the essence of the object. Hence the knowledge of the object is part of the object itself

[*For Marx*, 'Glossary', 251].

This identification of what is immediate and concrete with what is real prevents the achievement of *objective* knowledge of reality, because both subject and object fuse in a single process, namely history. The essence of objective knowledge is abstraction and the possibility of rigorously separating subject and object.

All ideologies are empiricist because they fail to make this separation, owing to their domination by 'practico-social' rather than 'theoretical' considerations. This apparently means that they treat social reality as a given and as homogeneous, and then attempt to grasp its essence, but only end by reading into reality the answers that are required by the particular ideology. Thus the empiricism of ideologies makes them circular, because they have no way to recognise and control the practical purposes which lie behind the enquiry. They always formulate problems on the basis of answers they already possess, answers that are 'imposed in advance by practical, religious, ethical and political interests'.[7]

But science radically excludes practical interests, and so moves beyond ideology, the mere reflection of aspects of reality, and achieves knowledge. It is not surprising therefore, that Althusser claims that science, unlike ideology, is not part of the 'superstructure' and so not subject to 'determination by the economy in the last instance'.[8] Such emancipation from the interference of practical interests is the result of a specific practice, theoretical practice, and of a specific theoretical achievement—the construction of an abstract system of concepts. There are three aspects of theoretical practice: Generalities I are 'the abstract, part-ideological, part-scientific generalities that are the raw material of the science'. Generalities III are 'the concrete scientific generalities that are produced', while Generalities II are 'the theory of the science at a given moment'.[9]

The emphasis which Althusser places on the need for theory

[7] *Reading Capital*, 53.
[8] cf *Reading Capital*, 133.
[9] *For Marx*, 'Glossary', 251.

as the only way to produce knowledge and avoid empiricism echoes in some ways that of Talcott Parsons in *The Structure of Social Action*.[10] Thus Parsons likewise scorned a naive empiricism which believed that significant results could be obtained merely by collecting and measuring 'facts' without any prior conceptualisation, since this simply made the concepts that were implicitly employed inaccessible to scientific assessment. Parsons too was concerned to found sociology as an objective science, neutral as regards values and practical interests, and therefore to distinguish it from ideology, which he was later to define as 'deviations from social science objectivity'. Like Althusser, he sees no difference in the basic method and assumptions of social and natural science—science becomes the only path to knowledge, and each science is distinguished by the way in which it conceptualises its object. The heart of science is thus its system of concepts. As Althusser puts it:

> (Science) can only pose problems on the terrain and within the horizon of a very definite theoretical structure, its problematic, which constitutes its absolute and definite condition of possibility, and hence the absolute determination of *the forms in which all problems must be posed*, at any given moment in the science [*Reading Capital*, 25].

Now while it is true that knowledge is not possible without a theory, what is really important is the status of that theory. What theoretical assumptions can one start with that are real? The argument of this book is that the only real starting-point is that which Marx chose—that men are purposive and social by nature. Althusser moves objectivity from man as such to science, and therefore to a particular group of men—the scientists. But he does not ask, why are not all men scientists? *His theory merely reflects the division between mental and manual labour and perpetuates it*, by holding up the possibility of an objective science which possesses its own intrinsic criteria of validity and excludes all practical interests.

[10] Althusser cannot be written off as a Marxist Parsons, however. Parsons adheres to an empirical concept of structure, whilst for Althusser, as we show below, a structure is never directly present in empirical reality.

Althusser suggests that Marx founded the science of history, by producing a theory that was a radical epistemological breakthrough, the first *scientific* theory of society, in contrast to ideology. Althusser's reading of Marx and his account of the theoretical revolution that Marx achieved, is analogous to Thomas Kuhn's theory of scientific revolutions, particularly regarding the transition from the pre-scientific stage to the scientific one.[11] The main feature of this change for Kuhn is that scientists agree on a *paradigm*, which not only creates a specific object to be studied, but also suggests the ways in which the paradigm itself can be articulated and developed through the 'puzzles' it sets up to be solved. Althusser understands Marx's theory to have done the same. What are the difficulties in this view?

First, Kuhn is careful to note that the choice of a paradigm is not itself a *scientific* matter, i.e., it is not a case of choosing one theory rather than another because it is more true, a more faithful representation of nature. This is because, as Kuhn convincingly argues, different paradigms are not directly comparable— their results cannot wholly be translated into each other's terms, because they do not merely interpret some fixed reality from different perspectives, they actually constitute that reality and constitute it differently:

> I do not doubt ... that Newton's mechanics improves on Aristotle's and that Einstein's improves on Newton's as instruments for puzzle-solving. But I can see in their succession no coherent direction of ontological development
>
> [Kuhn, *The Structure of Scientific Revolutions*, 206].

Kuhn argues that the principal factor in the choice between paradigms is the promise of success that each holds out in generating and solving puzzles. A science is defined as a practice by the existence of a community of scientists who accept a certain paradigm and strive to articulate it in their research. Now clearly this does not fit the case of Marxism or of any *social* science. None have reached the scientific stage in the sense that there is gen-

---

[11] T. Kuhn, *The Structure of Scientific Revolutions*, Chicago, 1962, 1970. Althusser mentions the influence of Bachelard's philosophy of science.

eral agreement on a paradigm, and that there exists a community of scientists whose work is guided by it. The most furious debates still continue about the object of social science and the methods it ought to use. Thus in Kuhn's sense of a social community, Althusser's science of Marxism does not exist; and even if it did, there is no *a priori* reason for supposing that it is a more faithful representation of social reality than its competitors. All one can say is that it may explain more because it allows the solution of more problems.

To assert more than this, Althusser would have to adopt the empiricist position which he explicitly repudiates, namely that his concepts are thrown up by the study of the facts. It follows that, in terms of the problem of knowledge, he is up in the air. His invocation of science hides the arbitrariness of his theory. His arbitrariness is revealed by the diversity of approaches even within Marxism. Althusser is appealing to Marxists to bury their different methods and paradigms and accept his; and it is true that were all Marxists to heed him, then we could certainly come to speak of a Marxist science—a body of Marxist theorists who all accepted a single paradigm for the investigation of social reality. But there is no such consensus, and little likelihood that Althusser's paradigm will be accepted. The reason is not hard to find. Historically, according to Kuhn, the reason for the birth of different sciences is that acceptance of a given paradigm in an area of enquiry has offered enormous scope for measurement and puzzle-solving, because it has meant that results of different experiments are comparable. Normal science is precisely the activity of exploring a given paradigm and solving the puzzles that it throws up. But the study of society offers no comparable rewards for initial agreement on a paradigm. Even less than in normal science are there agreed procedures for what will count as verification and falsification. And the link between different theories and different 'facts' is even more obvious than in natural science. Thus there is understandably some doubt as to whether social science should be modelled on natural science at all, and certainly no incentive to adopt one paradigm of social reality and call it true, merely because it is cast in the logical form of a scientific theory.

Thus what vitiates Althusser's whole enterprise is its scientific status. How do we know that Marxist theory in the form that he presents it to us is true? Althusser answers—because of its *'scientificity'*, the procedures it uses to establish its results. But that is precisely what gives us no criterion at all. It amounts to saying this theory is true because it is scientific, as though the consensus on a paradigm already existed, or as though Althusser had somehow managed to surmount the familiar objections to the criteria of verification developed by philosophers of science.[12] Althusser gives no reply to these questions. As we shall see, he rules out any appeal to social practice to validate his theories, and he also rules out philosophical anthropology as unscientific. Science is enough for him. It stands outside the social process, sufficient to itself, endowed with its own practice and itself responsible for the validity of its results. But let us enquire a little closer into the basis for this 'science'.

Althusser's claim that he has purged knowledge of ideology is the claim that judgements of fact and judgements of value can be distinguished. Ideology becomes the realm of value, of purposes and choices, and as such constitutes a distinct form of practice which will exist in socialist just as much as in capitalist societies,[13] whilst science is the realm of fact, of knowledge. He does not couch his argument for this separation in the normal positivist manner, i.e., he does not believe that there are myriads of neutral value-free facts swarming around only waiting to be netted by the conscientious investigator; indeed he *correctly* insists on the primacy of a conceptual scheme, for there are indeed no facts without theories, and reality can only be understood in terms of good or bad theories. Althusser believes, however (and here he goes even further than Weber), that the choice of a conceptual scheme is a scientific objective matter, and not one influenced by the scientist's purposes or the purposes of the group to which he

[12] A good account of these is given by Paul Piccone, 'Structuralist Marxism', *Radical America*, vol. 3, no. 5 (Sept. 1969), 25–32. Althusser's criteria are merely pragmatic. They amount to saying that what is transpersonally replicable is what is to count as Marxist science.

[13] See *For Marx*, chapter 7, 'Marxism and Humanism', for an account of humanist ideology in the Soviet Union and an argument that *ideology will be necessary in socialist societies!*

belongs. He regards it as a 'theoretical scandal', for instance, that the mass of intellectuals have not yet recognised the importance of Marx's work:

> They are still 'dabbling' in political economy, sociology, ethnology, 'anthropology', 'social psychology', etc. ... even today, 100 years after *Capital*, just as some Aristotelian physicists were still 'dabbling' in physics, 50 years after Galileo
>
> [Althusser, 'The Politics of Philosophy', 7].

In his next paragraph he says it is no scandal at all, but only a consequence of the ideological class struggle. But that is to suppose that it is only ideology that prevents all intellectuals, if they are honest, from recognising the truth of Marx's work; which means he is claiming that there do exist objective *theoretical criteria* for saying that Marx's work is true. There are in fact such theoretical criteria, but they depend on recognising the fact that man's distinguishing characteristic is that all men have purposes, and that the dialectics of labour when applied to history reveal the forces that shape and constrain this purposive nature. Lacking such premises, Althusser has no answer to Kuhn's position that one reason why all physicists were not immediately won over to Galileo's theory was that the two paradigms were in certain respects incommensurable, and the Aristotelians were seeking the answer to questions that could not be posed under the new paradigm.

But the substitution of one theory for another in natural science cannot be fully explained without reference to the practical interests that lie behind the scientific enterprise. Habermas has argued that the practical interest that governs science is technical control of the natural environment, whether or not this is the subjective meaning of their work for individual scientists.[14] In the long run those paradigms that advance this purpose are likely to triumph over others that are not so successful in this regard. (This approach stresses the dialectics of labour, whatever Habermas' own position may be, as it is applied to nature, and, incidentally, supplies a useful corrective to Kuhn's slide into rela-

---

[14] J. Habermas, 'Knowledge and Interest', *Inquiry*, vol. 9 (1966), 285–300.

tivism.) The interest governing the human sciences, however, is not technical control but *emancipation*. This is a form of rational control, but a very different kind of rational control from rational control exercised over the environment, because it involves the idea of realising species being, of overcoming the constraints that prevent the full expression of man's social being. Now it is no secret that much contemporary social science does not have this aim at all, but on the contrary treats society in the same way that the natural sciences conceive the environment—as an object to be manipulated. This has produced not only the machine language, but also the characteristic social engineering approach of orthodox sociology.

Now Althusser's work cannot be identified simply as a Marxist version of social engineering, if only because of his rigorous separation of theoretical practice from other forms of practice, and the resistance by both him and his 'orthodox' followers to those who try to turn his theory into a technology.[15] But there remains an 'absence' in his thought—the precise character of the Marxist science he is proposing, since he refuses to found it on any practical interest or any dialectical anthropology. At its most basic level, his theory is indeterminate. By *assuming* that he has an objective basis in science for his concepts, Althusser neglects to provide any adequate solution to the basic problem he sets his philosophy, namely 'to draw a dividing line between true ideas and false ideas'.[16] He thus provides no real justification for his choice of concepts like overdetermination and his rejection of others like alienation. He would reply of course that to provide a justification in terms of man or anthropology is to revert to an ideological problematic, it is to posit a subject for history and so forth. But his only alternative is to raise the banner of science, of objectivity, of value neutrality, in order to deny the legitimacy of these other questions. At times, however, he even makes his admirers anxious. Andrew Levine, for example, who gives one of the best sympathetic accounts of Althusser's work in English, is forced to acknowledge Althusser's weakness. He argues that

[15] See Gane, 'Althusser in English', for an attack on David Fernbach's understanding of how to apply Althusser's theory.
[16] 'The Politics of Philosophy', 10.

Kant sought a 'transcendental deduction' of his categories in order to show not just that his categories were presupposed by scientific practice

> ... but also that, in fact, cognition necessitates these structures. Something like a transcendental deduction of this kind is attempted by Marx in the first part of the *German Ideology*, before the complete maturation of the science of historical materialism. The starting point of this deduction was ... the conflict between man and nature.... The production of the means of material existence, the reproduction of life, is man's most fundamental response to this aspect of the human condition, and so man's 'mode of production' determines his material, and therefore also, his mental life. This starting point is of course 'anthropological', and ultimately, if Althusser is right, incompatible with historical materialism. But perhaps in stressing this incompatibility, Althusser has overlooked an important connection: a connection that alone can make his programmatic reading of Marx, his notion of determination in the last instance, entirely adequate. Althusser has shown the radical break between the conceptual scheme of historical materialism and Marx's early philosophical anthropology, an 'epistemological rupture' separates science from philosophy. But perhaps there is nevertheless a connection between the philosophy of historical materialism, dialectical materialism, and the anthropological situation in the early work.
>
> [Andrew Levine, 'A Reading of Marx', 12].

What Levine raises here is precisely the question of the status of Althusser's theory, how we can judge between different theories on theoretical grounds. Marx of course solved this question for himself in his early works, most notably in the 1844 manuscripts. To assert this is quite different from arguing that in *Capital* Marx merely filled out with detailed historical and economic analysis the theory he developed in the manuscripts. Clearly new and very important concepts are worked out in his later work, in particular the theory of surplus value. But the break between the early and the later works is not the epistemological rupture of the Althusserians, but the difference between concern with 'man in general' or 'man as such' and with 'man as modified in each particular epoch'; that is, between the distinctive character of man as a species, and the particular social formations and modes of production that have appeared in history. But the first of course is a *precondition* of the latter. Marx's scientific achievement, his ability to forge concepts like surplus value to explain the laws of motion of the capitalist mode of production was only possible given his original understanding that man was on the one hand a purposive being who created himself and his world while attempting to satisfy his needs, and on the other, a social being that only developed fully in society. He therefore divided human history and human societies according to the different ways in which labour was organised in them, and showed how there had been a progressive development in human history, so that the opportunity for the realisation of man's full social being increased enormously in the capitalist mode of production. For the first time the material conditions existed which could potentially free man from the constraints imposed on his labour by the necessity of spending most of his time meeting material needs. Marx therefore had no need to split fact and value. He had no need of subjective and external ethical judgements about the desirability of socialism, because his values and the interests behind his work were inherent in his premises and therefore immanent in his theory.

Part 3: Theory and Practice

Another notable feature of Althusser's reading of Marx is his conception of the relation between theory and practice. As outlined above, the role of philosophy is to supervise the 'practice' of historical materialism. But in his latest formulations[17] Althusser argues that this is no mere theoretical understanding and clarification of scientific method, it is also a political intervention:

> Philosophy represents the class struggle in theory. In return it helps the people to distinguish in *theory* and in all *ideas* (political, ethical, aesthetic, etc) between true ideas and false ideas. In principle, true ideas always serve the people; false ideas always serve the enemies of the people
>
> ['The Politics of Philosophy', 10].

[17] See footnotes 5 and 6.

Thus philosophy guarantees that the concepts which Marxists use are 'scientific'. But where does this dividing line between true and false ideas lie? In Althusser's own words:

> ... by what mechanism does the process of knowledge, which takes place entirely in thought, produce the cognitive appropriation of its real object, which exists outside thought in the real world? [*Reading Capital*, 56]

Some schools of scientific Marxism have replied that the only test of the truth of ideas is whether they succeed in practice. Mao-Tse-Tung for example states:

> Generally speaking those (ideas) that succeed are correct and those that fail are incorrect
>
>> [Mao-Tse-Tung, *Four Essays on Philosophy*, No. 4, 'Where do correct ideas come from?', Peking 1966, 135].

This test is akin to the falsifiability principle; social practice becomes the ground for experiments to test the ideas that are elaborated in theory. But this kind of pragmatism is specifically rejected by Althusser and his followers, because it is an incorrect view of the relation between theory and practice. Althusser writes:

> It has been possible to apply Marx's theory with success because it is 'true'; it is not true because it has been applied with success [*Reading Capital*, 59].

And Paul Hirst, in discussing Althusser's philosophy says:

> The union of Marxist theory and the workers' movement is no immediate self-reflecting unity of 'theory-praxis'... Marxist theory produces no direct reading of the 'current situation', no 'scientific strategy'
>
>> [P. Hirst, 'Althusser and Philosophy', *Theoretical Practice* No. 2 (April 1971), 27].

For the Althusserians there is not a single opposition, theory/ practice, but a number of distinct and relatively autonomous practices, of which theoretical practice is only one. The others include political, economic and ideological practice:

Marxist theory is the result of a specific form of practice, Marxist theoretical practice, which is specific in as much as it works in the realm of ideas to produce knowledge. In this respect it is different from political and economic practice through the distinctiveness of its raw material

[Editorial, *Theoretical Practice* 1 (Jan. 1971), 1].

When this complex unity of autonomous practices, each with its own distinctive 'raw material', is replaced by a crude distinction between theory and practice or theory and action, the result is that:

... theory ceases to be a developing and determinate scientific guide to political practice. Instead, it is transformed into an ideological tool, in order to distinguish one Marxist group from another [*Theoretical Practice* 1, 2].

This certainly identifies a real problem. But what is the magic key that Althusser offers us which will enable us to move beyond, for example, debates on the nature of the Soviet system? The answer he gives, of course, is the 'scientific' character of historical materialism when it is guided by dialectical materialism, i.e., science produces its own criteria of validity. But this is an arbitrary procedure unless he can specify the ways in which particular concepts and analyses can be established as correct *unambiguously*. Otherwise he is just as likely as other Marxists to be reading into reality his own ideological purposes. Indeed there is some evidence that this is the case.

This appears when we ask what are the uses to which a Marxist science of the Althusserian kind can be put. The answer Althusser and his followers give is that such a science is an important and indispensable aid in building a revolutionary party. The practice of Marxist science becomes institutionalised in the party apparatus and enables the party militants to make correct decisions in the various levels of practice in which they are active, whether political, economical or ideological. As an editorial in the Althusserian journal *Theoretical Practice* expresses it:

The essence of Scientific Socialism is that its political positions are founded on the knowledge of a science, Historical Material-

ism. This knowledge indicates the place and the task of proletarian political struggle within the capitalist social formation.
Theoretical-political deviations, deviations from Scientific
Socialism, necessarily lead to an incorrect and unscientific
politics, and therefore an ineffective politics, which is objectively reactionary [*Theoretical Practice* 2, 1].

So not only theory but politics too must be 'scientific'. This means
that Marxist theory must not reflect the struggles that arise spon-
taneously, but transform them on the political level, translating
these 'partial, sectoral demands into a revolutionary proletarian
political programme'.[18]

Science of course, being the result of a practice, theoretical
practice, cannot be assessed merely by looking at the uses to
which it is put in other practices, such as politics. This is the
fallacy of the 'Ultra-egalitarians' and the 'Social Democrats' and
while not wishing for a moment to be seen in their company, we
should like to examine some of the links between a scientific
theory and a scientific politics. For it does seem to be the case
that such a Marxism requires a party of the Leninist type if it
is to be effective at all in guiding other kinds of practice. We are
cautioned that science is not 'an open book', and that there is 'a
real inequality in knowledge and technical level' between people.[19]
So science, and hence knowledge, is an activity for specialists. Its
objective truths, which are revealed by the party's theoreticians
(who may also of course, like Lenin, be active political militants)
provide the essential means whereby democratic centralism can
operate, since it provides a tool that can distinguish between true
and false ideas, and so can guide the activities of the party at all
levels.

Thus, aside from the question of whether it is true, Althusser's
science, his restating of the philosophical prerequisites of a Marxist science, appears to be linked to a Leninist political strategy
that puts the greatest emphasis on the need to build a revolutionary party that is highly disciplined and hierarchically organised. The existence of such a party then itself supplies the motive
for revolutionary activity in the various levels of practice. The

[18] *Theoretical Practice* 2, 2.
[19] *Theoretical Practice* 2, 4.

reason for engaging in theoretical practice, for example, cannot be derived from historical materialism itself, since science cannot underwrite values and choices without admitting an ideological element.[20]

> Communists struggle for the suppression of *classes* and for a communist society, where, one day, all men will be free and brothers [Althusser, 'The Politics of Philosophy', 10].

But on Althusser's own account of science, science itself cannot give men sufficient reasons to struggle for the suppression of classes rather than for any other goal. What does is the existence of an organisation, the party, that is pledged to aims that are taken from its scientific theory. Thus the party justifies the science and the science justifies the party. People join the party for various personal reasons, but the existence of the party itself is not subject to choice, and so the symbiosis of the party and its science is not in question. The Althusserians are Marxist-Leninists, or potential ones when no party is available, because they believe that Lenin

> ... provides the concepts to think the political practice of the proletarian position, its organisational forms (the party) and the major forms of deviation from that practice
>
> [*Theoretical Practice*, 2, 2].

Lenin's importance, for them, is that he correctly determines how political practice is to be organised on the basis of his knowledge of historical materialism. He shows how political practice can be guided and controlled by Marxist theory when the latter is institutionalised in an organisation of revolutionaries.

The Althusserians might well say that if Marxist theory is not used as a science which is true not because of how it is applied but because of the way it is produced, then the attempt to obtain knowledge will be abandoned and we will be left with speculative ideologies, in the manner of the Frankfurt School. But this is to stay the prisoner of a partial conception of science, and to deny the range of alternatives that exists. ... Thus, if we have read

---

[20] Engels also believed in the separation of fact and value. See chapter 4.

Marx correctly, Marx offers us a 'science' of social reality that is rooted firmly in an ontology, an image of man, and which is aimed not merely at producing an objectively valid knowledge, but at providing knowledge which can help in emancipating man and dereifying the world. For this purpose the concept of aliena-tion is indeed crucial, because alienation creates the structures that transform men into things; because men under capitalism interact not as human beings but as things, commodities, it be-comes possible to quantify and measure certain aspects of this social reality, i.e., a science in Althusser's sense can only exist so long as there is alienation, which is certainly not merely a pheno-menon of consciousness:

> What Marx means by 'human science' is a science of concrete synthesis, integrated with real life. Its standpoint is the ideal of non-alienated man whose *actual human*—as opposed to both 'speculatively invented' and to practically dehumanized, 'abstractly material'—needs determine the line of research in every particular field. The achievements of the particular fields —guided right from the beginning by the common frame of reference of a non-fragmented 'human science'—are then brought together into a higher synthesis which in its turn deter-mines the subsequent lines of investigations in the various fields
>
> [I. Meszaros, *Marx's Theory of Alienation*, London 1970, 101].

If this is not the 'interest' that governs the science and the pro-duction of a knowledge, then it will either be the technical control and manipulation of society sought by bourgeois sociology, or some other, such as the Althusserian belief in the need for a party organised on scientific principles which can become one of the causes of a revolution in a situation of overdetermination. One of Marx's achievements was indeed to show that the realm of theory could not be made independent of other kinds of practice; this is not to claim that theory fuses with practice or that its results have to be directly validated by practice—only that by themselves all theories are incomplete. *They cannot exhaust reality, so their objectivity, their 'truth', and their meaning, depend on the interests that govern them.* This is no less true of Althusser's theory. Under the cloak of being an objective science the theory hides the real interest that governs it. Althusser refuses to found it on a philosophical anthropology, and thereby makes his theory indeterminate. The situation is rescued by introducing the party as the practical interest that the theory advances. This does not invalidate it, but at least the recognition of the role that the party plays demystifies Althusser's thought, and enables us to judge it more clearly.

It is not intended to argue here that the Leninist party is an incorrect form of organisation. There are situations where it is very appropriate. All we would question is that Marxism as a science lays down one and only one kind of revolutionary organisation. Revolution certainly demands a revolutionary movement, but there is no good *a priori* reason why this should only take the form of a Leninist party that is guided by an objective science of history. Whether a revolutionary movement is going to be truly liberating in all areas of human experience will depend on just how it establishes communication between people—how people learn from one another, and how they develop together. Althusser's theory and Althusser's party seem designed to frustrate the attempts to see the world and see it whole, and encourage the notion that only scientists can really make the revolution.

Part 4: The Concept of a Social Formation

Structure and History

Althusser's view of scientific explanation is the structuralist one, although he has some reservation about certain of the structuralist concepts.[21] The structuralist approach is set out very clearly by Maurice Godelier.[22] There are two main questions that concern us here. Firstly, the structures that are isolated are *conceptual* rather than *empirical*, and secondly, the study of structures has priority over their origin and evolution. Godelier explains the first point as follows:

> For Marx, as for Claude Lévi-Strauss, 'structures' should not be confused with visible 'social relations', but constitute a

[21] In particular the concepts of synchrony and diachrony, which Althusser rejects.

[22] M. Godelier, 'System, Structure and Contradiction in *Capital*', *Socialist Register* 1967.

level of reality invisible but present behind the visible social relations ['System, Structure and Contradiction', 92].

Therefore:

... the scientific conception of social reality does not 'arise by abstraction' from the spontaneous or reflected conceptions of individuals. On the contrary, it must destroy the obviousness of these conceptions in order to *bring out* the hidden internal logic of social life

['System, Structure and Contradiction', 93].

This is why Lévi-Strauss rejects Radcliffe-Brown's concept of structure, because it makes structure a part of empirical reality. It is not hard to see the closeness of this argument to Althusser's distinction between ideology and science. For ideology is precisely the failure to develop a sufficiently abstract conceptual system which is not merely a reflection of people's consciousness. As a result analysis remains on the level of the 'given', of appearance, and therefore cannot explain reality, but only 'interpret, systematise and defend' what already exists.

Some critics of structuralism have noted that the structuralist method is really the same as ordinary scientific method,[23] in the sense that all social theory tries to identify those elements of a society that can best explain how it works. Lévi-Strauss, for example, constructs abstract models by breaking down the object under study and subsequently reconstituting it in terms of essentially relational properties. But as Runciman argues, this is what science always does, and he quotes Merleau-Ponty: 'The objects which science constructs ... are always bundles of relations'.[24]

So the real difference between structuralism and other scientific methods is not the role of abstraction, the rejection of the given, the isolation of structures, but how these structures are chosen and validated. Since the structuralists reject the empirical conception of structure, they also reject the idea of linear causality between structure and events. They propose a new concept of causality, namely that the structure is immanent in its effects.

[23] In particular W. G. Runciman, 'What is Structuralism?', *British Journal of Sociology*, vol. 20, no. 3 (Sept. 1969), 253–265.

[24] 'What is Structuralism?', 257.

'The whole existence of the structure consists of its effects'.[25] Such a notion, however, seems to rest ultimately on a coherence view of truth—a structure has been identified correctly if it permits explanation of the largest possible number of 'effects'. But other Marxists also use a coherence view of truth, so how are we to judge between two theories that identify different structures in order to explain the same phenomena? Runciman asks, 'Why is Lévi-Strauss' mythography not itself a myth?' and we might well ask, 'Why is Althusser's science not itself an ideology?' This is not to subscribe to a relativist position; it is merely to point out that Althusser's attempt at avoiding relativism is a pseudo-solution, because his idea of science gives us no clear criteria for choosing between theories at the conceptual level.

The second principle that Godelier raises is that the parts of a structure should always be studied before the origin and evolution of the structure. This opposition between structure and process is often expressed as the distinction between synchronic and diachronic analysis. But Althusser himself rejects these terms. He points out that synchronic knowledge is sufficient:

> What the synchrony aims at has nothing to do with the *temporal* presence of the object as a *real object*, but on the contrary, concerns a different type of presence, and the presence of a *different object*: not the temporal presence of the concrete object, not the historical time of the historical presence of the historical object, but the presence (or the 'time') *of the object of knowledge of the theoretical analysis itself*, the presence of *knowledge*. The synchronic is then nothing but *the conception* of the specific relations that exist between the different elements and the different structures of the structure of the whole ... the synchronic is eternity in Spinoza's sense [*Reading Capital*, 107].

Diachrony then loses its 'concrete' sense, and becomes a category of the synchronic:

> Diachrony is ... merely the false name for the *process*, or for what Marx called the *development of forms*. But here too we are *within knowledge*, in the process of knowledge, not in the development of the real-concrete [*Reading Capital*, 108].

[25] Althusser and Balibar, *Reading Capital*, 189.

Thus the only knowledge there is is synchronic, which is scientific because it is atemporal in the sense that it suppresses time as it is experienced by men in their practical activity, in order to make its object amenable to identification and isolation and hence to generalisation and prediction. This has been the standard procedure of natural science, which takes the world *sub specie aeternitatis* and so derives explanatory models with predictive certainty. If we apply such a method to society, it follows, as Godelier puts it, that

> ... the genesis of a structure can only be studied under the 'guidance' of a pre-existing knowledge of that structure
>
>   ['System, Structure and Contradiction in *Capital*', 98].

And each structure, according to Althusser, has its own independent history:

> Just as there is no production in general, there is no history in general, but only specific structures of historicity, based in the last resort on the specific structures of the different modes of production [*Reading Capital*, 108].

Thus we can only know a history through its structures or forms, which are not present in reality, but are the result of theoretical practice:

> An event falling within one of these forms, which has the wherewithal to fall within one of these forms, *which is a possible content for one of these forms*, which affects them, concerns them, reinforces or disturbs them, which provokes them or which they provoke, or even choose or select, that is a *historical event* [Althusser, *For Marx*, 126].

Now it is clear how this view of studying history differs from the practice of orthodox historians who believe that they have no need for science or theory in understanding the past, but instead try to describe the past 'as it really was' or how it appeared to men at the time and so forth.[26] But they are not really Althusser's target. His main attack is on that other empiricist and ideological conception of history—Hegel's.

[26] Cf G. Stedman Jones' critique of English historiography, 'The Pathology of English History', *New Left Review* 46.

Hegel is accused of the following. Firstly, he tries to grasp the movement of the real with the concepts, and therefore fails to distinguish between knowledge of the object and the object itself. Secondly, his starting point is the individual or subject. History becomes the result of the complex interplay between individuals, whether these are concepts, as in Hegel, or men, as in the early Marx. This conception of history, says Althusser, is common to Hegel, the young Marx, the political economists, Lukacs, and Sartre, amongst others. The individual, the empirical subject, becomes the given of the theory, but since any conception of such an individual must be metaphysical, it follows that the qualities which are given to him, his essence, can only be ideological, i.e., can only be what the theory in question requires them to be. But this ideological element, once it has crept in, vitiates the whole analysis, and prevents the attainment of knowledge, for the isolated individual cannot be understood by means of a structure or form. What happens is that the analyst starts from the individual and his consciousness, and then deduces from this the historical development of society, in order to grasp the mediations between individual experience and the social structure men create. But, says Althusser, this is to confuse the level of scientific concepts—social structure—with the level of empirical reality—the individual and his consciousness. The result is not a knowledge, but an ideology of history, because values, in the form of different conceptions of human nature and the essence of the individual, are smuggled into the analysis.

Althusser can quote in support of his view Marx's criticisms of the abstract 'man' of the Young Hegelians, and the 'economic man' of the political economists, but it is clear from the way in which he makes his attack that he has not really grasped Marx's philosophical anthropology at all. He has read into it his own ideology of science. For it is ludicrous to suppose that Marx in his early works conceives of man as an isolated subject. Yet Althusser has no hesitation is stating the following:

If the essence of man is to be a universal attribute, it is essential that *concrete subjects* exist as absolute givens; this implies an *empiricism of the subject*. If these empirical individuals are to be men, it is essential that each carries in himself the whole human essence, if not in fact, at least in principle; this implies an *idealism of the essence* [*For Marx*, 228].

Recent scholarship on the early works has shown conclusively that Marx's concept of man as a social being cannot be reduced to the above terms. The 'concrete subjects' of his theory do not exist as absolute givens; on the contrary, they are only intelligible in terms of the 'ensemble of social relations'. They do not carry around with them the human essence. Species being, or man's full sociality, exists only in relation to a whole society, and determinate modes of production. When Marx talks of man, he means of course not man as an individual, but mankind, the human species. As Meszaros puts it:

This approach ... carries with it that what emerges as the 'essence of human nature' is not *egoism*, but *sociality*. ... 'Sociality' as the defining characteristic of human nature is radically different from those criticised by Marx. Unlike 'egoism', it cannot be an abstract quality inherent in the single individual. It can only exist in the relations of individuals with each other [*Marx's Theory of Alienation*, 149].

What Marx argues for is a 'science' of history that understands history as the transformation of man through man's own activity in satisfying his needs and creating new ones. Thus he distinguishes between 'human nature in general' and 'human nature as modified in each particular epoch'. What he isolates are the conditions or the structure of human actions, how we distinguish human activity from animal activity. He does this in his concepts of labour, social being, and species being. But these are not attributes and qualities which constitute man's 'essence'—on the contrary, they are the concepts that allow us to recognise *human acts* as human. Marx can then analyse the history of specific societies as the development, satisfaction and creation of human needs. These needs, and the way men seek to realise them define what man is:

As men express their life, so they are
[*The German Ideology*, London 1965, 32].

History is nothing but the continuous transformation of human nature [*The Poverty of Philosophy*, London 1956, 147].

Thus Marx insists that what men are cannot be deduced from a few principles of human nature, a procedure he criticises throughout his early writings. His philosophical anthropology defines the method and the status of his historical and economic studies. In particular, *it establishes why the social relationships established around material needs should be more important than any other in explaining historical change, through its account of the preconditions for human history.*

Althusser, however, *has no similar way of demonstrating his dictum that the economy is determinant in the last instance, other than resorting to some metaphysical principle of the primacy of matter over spirit.* It remains a profession of faith. He stresses the autonomy of all the various levels in the 'social formation', which, he argues, is for Marx a complex structured totality, in which there is not a single simple contradiction that unites the whole. Instead, each level is relatively autonomous with its own contradictions. In place of a dialectical totality we have a totality that is the sum of relatively autonomous parts. The only unifying factor is the ultimate dominance of the economy over the other levels. But as Althusser himself confesses, 'From the first moment to the last, the lonely hour of the "last instance" never comes',[27] yet the belief that it does is crucial to Althusser's theory, as Andrew Levine explains:

> To deny that some level is determining in the last instance would be to undermine the possibility of a dialectical under-standing of the social totality. Historical materialism would then be a positive science like any other, and dialectical materialism would give way to an empiricist philosophy of science ['A Reading of Marx', 11].

Because the principle really is arbitrary and lacks an ontological foundation, its application in actual analysis has interesting, if rather crude, consequences, which we shall later examine.

One of the reasons why the last instance never comes is that the contradictions in the autonomous structures are external rather than internal, that is, they have most significance when they arise between structures rather than when they develop

[27] *For Marx*, 113.

within a single structure. We find Godelier, for example, arguing that the contradiction which Hegelians often make the central contradiction of the totality is that between capital and labour. But this is a contradiction only within one structure—the relations of production. As a result it can be managed; hence it gives rise to no more than trade union consciousness. A much more important contradiction, says Godelier, is that between the two main structures in the economy, the relations and the forces of production, which develop at their own speeds and according to their own historicity, and so are sometimes in harmony and sometimes not. (For example, bourgeois relations of production are in harmony with the new techniques of the capitalist mode of production in the early years of capitalism—only later does a contradiction arise between them.)

> ... (the contradiction) is unintentional and without teleology, but transparent to *science* because it is 'significant'. It signifies the *limits* within which it is possible that capitalist relations of production, based on private property, may correspond to the development of the productive forces to which they have given birth
>
> [Godelier, 'System, Structure and Contradiction in *Capital*', 105].

And we have to understand these limits as objective and immanent features of the capitalist mode of production, and not of capitalists or workers as individuals or economic agents.

But this attack hits no target, for all Marxists have grasped Marx's insight that capitalist social relations cannot be reduced to the wills of individual actors. Thus, while Godelier usefully isolates some of the different kinds of contradiction to be found in *Capital* which belong to the capitalist mode of production as a system, he fails to understand what the wider debate is about when he writes:

> ... it is no longer possible to read into the historically determined contradiction of capitalist relations of production with a determined level of the productive forces the philosophical drama of the revolt of the 'true essence' of man against the 'dehumanised existence' imposed on the workers by the bourgeoisie ['System, Structure and Contradiction', 106].

Godelier attempts to dispose of concepts like alienation by reducing them to epiphenomena. By denying that alienation is a structural question, and implying instead that it is merely a matter of consciousness it can be relegated to ideology. For Marx, however, alienation and 'dehumanised existence' are not conditions imposed on workers through the personal malevolence of capitalists as individuals. Alienation is rooted in the conditions of capitalist production, which continually reproduce it.

> By the introduction of machinery the division of labour inside society has grown up, the task of the worker inside the workshop has been simplified, capital has been concentrated, human beings have been further dismembered
>
> [Marx, *The Poverty of Philosophy*, 141].

> ... the character of independence and estrangement which the capitalist mode of production as a whole gives to the instruments of labour and to the product, as against the workman, is developed by means of machinery into a thorough antagonism. Therefore it is with the advent of machinery that the workman for the first time brutally revolts against the instruments of labour [*Capital*, vol. I, Moscow 1954, 432].

> ... within the capitalist system all methods for raising the social productiveness of labour are brought about at the cost of the individual labourer; all means for the development of production transform themselves into means of domination over, and exploitation of, the producers; they mutilate the labourer into a fragment of a man, degrade him to the level of an appendage of a machine, destroy every remnant of charm in his work and turn it into a hated toil; they estrange him from the intellectual potentialities of the labour-process in the same proportion as science is incorporated in it as an independent power; they distort the conditions under which he works, subject him during the labour process to a despotism the more hateful for its meanness; they transform his life-time into working time, and drag his wife and child beneath the wheels of the Juggernaut of capital [*Capital*, vol. I, 645].

Alienation is much more than a psychological disorder or a speculative philosophical notion. It is one of the general concepts of Marx's theoretical system, which he uses to analyse the various ways in which labour has been constrained in history. Godelier is correct in stating that the fundamental contradiction is not between workers and capitalists, but belongs to the limit set to the indefinite expansion of capitalist production by the contradiction between the forces and relations of production, which expresses itself in the tendency of the rate of profit to fall. But he fails to notice that the *economic struggle between workers and capitalists is one of the crucial factors in explaining why there is a tendency for the rate of profit to fall*. When workers press on profit margins, one reaction of the capitalists can be to introduce new techniques in an attempt to raise *relative surplus value*, and this naturally raises the organic composition of capital, which causes the rate of profit to decline. We will discuss these matters more fully in our final essay, but at least we must avoid thinking that contradictions arise only because of uneven development between structures that otherwise are quite independent of one another. We cannot understand what causes crises and how the capitalist system develops without understanding not merely the relative autonomy but also the relative dependence of structures.

Althusser expresses his own thinking on contradictions in his concept of *overdetermination*, which he contrasts with both the 'Hegelian' dialectic and the 'Hegelian' concept of contradiction. In the latter the solution to contradictions is always internal (*Aufhebung*), superstructures are not autonomous, and there is an internal teleology which governs the evolution of nature and history.[28] For Althusser, however, contradictions occur at different times at different speeds in different parts of the social formation and independently of one another. Contradictions can thus accumulate, as in Russia by 1917, until their weight becomes too great and the system snaps. The situation has become overdetermined. Breakdown when it comes is often due to accidents—the most important causes are frequently unrelated to economic contradictions. The task of the revolutionary party is to foresee such breakdowns, and use the opportunity to force a historical 'rupture' by seizing power.

[28] Cf Godelier, 'System, Structure and Contradiction'.

Now it is easy to understand the reasons for this approach, apart from its importance for political strategy. It allows Marxists to incorporate all the unique and particular and freaky facts into their analyses. It is a move away from eschatology—the sort used by Marx in the *Communist Manifesto*—which proclaims the circumstances and the sequence of events that will accompany the leap into freedom. But however realistic this may be, it makes a *science* of history very difficult, since suddenly we are faced with a whole set of facts and events which cannot be generalised, quantified, compared etc.—in short, cannot be foreseen. It acknowledges the openness of the future. It also changes what we understand by a revolution. Revolution now depends on a change in structures which may or may not affect consciousness and purposes. Its agency is the party which presides over the rupture in history and presumably is alone able to comprehend it. Everyone else is pursuing their own ends and sees something quite different in what is taking place.

Althusser intends the concept of overdetermination to be the scientific version of the theory of the weakest link. He says that it enables us to account for all the other revolutions that should never have happened, such as the Paris Commune. But in that case his analysis is well on the way to becoming ex post facto explanation in the manner of orthodox non-Marxist historians. Revolutions occur because the situation is overdetermined, but how do we know when one situation is more overdetermined than another before a revolution occurs to show us?

This is not to deny that the emphasis on the role of accident is important in looking at actual historical situations. Marx himself drew attention to the significance of accidents in a letter he wrote to Kugelmann about the Paris Commune:

> World history would indeed be very easy to make, if the struggle were taken up only on condition of infallibly favourable chances. It would on the other hand be of a very mystical nature, if 'accidents' played no part. These accidents themselves fall naturally into the general course of development and are compensated for, again, by other accidents. But acceleration and delay are very dependent upon such 'accidents', which include the 'accident' of the character of those

who at first stand at the head of the movement. The decisive, unfavourable accident this time is by no means to be found in the general conditions of French society, but in the presence of the Prussians in France and their position right before Paris...

[K. Marx, F. Engels, *Correspondence*, London 1934, 310–11].

But if the concept of overdetermination is designed merely to take account of the accidents that can precipitate a revolution it does not have much precision as a scientific concept. It does have other consequences, however. One of these, a rigid insistence on the independence of contradictions, we have already noted. But it also implies that for socialism to come into existence, not all the levels of the social formation have to be transformed. Thus we find Althusser writing about Stalinism as follows:

... everything that has been said of the 'cult of personality' refers exactly to the domain of the *superstructure* and therefore of State organization and ideologies; further it refers largely to *this domain alone*, which we know from Marxist theory possesses a 'relative autonomy' (which explains very simply, in theory, how the socialist *infrastructure* has been able to develop without essential damage during this period of errors affecting the superstructure) [*For Marx*, 240].

Now since determination in the last instance by the economy is what characterises social formations of the capitalist type, we might, as foolish anti-Stalinists have, expected the arrival of socialism to transform the relative autonomy of the superstructures into a real autonomy. Certainly the Althusserians rarely seem to accord real autonomy to the superstructures when they are analysing capitalist societies.[29] But all we need to note here is

---

[29] Apart from the case discussed in the next section, another example is an unpublished paper by Gilles Bourques and Nicole Laurin-Frenette: 'Social Classes and Nationalist Ideologies in Quebec 1760–1970'. Using an Althusserian framework, they treat all nationalist ideologies as the direct expression of social classes, thus making the level of ideological practice completely determined by the economic level.

how mechanistic the analysis becomes when we divide the levels of the social formation in this way, and what dubious ideological and practical implications it can have.

Part 5: English History and Althusser's Model

The actual application of the Althusserian theory can be studied by looking briefly at the recent debate on English history between Perry Anderson, Tom Nairn, Edward Thompson, and Nicos Poulantzas.

The Anderson-Nairn interpretation of English history[30] was intended to account for some of the peculiarities of this history. Why did England, the first industrial country, fail to have a clearcut bourgeois revolution, but was instead governed throughout the nineteenth century by a ruling class that was aristocratic in its way of life and its ideology? And why did Marxism never develop a strong base in the English working class,

The first question they trace to the English civil war, 'the first, most mediated, least pure bourgeois revolution of any major European country'. They distinguish between the various contradictions that caused the civil war and determined its particular history, and the objective consequences of the upheaval. Thus they state that the conflict was between two segments of the landowning class neither of whom were direct representatives of economic interests. The main ideologies of the struggle were religious, and the main issues concerned the political, religious, and economic role of the monarchy. But the objective results of the civil war, which were not consciously intended by any of the participants, were to remove all the juridical and constitutional obstacles to rationalised capitalist development, to leave the social structure intact, and to destroy militant puritanism as an ideology of any consequence. This created a landowning class which used capitalist methods in the countryside to maintain

[30] Perry Anderson, 'Origins of the Present Crisis', New Left Review 23 (Jan.–Feb. 1964); T. Nairn, 'The English Working Class', New Left Review 24 (Mar.–Apr. 1964); T. Nairn, 'The Anatomy of the Labour Party', New Left Review 27 and 28 (Sept.–Oct. and Nov.–Dec. 1964); P. Anderson, 'Socialism and Pseudo-Empiricism', New Left Review 35 (Jan.–Feb. 1966).

itself. In the course of the nineteenth century, this class came to terms with the new industrial bourgeoisie, and fused in a 'hegemonic bloc', a bloc in which however the aristocratic section retained its ideological and political dominance.

The answer to the second question—why did the English working class never embrace Marxism?—follows from the answer to the first. Since the industrial bourgeoisie 'lost its nerve' and fused with the old ruling class, it never developed its own coherent ideology and so never remade society in its own image. As a result, the working class was stunted in its growth, because Marxism only develops in reaction to a fully fledged bourgeois ideology. The working class never had a bourgeois vision and bourgeois institutions to oppose; hence it never developed a hegemonic but only a corporate consciousness:

> If a hegemonic class can be defined as one which imposes its own ends and its own vision on society as a whole, a corporate class is conversely one which pursues its own ends within a social totality whose global determination lies outside it
>
> [Anderson, 'Origins of the Present Crisis', 41].

What Anderson and Nairn are attempting in their account of the civil war is to distinguish between the intended and the unintended consequences of social action. They thus emphasise that the structural reality can often be other than men's consciousness. They resist the kind of Marxism that attempts to make all the superstructures transparent and direct reflections of the economic base. But they then proceed to argue that gaining consciousness of the structural reality is a major prerequisite for the formation of a hegemonic class, and that the failure of the bourgeoisie to become hegemonic in this sense contributed to the failure of the working class.

Poulantzas criticises the interpretation with a framework largely derived from Althusser and, in doing so, gives us some insight into how the Althusserian concepts can be applied.[31] As might be expected, he largely welcomes the account of the civil war, for it distinguishes between the manifest and the latent func-

---

[31] N. Poulantzas, 'Marxist Political Theory in Great Britain', *New Left Review* 43 (May–June 1967), 57–74.

tions of the conflict—and the war can be treated as the result of an over-determined situation. What Poulantzas objects to is the concept of hegemony that Anderson and Nairn employ, because it includes the consciousness that a class has of its situation and its goals. He therefore condemns it as historicist and subjectivist. He represents Anderson and Nairn as saying that the superstructures are produced by the conscious will of the hegemonic class, and that as a result a class that is economically dominant cannot be politically dominant unless it produces new state superstructures through its praxis and its consciousness. So Anderson and Nairn, because they find that ideologically the aristocracy is still dominant in the nineteenth century wrongly conclude that the aristocracy must still be politically dominant. (If they were consistent historicists, however, we might, extending Poulantzas' argument, expect them to argue that the aristocracy was still dominant economically also, that despite appearances the mode of production was still feudal. The fact that they do not shows that while they do accord some autonomy to the superstructures, they are still incapable of saying what relationship this has to the economic base.)

Poulantzas simplifies the Anderson-Nairn position somewhat. What does he offer in its place? He sets out to provide the scientific version of English history, drawn from the two ideological accounts of Anderson and Nairn on the one hand, and E. P. Thompson on the other. Thompson had criticised Anderson for evaluating English history according to a model drawn from French experience of what a proper bourgeois revolution and working class movement should be like.[32] He had argued that the aristocratic elements in Victorian England were only vestiges, a ceremonial façade to secure the people's deference, and cited evidence to show not only the predominance of the bourgeoise in politics but also in ideology (political economy and utilitarianism). Poulantzas, however, employing the well-known Hegelian principle of the identity of opposites, consigns him to the same bin as Anderson and Nairn, for he says that Thompson shares the same problematic—he tries to deduce who dominates politi-

[32] E. P. Thompson, 'The Pecularities of the English', in J. Saville and R. Miliband (eds.), *Socialist Register 1965*, 311–362.

cally by showing who dominates ideologically, that is he treats consciousness as a part of structure.

Poulantzas wishes to show that consciousness has nothing to do with structure, which is purely a theoretical construction and has no existence in the minds of real men. So how does he proceed? He has a concept of the social formation with its three main levels of practice—economic, political, and ideological. The economic is dominant in the last instance, but otherwise the levels are relatively autonomous, and each is governed by its own structures. Given this starting point, Poulantzas can say that the Anderson-Nairn thesis is mistaken, because the fact that the dominant ideology in Britain does not represent a coherent bourgeois world view does not mean that this ideology does not in fact correspond to the political interests of the bourgeoisie, nor that the bourgeoisie could not be in a hegemonic position.[33] Poulantzas therefore puts forward his own scientific thesis on British history:

> ...given the peculiarities of capitalist formation in Britain, the dominant ideology is deeply impregnated with elements relating to an aristocratic life style, as Anderson and Nairn show; however its internal coherence, comprehensible if related to the overall unity of the formation, corresponds to the 'political hegemony'—not to the class consciousness—of the bourgeoisie, which explains those bourgeois features that Thompson insists upon.[34]

Thus all three theories agree that the bourgeoisie dominates in the economy. Anderson and Thompson disagree about which class dominates in the ideological level and therefore also in the political level. Poulantzas argues that the bourgeoisie dominates in the political level, and that in the ideological level the dominant ideology, although not in the form of a coherent bourgeois world view, conforms to the political interests of the bourgeoisie. Which is to say that the bourgeoisie dominates at every level of practice.

[33] Poulantzas, 'Marxist Political Theory in Great Britain', 67.
[34] 'Marxist Political Theory', 68. For Poulantzas relative autonomy of the superstructures appears to mean only that the class which dominates politically may draw its support from other classes. At the structural level all levels are determined by the economy.

Thus despite the much vaunted autonomy of levels, Poulantzas ends by finding less real autonomy than Anderson and Nairn.

Is this perhaps because this *is* the correct explanation in this case, or has Poulantzas misapplied Althusser's conceptual scheme? The problem seems to be that there is no other way the principle of determination by the economy in the last instance could be followed except by assuming that the economy is also determining in the first instance, and that if the structures of the economy are bourgeois, then the dominant ideology and politics must conform to the interests of the bourgeoisie at the structural level. Otherwise the 'economy' can have no causal impact at all, and the three levels must be treated as completely independent. Given Poulantzas' thesis, what conceivable evidence about the dominant ideology could persuade him that it was *not* in the political interests of the bourgeoisie?

If the principle of determination by the economy in the last instance is abandoned, then the capitalist social formation loses its defining characteristic. Althusser's structuralism then is deprived of its distinctiveness and would become a social theory of the more orthodox functionalist type, in which it is held *a priori* that there are a number of structures, all of which have equal status theoretically as possible factors which unify the structures into an interrelated whole. It is made a question of balance. Faced by this threat, Althusser needs his principle of the last instance for his concept of the social formation to remain a Marxist one. But he lacks any means of establishing it, and this helps to make his concept of structure and overdetermination rather mechanistic. The social world loses some of its contingency, its status as a *human product* rather than just an object of science. Thus, whatever Althusser's intentions, the use of the principle of the last instance in actual analysis will tend to mean that what the investigator finds will be either an all-pervading dominance of 'economic' relationships, or none at all, because in the absence of clear criteria as to how it should be applied most analysts would probably opt for consistency and stick to one end of the scale rather than float about in the middle. What his analysis does is reify concepts such as 'economy', 'base', 'super-structure', and then discover problems regarding which deter-mine, balance, or correspond with a description of a particular historical period. Such 'theory' becomes obsessed or fetishistic over how to characterise particular instances of human history. Yet such theory mystifies, for it rarely confronts the central problems of Marxism. To give but one instance, contemporary conditions in the Soviet Union require an analysis which uses concepts and theories which tackle the constraints on labour and freedom, and such questions must start with the limitations upon the development of free activity which such a society requires for its maintenance.

Part 6: Conclusion

Althusser's strength is that he insists on the centrality of the theoretical. He recognises that from the point of view of contemporary Marxism, textual exegeses of Marx's work have little interest. What is important is to understand Marxism as a theory, to look for the coherence and the absences in Marx's system of concepts, and to grasp the object these concepts create. But this strength turns into a weakness when Althusser concludes that what Marx achieved was merely an objective *science* of history. For this leaves out Marx's own premises, and so resurrects the familiar division between fact and value, encounters all the familiar problems of verification, and obscures the practical interests that govern knowledge.

Althusser is also right to emphasise that capitalism must be seen as a system, but so keen is he to divest himself of the ideology of humanism that he produces a thoroughly mechanistic account of how structures are related in the social formation, and never seems to realise that if we cannot understand the origin of a society without knowing its structure, we likewise cannot understand the structure without knowing its origin. What is the use of a knowledge of abstract structures? The contradictions between the forces and the relations of production is only significant because it raises the question of the relationship between social organisation and technical possibilities. Similarly, what is meant when we talk about determination by the economy in the last instance? The economic level is always a specific organisation of labour, and it is the particular way in which labour is organised under capitalism that gives rise to the central contradiction of the capitalist system, the barrier to its indefinite expansion. This is the conflict between the productivity of labour power and the distribution of this product according to labour time.[35]

Marx was able to discover this contradiction and to show that it could be overcome because he understood that capitalism was only a specific historical mode of production, one particular way of organising labour. This insight stemmed directly from his anthropological premises. It is because Marx sees purposive social activity as the distinguishing characteristic of man, that he sees it also as the ever-present liberating potentiality in human action. To set out the problem in this way is at the same time to indicate the area for theoretical enquiry—namely what prevents this liberation, this full human development? Marx's whole work is an analysis of the different social and production constraints that govern human behaviour. He shows how capitalism is the first mode of production that creates the objective possibility of overcoming the production constraints, the performance of necessary labour. The barrier that it erects is the relations of production, which determine how the product is distributed. At the same time the capitalist mode of production represents the most complete form of alienation, because it alienates the worker from his product, from his work, and from his fellow men.

Marx, however, did not *deduce* all the concepts of his theory from his anthropological premises. On the contrary, he devoted his life to a critique of political economy in order to uncover the precise ways in which capitalism works, and its precise limits and contradictions. Althusser is certainly right to point out that, from one angle, Marx's achievement was to move beyond the Young Hegelians; instead of engaging in a purely speculative criticism of existing institutions, he began to study the evolution, structure and the future development of the capitalist system. As the Russian reviewer of *Capital* put it:

> Marx treats the social movement as a process of natural history, governed by laws not only independent of human will, consciousness and intelligence, but on the contrary, determining that will, consciousness and intelligence
>
> [quoted by Marx, *Capital* vol. I, 18].

[35] We deal with these questions at greater length in chapter 7.

Marx accepts that liberation is not merely a question of consciousness, that the constraints that govern men cannot be overcome through the exercise of will alone, but that they are continually reproduced because they result from the interaction of man and nature under specific social conditions. But this is the starting point that Marx reached in his early works. The break in his writings is not an epistemological rupture, for without the premises developed in the early works, Marx's method and the meaning of his researches lacks any real basis. What the Althusserians never answer satisfactorily is what led Marx to exchange ideology for science? Was it new facts, a new method, or did the new science drop from the skies? If our reading of Marx is correct, then it was precisely Marx's formulation of the real starting point for the study of society that defined for him the area and the methods for such a study. Althusser admits that the early works and the 'works of the break' were important in leading Marx to create the new science, but he believes that once the new science was launched, its antecedents are set apart as belonging to the old pre-scientific problematic, and are of interest only for the light they shed on Marx's intellectual development, and are therefore a hindrance rather than an aid to contemporary Marxism. It is this thesis *with all its consequences* that we believe to be mistaken.

6

MARX, ADAM SMITH AND POLITICAL ECONOMY[1]

Introduction

The most passing acquaintance with Marx's writings would show the significance he attaches to political economy. From the days in 1844 when he first began copying down passages from the political economists in his notebooks to his great works on economics, he wrestled with this obscure and dismal science. He saw his work both as a critique of political economy and as 'a critical analysis of capitalist production'.[2] But the political economists, whatever their failings and errors and bias, were in his view dealing with the right subject matter. Marx seems to have originally thought that he could have dealt with political economy in a very short time and move on to the subjects that interested him more. He wrote in 1851 about his studies that:

> ... in five more weeks I will be through with the whole economic shit. And that done, I will work over my *Economics* at home and throw myself into another science in the Museum. I am beginning to be tired of it. Basically, this science has made no further progress since A. Smith and D. Ricardo, however much has been done in individual, often very subtle, researches [quoted in McLellan, *Marx's Grundrisse*, 5].

But he never did get through with the economics shit. Indeed, his economic works are now known to be only a part of what he planned.

Despite his very evident obsession with political economy, Marx's relationship to the political economists is probably the

[1] An early version of this essay is contained in an MA thesis, University of Durham, in 1969, by one of the authors, Andrew Gamble. The original title was 'The Social Bond and Civil Society: A Study of Karl Marx and Adam Smith'.

[2] This is the sub-title of *Capital*.

most neglected area of the current flood of writing on Marx. Marx's relationship to Hegel, the philosophical, historical and political aspects of his work have been exhaustively discussed, but not his economics.

Political economy as a separate branch of study was still very new when Marx took it up. The economic aspects of human activity had often been treated by philosophers such as Locke and Hume but it was Quesnay in his *Tableau Economique* who produced the first distinctive work of political economy, because, for the first time, it made an understanding of economic activity central to an understanding of society. In this connection it is interesting to observe the development of Adam Smith's studies. He held the Chair in Moral Philosophy at Glasgow, but moral philosophy encompassed all areas of human activity and his lectures were arranged in four parts; Natural Theology, Ethics, Justice and Expediency. The second part, 'Ethics', he later published as *The Theory of Moral Sentiments*.

Under 'Expediency', Smith dealt with what he termed 'Police', by which he meant the political institutions governing commerce and finance, and ecclesiastical and military establishments. In the introduction to his lectures[3] he defined 'Police' as the second great object of law. It was concerned with the cheapness of commodities, public security and cleanliness, and the opulence of states. It was this part of his lectures that, when he retired from his chair in 1764, he expanded into *An enquiry into the Nature and Causes of the Wealth of Nations*, which was published in 1776. Thus, although he began as an orthodox moral philosopher, he ended by abandoning moral philosophy as a general account of human behaviour and instead concentrated on one area, economics. But his economic investigations, because of his background in moral philosophy, were cast in a much wider frame than those of many of his successors and give rise to certain tensions in his thought.

Smith's work, however, and the extent of its influence, cannot be properly understood without knowing the practical interest that lay behind it. His economics was based on his observation

[3] Students' notes of Smith's lectures were discovered in the 1890s and were edited by E. Cannan.

of the new industries that were growing up in Glasgow, and it was his grasp of the new form of economic organisation that these represented that led him to inveigh against the mercantilist institutions which were preventing the emergence of the new economic order, or system of natural liberty, as Smith called it. Although industrial capitalism existed only in a few places and on a small scale when he wrote, Smith was the first to grasp its enormous potentialities for increasing the wealth of nations. He achieved this because he developed a theory of value which held that labour was the only source of wealth and this meant he broke with the economics of the physiocrats and the mercantilists, who held that wealth resided in land and gold respectively. This insight was not, of course, separate from the different political policies that he favoured. Once labour is made the only source of value, and the goal of economic activity is defined as increasing the wealth of the community, then attention is focused on how the *productivity* of labour can be increased; hence Smith's characteristic concern with the division of labour, the role of machinery and the size of the market. Since manufacturing industry offers the greatest opportunities for increasing productivity by these means, Smith naturally appears as the spokesman of the rising industrial bourgeoisie and as the opponent of the mercantilists (because of their restrictive trade policies) and the physiocrats (who were attempting to bolster the position of the landed aristocracy).

Smith was thus both critical of existing economic arrangements and of the political economy that defended and justified these arrangements. The measure of his achievement was that he not only founded the science of political economy but also helped to change the terms in which debate on economic and political matters was conducted within the political community, so that even the representatives of the landowners, like Malthus, conducted their argument in terms of the new political economy. It was not just that Smith spoke for different groups from the mercantilists and physiocrats. His theories were demonstrably superior to theirs in understanding how modern economics worked; and nowhere was this more true than in his labour theory of value.

Marx, of course, also began his studies in philosophy, but the

German philosophical tradition was rather different from the English. Throughout his early writings, Marx is seeking a truly *critical* outlook on reality, one that will not only permit understanding but will show how that reality can be changed. He wrote to Ruge in 1843: 'We want to act on our contemporaries. . . . How to go about it? That is the question.' In Berlin he joined the Young Hegelians, whose main criticism of Hegel was that he limited his philosophy to understanding forms of life that were past, and left theology outside the critical self-consciousness of the philosopher.

The Young Hegelians wished to put into practice in Germany the ideals of the French Revolution. They therefore rejected Hegel's dictum that the rational is real, and sought to criticise existing reality in terms of its potentialities. But Marx came to realise that they had not succeeded in creating a real philosophy of praxis but, like Hegel, continued to treat man's reflective thought, his self-consciousness, as the basic determinant of reality.

Following Hegel, they recognised that the material conditions of life, civil society, were dominated by egoism and hence by particularistic and antagonistic interests, but they argued that this private existence of man was transcended in his public existence as a citizen of the state, where he was free, equal and lived in harmony with his fellows. The state represented the interests of all members of civil society and so represented the universal interest. It restored unity and coherence to man's experience and gave man a truly universal existence, such as there had been in the Greek polis, with complete unity between the individual and the community.

Marx, however, argued that true universality, real harmony of interests, had only been attained in thought and not in the daily life and activity of men in society. Thus the task for a critical theory that wished to do more than rationalise what was already in existence was to discover the real basis of social life. At this point, Marx naturally turned to Feuerbach, who offered a radical inversion of Hegel's system instead of a mere extension of it.

History for Hegel was the unfolding, the self-determination of certain concepts, Ideas, such as Spirit and the Will. Feuerbach argued that as a result the real activity of men in history became only moments in the realisation and unfolding of these Ideas. The real relation was the reverse of what Hegel put forward. Concepts like Spirit and the Will were only products of man's mind, of consciousness. They were organising principles of thinking but did not have an independent existence; rather they themselves were dependent on men's practical activity. Once the latter was treated as the basic determinant of reality, instead of consciousness, then it was apparent that the ideal harmony and coherence that consciousness described was far from being achieved. Feuerbach applied his transformative method to religion, and Marx applied it to Hegel's analysis of the state.

Marx noted that in Hegel's system, the German *Stände* gave equal representation in the state to all the interests and classes of civil society. The proletariat, however, was represented by the bourgeoisie. Their interests were diametrically opposed. Thus, concluded Marx, Hegel made the state represent the general interest only by leaving outside it the most numerous class of all.

Yet it was on the labour of this class that civil society rested. The interest and needs of the proletariat were therefore the real universal needs and interests. To explain and judge the nature of existing social reality required an analysis of the proletarians' conditions of life, wage labour. This social relation was the basis of civil society and so of all social life. Political conditions, wrote Marx, were only the official expression of civil society, and could not overcome but only conceal its antagonisms and lack of real freedom. He commented on the American constitution:

> Let us notice first of all that the so-called rights of man, as distinct from the rights of the citizen, are simply the rights of a member of civil society, that is, of egoistic man, of men separated from other men and the community. . . . Man is far from being considered, in the rights of man, as a species-being; on the contrary, species-life itself—society—appears as a system which is external to the individual and a limitation of his original independence. The only bond between men is natural necessity, need and private interest, the preservation of their property and their egoistic persons.
>
> [T. B. Bottomore (ed.), *Karl Marx, Early Writings*, London and New York 1963, 24–26].

The antagonistic nature of civil society destroyed real social harmony based on a community of interests and relations that were not forced but free and equal.

Marx uses Feuerbach's method, but in the process moves far beyond him.[4] For in seeing that real human emancipation depends on the proletariat, he sees that what is required is a study of political economy. He begins this in the *Economic and Philosophical Manuscripts of 1844*. The real significance of this work is that here Marx begins to develop the premises which guide all his later studies. Feuerbach's transformative method does not have a big role. Instead, in these manuscripts, Marx tries to integrate his knowledge of Hegel with the 'facts' of political economy. What emerges is a new conception of the nature of human rationality and human activity.

This leads him to break with Feuerbach, for he sees that Feuerbach in the most important respect is no different from the other Young Hegelians, because like them he failed to develop a truly critical outlook. Feuerbach's premises are not the real, empirical premises of social action that he believes them to be and so, despite his intentions, he cannot get beyond a mere contemplation of the world. Despite his transformative method and his emphasis on deriving ideas from men's sensuous activity, his critical outlook on the world remains entirely within reflective consciousness. It is only a reordering of what already exists. It cannot provide the basis for an understanding that will change what exists. This is why Marx says that 'Philosophy and the study of the actual world have the same relation to one another as onanism and sexual love'.[5] Without the real material premises of human history, philosophy, in so far as it seeks to change the world, is doomed to become an argument about the moral attitudes that should be adopted:

German philosophy, because it took consciousness alone as its point of departure, was bound to end in moral philosophy,

---

[4] Engels was a much more wholehearted disciple of Feuerbach than Marx. See his eulogy of Feuerbach in the part of the *Holy Family* written by him; reprinted in L. D. Easton and K. H. Guddat, *Writings of the Young Marx on Philosophy and Society*, New York 1967, 384 ff.

[5] Marx-Engels, *The German Ideology*, London 1965, 259.

where the various heroes squabble about true morals. Feuer-bach loves man for the sake of man, Saint Bruno loves him because he 'deserves' it ... while Saint Sancho loves 'every-one', because he likes to do so, with the consciousness of ego-ism [*German Ideology*, 409].

Throughout the *German Ideology* Marx shows that what is really at stake in developing a critical theory is what premises are to be adopted, which conception of man is to be chosen:

Philosophers have declared people to be inhuman, not because they did not correspond to the concept of man, but because their concept of man did not correspond to the true concept of man, or because they had no true knowledge of man [p. 485].

He rejects the Young Hegelian search for presuppositionless thinking, but he does not view the choice of premises as an arbi-trary matter. In the section on 'True Socialism' he criticises Her-mann Semmig's conception of the special nature of man, because it leaves out the interaction between man and nature:

... 'independence of things' is claimed in respect of activity and enjoyment. Activity and enjoyment are determined by 'the peculiar nature of man'. If he had demonstrated this peculiar nature in the activity and enjoyment of the men who surround him, he would very soon have found how far the products ex-ternal to us have a voice in the matter too; but instead, he states that 'both activity and enjoyment' coincide in the 'peculiar nature of man'. Instead of visualising the peculiar nature of men in their activity and their manner of enjoyment, which is conditioned by their activity, he explains both by in-voking 'the peculiar nature of men', which cuts short any fur-ther discussion [*German Ideology*, 524].

It is in this context that Marx grasps the importance of political economy. For any theory that seeks to provide knowledge that can help men to liberate themselves must offer a concrete analy-sis of men's social being, their material life. Marx is above all concerned to find a critical outlook on society that has a univer-sal character, and is not doomed to become 'a mere phrase ... a sophistical embellishment of existing society'.[6] He therefore saw

[6] *German Ideology*, 470.

that philosophy could not provide any of the answers that he wanted. What was required was a critical analysis of the science that sought to describe and explain the material life of man, how wealth was created and distributed. He therefore turned to political economy, and abandoned the speculative philosophical framework he had employed up till then, but not before he had evolved the basic premises of his method:

> ... the materialistic outlook on the world, an outlook which is *not without premises*, but which empirically observes the actual material premises as such and for that reason is, for the first time, *actually* a critical outlook on the world. This path was already indicated in the *Deutsch-Französische Jahrbücher* —in the *Einleitung zur Kritik der Hegelschen Rechtsphiloso- phie* and *Zur Judenfrage*. But since at that time this was done in philosophical phraseology, the traditionally occurring philo- sophical expressions such as 'human essence', 'genus' etc., gave the German theoreticians the desired excuse for mis- understanding the real trend of thought and believing that here again it was a question of merely giving a new turn to their worn-out theoretical garments [*German Ideology*, 259].

It is no surprise then that when Marx turned to political economy, he spent a lot of time examining and criticising the premises of this branch of knowledge also. Political economy described the material conditions of existing societies, but it also mystified them. For it tried to present the system of natural liberty, the society of free exchanges, as the form of society that was most in accord with nature and so the final stage of history.

This nature was not to be understood by the reason of man but by the reason of God. God was the ultimate guarantor of harmony and intelligibility in the world of men. But he did not intervene in men's affairs. The social world and the physical world were alike conceived as natural orders, sufficient unto themselves, and governed by the laws that God had given them when he established them. God was thus banished from the *workings* of matter and of society, and this legitimated the growth of sciences that uncovered the laws of the universe and of history. But if teleology was taken away from God, it was not given to men. Instead it was returned to God, as the creator of the natural order of which men were a part. For political economy this meant that a particular set of social relationships which made up the market economy was sanctified as natural, hence in origin divine, and so not capable of being improved by men. The laws that political economy discovered were thus natural necessities, rooted in the human condition. If they were deified or ignored, only misery, poverty and strife could result. But if they were heeded, then there was the hope of social harmony and prosperity. One of these natural necessities was the existence of private property. Marx was therefore bound to include in his critique of political economy an attack on its conception of man, for what was at stake was what was to count as rationality in the analysis of material conditions. It was Smith's conception of man that marked out the terrain of political economy and was implicit in the work of the school that he founded. Like Marx he did not try to separate fact from value. Crucial to his approach is not only the idea that man is purposive but also which kinds and which organisation of purposes ensures men's full human development.

PART I: ADAM SMITH

1. *The Springs of Human Action*

(a) *Self-love*

Smith was concerned in his moral philosophy to explain the springs and motives of human action, and how virtue was attained. The springs of human action were the passions, which were inborn and pre-social. The two chief ones were the desire for self-preservation and the desire to reproduce. Self-preservation had two aspects; it was the desire to avoid death and the desire to better one's condition. Smith considered that the latter was stronger than the former, provided men had reasonable security.[7] These passions were pre-social, but men's purposes and activities were always social. The passions, however, were the

[7] Smith followed Hobbes fairly closely in his account of the basic passions, but differed from Hobbes in seeing the desire to better one's condition as stronger than the fear of death. This led him to a very different explanation of social life.

reason men acted at all, and determined the direction of their actions. Motives which drew their strength from the basic passions were motives of self-love, and they found expression chiefly in economic activity—the production and consumption of the goods necessary for man's survival and the satisfaction of his material needs.

Self-love was neither good nor bad in itself. It was the manner of its expression that made it a virtue or a vice. Smith emphasised, however, that since it drew its strength from man's most basic passions, it could not be eradicated from human life and would always find an outlet. If the social conditions were right, then the expression of self-love would be virtuous. Smith thus directed attention to the institutional arrangements in society that would make man's natural and inevitable expression of self-love a virtue and a contribution to social welfare.

Self-love, however, was not the highest but the lowest of the virtues. The business of producing and exchanging the goods necessary for human existence was for Smith only a means to creating the conditions for the good life. It was not the true end of human activity, but it also could not be ignored. Smith criticised his teacher, Francis Hutcheson, for making benevolence the principal bond between men, thus presenting the ideal as the real and as a matter of conscious choice. Smith argued that men were not free in this way, because their actions were determined by the nature of their being and the strongest motive in men was not benevolence but self-love. If a man experienced a conflict between self-love and benevolence the former would always prevail, because of the character of man's basic passions. This, said Smith, was a matter of simple observation:

It is not from the benevolence of the butcher, the brewer or the baker, that we expect our dinner but from their regard to their own interest. We address ourselves, not to their humanity but to their self love, and never talk to them of our own necessities but of their advantages. Nobody but a beggar chooses to depend chiefly upon the benevolence of his fellow citizens

[Adam Smith, *The Wealth of Nations*, ed. E. Cannan, London, 6th ed., 1950, 18].

(b) *The natural basis of society*

Smith rejected the notion that benevolence could be the basis of society, partly because of his realism and partly because he held that the passions rather than reason were the springs of action. All knowledge came through reflection on the impression of the senses. But the senses were primarily instruments of the passions. As a result, reason was greatly handicapped and its knowledge of the external world necessarily imperfect. The imperfection of knowledge made any attempt by reason to control or direct the passion mischievous. Smith regarded the exercise of reason and the accumulation of knowledge as the peculiar excellence of the human species, but resolutely opposed any attempt to reconstruct society according to reason. Such a course would be irrational, because it would ignore the reality of the human passions. The order Smith detected in history was not the order of human reason. History was primarily the expression of man's passions rather than a conscious planned process.

As a result, Smith, like Hume, disputed the contract theory of society and government. Society, he argued, was not a matter of conscious choice, of consent. It arose because man found it useful to co-operate with others in their struggle for survival. It was on this natural basis, the interplay of men's passions, that institutions such as social hierarchy, private property and government arose. Social prestige and authority were the recognition of some men's superiority in particular activities and qualities. The same was true of private property—it was an acquired right, which depended on social acceptance. 'Occupation seems to be well founded when the spectator can go along with my possession of the object and approve me when I defend my possession by force.'[8] Government was then instituted to 'secure wealth and defend the rich from the poor'.[9] Smith presents the history of society and the origin of social institutions as a natural process founded on men's passions. Every man is endowed with the same basic passions and so every man has an equal right to pursue the means of life and preservation, free from interference.

[8] Adam Smith, *Lectures on Justice, Police, Revenue and Arms*, ed. E. Cannan, Oxford 1896, 108.
[9] A. Smith, *Lectures*, 15.

This assumption is the source of many later difficulties and tensions in Smith's theory, because in employing an image of man that assigns to men characteristics that are prior both to society and to history, he tends to reduce all social and historical events to epiphenomena of man's basic passions.

(c) Social being—The concept of sympathy

From one angle, therefore, Smith's theory is rooted in an individualist conception of man. Man's fundamental characteristics belong to him as an individual, prior to any contact with society. Smith, however, also regarded man as inescapably a social being. He criticised Hume for making utility the social bond because utility is a purely individual standard. To argue that society could be explained from motives of utility alone overlooked the need men had of social approval. Self-love was not individual selfishness, activity undertaken with no regard for the interests and desires of others;[10] on the contrary, its expression was always moulded by men's desire for social approval. Social approval was a sentiment which judged actions not only according to their utility in respect of a particular goal, but also according to their propriety. What was considered proper varied from society to society and as civilisation developed so men's idea of propriety became more refined.

Thus men, in acting from self-love, acted in ways which were approved by their fellows. In this way every man was the 'impartial spectator' of every other man's actions. This occurred through the operation of sympathy. The individual in imagination recreated in his own mind the situation and state of mind of the man whose actions he observed. The moral rules and institutions of a society were the result of countless single acts of sympathy. What was socially approved thus evolved in a constant interplay of actions and judgements.[11] Awareness of the opinions and standards of his fellows made the individual inter-

[10] See E. Fromm, *Man for Himself*, London 1948, 130–134, for an account of the change in the concept of self interest.

[11] Smith's conceptions have similarities with G. H. Mead's conception of the 'generalised other', see G. H. Mead, *Mind, Self and Society*, Chicago 1934.

nalise the rules and standards of his society as conscience. This was the 'impartial spectator in the breast'. The individual made the rules and prohibitions of society his own. At the same time, the impartial spectator was given an external existence in the form of laws and moral codes. What began as an activity of feeling, became at last an activity of thought and reflection. Smith regarded legislation as extremely important but observed that laws made without due regard for the operation of men's passions would be wasteful and unsound.

(d) Moral being

Thus although the sentiment of approval, the ability to sympathise, was a passion inherent in man, its development became an activity of reason. It was sympathy that Smith saw as the basis of moral judgement and he thought that during the progress of civilisation moral rules were steadily purified by the growth in men's understanding. The higher virtues, unlike self-love, were more products of a wide and sophisticated understanding than of the passions. Moral perfection and happiness consisted in actions that were guided by sentiments of benevolence and propriety, rather than self-love. Smith, however, never lost his hard-headed approach. Benevolence could only replace self-love when the demands of the primary passions had been met. Benevolence, says Smith, is 'an ornament that embellishes, not the foundation which supports the building'.[12] But he still thought of moral excellence as something quite separate from men's passions, because moral excellence was essentially a social quality. Since it was human judgement, by reflecting on every act of sympathy, that evolved moral rules and standards, virtue was not something innate in men. Good conduct was what was appropriate to man's nature, to what was judged socially to be virtuous and in Smith's view the highest place was reserved for acts of benevolence.

> To feel much for others and little for ourselves ... to restrain our selfish, and to indulge our benevolent affections, constitute the perfection of human nature; and can alone produce among

[12] A. Smith, *The Theory of Moral Sentiments*, London 1792, 49.

mankind that harmony of sentiments and passions in which consists their whole grace and propriety

[A. Smith, *Theory of Moral Sentiments*, 47].

To become virtuous was a matter of learning the customs and traditions of a society and of acquiring a mature judgement by exercising the mind on as many and as varied subjects as possible.

(e) Smith's image of man

Smith presents human motivation as a set of pre-social passions existing in every man and determining the greater part of human activity. Natural man, however, is not moral man. The source and arena of moral behaviour, for Smith, is society and truly moral behaviour results from the development of man's reason. Smith is thus committed, on the one hand to a portrayal of society as a natural, determined process which human reason can only frustrate but not alter, and on the other hand to a view of man as a social being who realises his human capacities and achieves the good life through developing his reason. Thus he comes to the conclusion, that although self-love is the actual social bond, it is not the true social bond. Yet he nowhere shows how a society based on self-love can change into one based on benevolence, since man's basic passions are unalterable. He even acknowledges that some of the consequences of a society based on the full expression of self-love actually destroy the conditions for moral behaviour among large sections of the people.

This ambivalence is reflected in the fact that, although men's motives are rooted in the passions, what turns these motives and the actions they inspire into virtues is the manner of their expression in society. For an action to be virtuous it must have social approval but it must also not infringe another man's natural rights. Thus Smith used a double standard for judging an action. The situation was further complicated because he did not merely equate a virtuous action with any action that is socially approved. The real standard of virtue and propriety was the degree of refinement and moral excellence that some groups in the society had reached. As a result, Smith always remained critical of economic activity and never treated it as an end in itself.

2. *The System of Natural Liberty*

(a) *The invisible hand*

Men's self-love, then, was for Smith the motive that drew men together and established society. The mutual adjustment of interests led to a set of economic institutions and a set of laws, a system of justice. Not every system of justice, however, was in accord with man's nature. Indeed many institutions blocked men's pursuit of their natural interests. Smith thought, however, that reason could uncover the institutions that agreed best with human nature. This was the system of natural liberty, the economic order that most increased the opulence of states.

Smith saw frugality as the great engine of industry. It was a stronger motive in man than prodigality. 'The principle which prompts to save, is the desire of bettering our condition, a desire which, though generally calm and dispassionate, comes with us from the womb and never leaves us till we go to the grave.'[13] Men will be frugal and industrious, said Smith, provided they have security. 'Our ancestors were idle for want of sufficient encouragement to industry.[14] But once the rule of law is established, 'that security, which the laws in Great Britain give to every man that he shall enjoy the fruits of his own labour, is alone sufficient to make any country flourish'.[15] Thus given the right conditions, the natural industry of men will make trade flourish. But the law must not overstep itself. It ought always 'to trust people with the care of their own interest; as in their local situations they must generally be able to judge better of it than the legislator can do'.[16]

The system of natural liberty is superior to any other arrangement, because the general, as well as individual, welfare is assured.

Every individual is continually exerting himself to find out the most advantageous employment for whatever capital he can command ... the study of his own advantage leads him

[13] *Wealth of Nations* I, 363.
[14] *Wealth of Nations* I, 357.
[15] *Wealth of Nations* I, 415.
[16] *Wealth of Nations* I, 407.

necessarily to prefer that employment which is most advantageous to the society [*Wealth of Nations* I, 475].

To establish this early functionalist assertion, Smith has no need to invoke the purposes of a supreme being. He has only to show that the social bond in the system of natural liberty is exchange relations between free, equal and independent citizens. Men that are equal and independent will only consent to those relations that are advantageous to them. Smith relied on men's self-love to ensure that all exchange relations would benefit both parties. Thus men pursuing their self-interest benefit not only themselves, but also all those with whom they make contracts. This is what Smith means by the welfare of society and by his metaphor of the invisible hand.[17] In addition, the activity of men, striving to do the best they can for themselves, is the process of competition, which forces men to moderate and adjust their interests to one another. Every man's self-love acts as a check on every other man's and the result is that all third parties to the relation, such as the consumer, benefit.

(b) *Exchange relations*

Promotion of both individual and social welfare therefore depends on exchange relations between independent and free in-

---

[17] Although there may be a theological element in his theory, Smith did not need it to explain how individual and social interests were reconciled. As Marx wrote about the theory:

The point here is not that, in following his private interests, everyone attains the totality of private interests, namely the collective interest. One could as well conclude from this abstract slogan that everyone reciprocally blocks the interests of the others, so that instead of a general affirmation, this war of all against all produces a general negation. The point is rather that private interest is itself already a socially determined interest, which can be attained only within certain socially ordained conditions and with socially given means, and which is therefore dependent on the reproduction of these conditions and means. It is the interest of a private person; but its content and the form and means of its realisation are set by social conditions independently of the individual.

[*Grundrisse*, cited in M. Nicolaus, 'The Unknown Marx',
New Left Review 48 (1968), 48.]

dividuals. If men are not independent, then the exchange relations will often be forced and will only benefit one party to them. In this case, only individual welfare will be promoted. Examples are strewn throughout Smith's work. 'Nothing tends so much to corrupt mankind', he declared, 'as dependency, while independency still increases the honesty of the people. The establishment of commerce and manufactures, which brings about this independency, is the best police for preventing crimes.'[18] If men are dependent, they will not be industrious, for their own interest will not be benefited. Smith contrasts free workmen with slaves. The former, he observes, were often over-zealous when they were paid by the piece: 'Mutual emulation and the desire of greater gain frequently prompted them to overwork themselves, and to hurt their health by excessive labour'.[19] Slaves, on the other hand, only worked through fear, and so required constant surveillance, for they would take every opportunity to avoid their work.

Under the system of natural liberty, it is every man's interest to be industrious and honest. Its foundations are the relations of exchange men freely contract among themselves.

> Whoever offers to another a bargain of any kind, proposes to do this. Give me that which I want, and you shall have this which you want, is the meaning of every such offer; and it is in this manner that we obtain from one another the far greater part of those good offices which we stand in need of
>
> [*Wealth of Nations* I, 18].

In this way, 'every man ... lives by exchanging or becomes in some measure a merchant, and the society itself grows to be what is properly a commercial society'.[20]

(c) The pursuit of wealth

Smith did not however believe that the system of natural liberty would be easy to attain. 'Nothing is more difficult', he wrote, 'than perfectly to secure liberty.'[21] The passion for self-preservation was so strong in men that free and equal exchange relations

[18] *Lectures*, 155.
[19] *Wealth of Nations* I, 92.
[20] *Wealth of Nations* I, 26.
[21] *Lectures*, 144.

were constantly in danger of being subverted into unequal power relations. If this happened, competition and industry would be destroyed. Smith had come to the conclusion that man's search for moral excellence and the good life could not outweigh the promptings of his basic passions. Hence moral excellence depended on the establishment in economic activity of relations between men that would turn self-love into a virtue. Only competition and the rule of law would guarantee the liberty of all. In this argument, Smith appears to assert the primacy of man's pre-social passions against his social being. He implies that the promptings of the passion to preserve oneself are stronger than any sanctions of social disapproval. Thus he stresses the role of external institutions and laws, rather than the sanctions of conscience.

A shift in Smith's views on this point is apparent between the *Theory of Moral Sentiments* and *The Wealth of Nations*, though it is not so great as to indicate a complete break between the two works. In the *Theory of Moral Sentiments* the reasons why men pursue wealth are of two kinds. In the first place, there is self-deception. Men pursue wealth and status because these have social prestige, and so appeal to their vanity. Such pleasures are in fact illusory, and not the real happiness of life, which is found in ease of body and peace of mind. 'The beggar who suns himself by the highway possesses that security which kings are fighting for.'[22] But the fact that some men, such as philosophers, can see that such pleasures are illusory, yet still approve the pursuit of wealth, means that for them there must be a second kind of reason. This is what Smith calls the contemplation of the universe as a great machine. 'Human society ... appears like a great, an immense machine, whose regular and harmonious movements produce a thousand agreeable effects.'[23] In this way philosophers can admire the accumulation of social wealth and devote their powers to the invention of new techniques.

Both these sentiments belong to the feeling for propriety which is involved in all sets of social approval. But the first is vanity; the second, due to the greater refinement of the philo-

[22] *Theory of Moral Sentiments*, 467.
[23] *Theory of Moral Sentiments*, 247.

sopher, is magnanimity. In *The Wealth of Nations*, however, Smith scarcely mentions this aspect of economic motivation. His concern is much more with utility, an emphasis for which he had earlier criticised Hume. Economic activity appears as a much more natural and determined process, rooted in men's passions rather than their reason. He tends to diminish the role of man as a social being, motivated by the desire for social approval. The social controls of conscience and other men's good opinion cannot withstand the claims of the passions. What Smith stresses in *The Wealth of Nations* is how men are stimulated to industry to better their condition and because of their passion for novelty, the desire to improve everything—another basic passion. Vying with these two is the passion in man for ease and security. In certain situations, some men have the opportunity to fulfil both sets of opposing passions, but only at the social cost of oppressing and plundering others, and destroying free exchange relations between equal and independent parties.

What Smith concludes is that no considerations of benevolence, justice or anything else will prevent men from plundering their fellows if they can. They will always obey the promptings of their passions. Thus a very elaborate set of institutions is required to ensure that all men are free to pursue their interests, yet in such a way that does not harm the interests of others. If men do not have the security they need to better their condition, then the other aspect of the passion for self-preservation, the fear of death, will dominate men's actions. Smith arrives at the paradox that, left to itself, the natural order will not establish the natural system of liberty. Only social judgement that perceives the nature of the world aright will do that.

(d) The division of labour

The precise means by which the system of natural liberty was to ensure a continual expansion of wealth is the core of Smith's economic theory and his labour theory of value. He discerned, in the new economic forms taking shape in Glasgow, a principle which could revolutionise economic activity, and break the connection between social wealth and agricultural productivity. This was the division of labour in manufacturing industry.

In some form the division of labour had always existed. The

specifically new development in Smith's England was that it was
extended to the workshop, to the different stages of the production of goods, rather than merely to different occupations, so
that work, which had formerly been done by one man, was now
done often by twenty or more, each specialising in one part of
the process. The result, as Smith showed, was a great increase in
the productive powers of labour, due to the increase in the individual workman's dexterity; time-saving and a faster rate of
inventions, because of the workman's application of all his
powers to such a minute area.[24] The barriers to raising production in agriculture did not exist in manufacture and so the new
form of the division of labour was potentially the creator of un-
limited wealth.

The flood of new manufactures would overwhelm the old self-
sufficiency of regions and countries and spread exchange relations. Entire nations and continents could become interdependent, linked by the exchange of the products of their labour.
Such an outcome, which was of much greater consequence than
the old forms of trade, Smith saw as an entirely natural process.
The division of labour itself arose not from human wisdom, but
from a propensity in human nature to truck, barter and exchange.[25] It is this propensity, says Smith, which more than any
other distinguishes men from animals. Not only is the division
of labour the great engine of economic progress, it is what allows
differences among men to appear. Differences in men's natural
endowment are not so much the cause as the effect of the division
of labour.

In the system of natural liberty, exchange relations become
the objective form of the social bond, and lead to a great extension of the division of labour, every man specialising in what
gives him the highest return. The division of labour allows all
men's different geniuses and talents to be brought into a common
stock, 'where every man may purchase whatever part of the

[24] *Wealth of Nations* I, 7–16.

[25] In this he differed from his contemporary, Adam Ferguson, who
saw commerce and the division of labour arising from differences of
physical and social situation and individual need. In other words, he
stresses social rather than presocial factors.

produce of other men's talents he has occasion for'.[26] The foundation of the disposition to barter is the art of persuasion, which enables men to negotiate with one another. Some men fare better than others because they are more skilful in persuading others or because they have more to put in the common stock.

At times, however, the form of bargaining endangers the principle of free exchange relations. This, Smith thought, was particularly true of the central social relation in the new society—that between capitalist and worker—because the interests of the two groups were opposed.

> What are the common wages of labour depends everywhere upon the contract usually made between those two parties, whose interests are by no means the same. The workmen desire to get as much, the masters to give as little as possible. The former are disposed to combine in order to raise, the latter in order to lower, the wages of labour [*Wealth of Nations* I, 74].

This was not in itself bad, since it meant competition. The situation of the workers, however, who generally had only their labour to trade for the basic necessities of life, gave the masters unfair advantages. In the event of a strike, they could starve the workers into submission: 'in the long run the workman may be as necessary to his master as his master is to him, but the necessity is not so immediate'.[27] Masters' combinations were also not illegal, unlike those of the workers. As a result the workers in desperation had recourse to 'the most shocking violence and outrage'.[28]

While noting these defects, however, Smith and the whole Scottish school did not lose their faith in the possibility of free exchange relations between equals as the social bond of the new society. Their view is well summed up by John Millar, the Scottish sociologist, when he denied that the relation between capitalist and worker was based on exploitation:

> Perhaps part of the profit of a manufacturer may also be drawn from the workman, who, however, will have a full equivalent for what he thus resigns. By working to a master he

[26] *Wealth of Nations* I, 20.
[27] *Wealth of Nations* I, 75.
[28] Ibid.

is sure of constant employment, is saved the trouble of seeking
out those who may have occasion for his labour, and avoids
the anxiety arising from the danger of being thrown occasion-
ally idle. In return for these advantages, he willingly relin-
quishes to his master some part of what he can earn while
employed

[quoted in R. L. Meek, *Economics and Ideology*,
London and New York 1967, 45].

The ideal of exchange relations which are contracted by free and
independent individuals, and proves mutually advantageous, is
untarnished.

(e) *The natural order and the moral order*

Smith regarded the Middle Ages as a period when there was no
rule of law, and so no incentive to industry. Men were forced
to survive as best they could and resorted to force and plunder.
The majority of men were not free to enter the occupations of
their choice, but were tied in traditional relationships, such as
serf to lord and apprentice to master. As a result, the system of
natural liberty existed nowhere and there was a general stagna-
tion both of social wealth and moral life. The conditions for the
extended division of labour did not exist.

Smith saw many artificial barriers, associated with mercantilism and the church, in the path of natural liberty in the Britain
of his own day, but he thought that the rule of law, with a few
interruptions, which had been maintained since 1500 had per-
mitted the steady unfolding of man's natural activitiy. Its most
important features were freedom of contract and security of property. As we have seen, it is a central proposition in Smith that,
given the right legal framework, and left alone, men will contract those exchange relations most advantageous to themselves.
Smith continually uses two levels of analysis. He contrasts the
ideal state of affairs, which exists only in limited form, with the
actual state of affairs. The ideal state of affairs for him in the
economic sphere was the system of natural liberty. Were it established universally, individual and social welfare would be maxi-
mised. The market would make capital and labour, producer and
consumer, the servants of one another. Exploitation would be an
aberration and certainly not a necessary consequence of the

market process. Smith backed the free market economy against mercantilism because he thought it the fairest and most efficient way of producing the goods society needed and in such a manner that the natural expression of men's self-love would become a virtue, because it did not infringe other men's rights but, on the contrary, was the means by which other men could assert their rights.

But the end of economic activity was not, for Smith, the end of human activity. He did not attempt to glorify the new economic order. He advocated it, because he thought it superior in certain respects to former economic systems, but he remained critical of some of its results, especially its effect on manners. Although it tended to increase men's honesty and punctuality, it also tended to confine the views of men, in particular of the workers. The cause of this was the division of labour:

> In the progress of the division of labour, the employment of the far greater part of those who live by labour, that is, of the great body of the people, comes to be confined to a few very simple operations; frequently to one or two. But the understandings of the greater part of men are necessarily formed by their employments. The man whose whole life is spent in performing a few simple operations, of which the effects too are, perhaps, always the same, or very nearly the same, has no occasion to exert his understanding ... he naturally loses, therefore, the habit of such exertion and generally becomes as stupid and ignorant as it is possible for a human creature to become. The torpor of his mind renders him, not only incapable of relishing or bearing a part in any rational conversation, but of conceiving any generous, noble or tender sentiment and consequently of forming any just judgement concerning many even of the ordinary duties of private life.... In every improved and civilised society this is the state into which the labouring poor, that is, the great body of the people, must necessarily fall, unless government takes some pains to prevent it [*Wealth of Nations* II, 302].

This passage exhibits the tension in Smith's image of men. The understanding of men is formed by their situations, by the variety of objects they encounter in their daily activity. 'When the mind is employed about a variety of objects, it is somehow expanded and enlarged.'[29] Smith observes that agricultural workers are much more receptive and intelligent than factory workers because of the nature of their environment and the varied tasks they must perform. Thus, although the factory worker becomes much more dexterous owing to the division of labour in the workshop, and is able to suggest improvements to the process he is engaged on, these very gains destroy the opportunities for the worker to develop his mind, which Smith sees as the foundation for the higher virtues and the moral life.[30] The neglect of education means that most workers have no ideas with which to amuse themselves. 'Their work through half the week is sufficient to maintain them and through want of education they have no amusement for the other but riot and debauchery.'[31] The military spirit of the people also declines because men have their minds employed on the arts of luxury. As a result they grow 'effeminate and dastardly'.[32]

Smith never satisfactorily resolves the paradox between his advocacy of the new economic order and the divisions of labour as means to the attainment of the good life and his observations of their effects on the majority of the common people. He suggested education as a remedy, but, as Marx commented, only in homeopathic doses.[33] He treats the problem as a necessary feature of an industrial economy, which cannot be altered without sacrificing the advantages such an economy brings. The upper classes were only slightly affected and the workers were incapable, on Smith's assumption, of becoming aware of what they were being deprived of. On the contrary, they were content for the most part because of the rising living standards.

Although he became their spokesman, Smith was no admirer of the rising capitalist class. He thought that their industry only lasted so long as competition made them insecure. 'People of the same trade seldom meet together, even for merriment and

[29] *Lectures*, 256.

[30] Although the intelligence of the workers fell, the collective intelligence of society rose, because the division of labour gave rise to a class of highly skilled technicians and inventors. See N. Rosenberg, 'Adam Smith on the Division of Labour', *Economica* 1965.

[31] A. Smith, *Lectures*, 257.

[32] *Lectures*, 258.

[33] K. Marx, *Capital* I, Moscow 1954, 362.

diversion, but the conversation ends in a conspiracy against the public, or in some contrivance to raise prices.'[34] He still held that the social bond of commercial society—exchange relations founded on self-love—was not the highest or most desirable social bond because it was based more on man's passions than his judgement. Natural liberty provided abundance, but not always the higher human qualities. Sometimes it encouraged selfishness and sloth. Smith judged it in terms of classical ethics. At the same time as he set out its advantages, he drew attention to its short-comings.

Reason remained for him subordinate to the passions. It could not fundamentally alter the world. Understanding could only seek to establish human institutions that were in harmony with man's driving passions. But the exercise of reason remained the essence of a truly moral and human life and for Smith the truly moral life conflicts with his account of the natural life. The gap between the two is rooted in the ambiguity of his assumptions about human nature, in the tension between his individualist conception of the basic driving forces in man and his notion of man as a social being who expresses and fulfils himself only in society.

Part II: Marx and the Labour Theory of Value

1. *The Critique of Political Economy*

In his early economic studies, Marx criticises political economy in terms of its own theory of value and its description of how wealth is produced and distributed. But what he also does is to criticise its starting-point and its conception of man. In the 1844 manuscripts, after a section in which he quotes extensively from the classical economists and comments on them, Marx says:

> We have proceeded from the premises of political economy. We have accepted its language and its laws. We presupposed private property, the separation of labour, capital and land

---

[34] *Wealth of Nations* I, 144. For this reason, Smith opposed joint stock companies. He never proclaimed the capitalists' interest as the general interest.

and of wages, profit of capital and rent of land, likewise division of labour, competition, the concept of exchange value, etc. On the basis of political economy itself, in its own words, we have shown that the worker sinks to the level of a commodity and becomes indeed the most wretched of commodities; that the wretchedness of the worker is in inverse proportion to the power and magnitude of his production; that the necessary result of competition is the accumulation of capital in a few hands and thus the restoration of monopoly in a more terrible form; that finally the distinction between capitalist and land-rentier, like that between the tiller of the soil and the factory worker, disappears and that the whole of society must fall apart into the two classes—the property-*owners* and the propertyless *workers*

> [*Economic and Philosophical Manuscripts of 1844*, Moscow 1959, 64].

Marx then proceeds to examine these premises. He seems to have thought at this stage that it was sufficient to expose the assumptions on which political economy rested, in particular the existence of private property, in order to provide a critical account of it. But the laws of political economy still provided an adequate description of how capitalism worked, once capitalism was placed in a historical framework and seen as a particular mode of production rather than as the natural way of organising economic activity:

> Economists have a singular method of procedure. There are only two kinds of institutions for them, artificial and natural. The institutions of feudalism are artificial institutions, those of the bourgeoisie are natural institutions. . . . When the economists say that present day relations—the relations of bourgeois production—are natural, they imply that these are the relations in which wealth is created and productive forces developed in conformity with the laws of nature. These relations therefore are themselves natural laws independent of the influence of time. They are eternal laws which must always govern society. Thus there has been history, but there is no longer any [*The Poverty of Philosophy*, London 1956, 120–21].

In the 1844 manuscripts, Marx shows that the institution of private property is not a law of nature, but in reality is nothing but alienated labour. Jaques Rancière has therefore argued that in these early writings, Marx merely criticises the anthropological assumptions of political economy with the aid of a different set of anthropological assumptions, which he takes from Feuerbach. This 'amphibology' is only possible

> through a special kind of encounter: the encounter of an explicit anthropological discourse and the anthropological discourse which is implicit in classical economics
>
> [J. Rancière, *Theoretical Practice* 1 (Jan. 1971), 26].

This view has a certain instant plausibility. For in all Marx's economic writings before 1850 no new *economic* concepts are introduced. Instead he does two things. He puts the laws of political economy into the perspective of his materialist conception of history, and he criticises its concepts in terms of his image of man. Thus he shows capitalism as a stage in man's alienation from himself and his labour, a particular stage in the development of the productive forces and therefore as a stage of history that will be superseded. For the rest he is content to let the classical economists condemn capitalism out of their own mouths. He merely draws attention to the negative and destructive side of the laws which they have discovered. Both he and Engels evidently believed for a time that industrial capitalism was being propelled towards a major crisis and that a proletarian revolution was consequently imminent. This conviction obviously dominates works like the *Communist Manifesto* and *Wage Labour and Capital*.

But the defeat of the 1848 revolution made Marx think again about political economy and in his later studies he saw that it was not enough to use the theory of value of the classical economists for understanding capitalism. The difficulties and confusions in the theory of value meant that it had to be replaced by what amounted to a new theory of value. The implications of this step for Marx's later work were enormous. Instead of criticising political economy immanently, by pointing out the conclusions it failed to draw from its own theory, Marx now criticised it from the vantage point of a new theory. But this does not mean that Marx abandoned his earlier critique of the premises of political economy. Rather his science and genius derived from the development of such premises, for without them his starting point would be arbitrary and his law of value would have no foundation. He did not substitute 'science' for anthropological criticism. In asserting this, Rancière shows that he does not know what theories of value are about. The truth is rather that in the 1850s Marx went back to his premises about man. The evidence is strewn throughout the *Grundrisse*. The difference is that this time, and for the first time, Marx really began to make use of his anthropological criticism, and fused it with his critical analysis of capitalist production. Before, it had been separate from it, and despite his intentions, it tended to appear as the application of morality to economics. This was because he criticised the political economists with their own theory, based on their own law of value. But now he was able to apply his premises about man to develop a new version of the labour theory of value, which in turn provided the basis for a new theory of capitalist development.

The fact that there had been no breakdown of the capitalist system and no proletarian revolution as he had expected, was not in itself sufficient to force Marx back to first principles. He could have attempted to devise a better theory of economic crises and remained within the framework of political economy. Instead, he went back to his earlier study of the nature of human activity and his theory of alienation and developed a line of enquiry that was implicit within it, but which he had not paid much attention to before. What he focused on was the nature of exchange, the heart of the classical theory, for he now saw that it was from his idea of exchange relationships that Adam Smith had fashioned his labour theory of value. In the 'Excerpt Notes' of 1844 Marx had written;

> Political economy understands the *common life of man*, the self-activating *human* essence and mutual reintegration toward generic and truly human life, in the form of *exchange* and *commerce*. Society, says Destutt de Tracy, is a *series of multilateral exchanges*. It is constituted by this movement of multilateral integration. *Society*, says Adam Smith, is a *commercial enterprise*. Each of its members is a *merchant*. It is evident that political economy *establishes* an *alienated* form of

social intercourse as the *essential, original*, and definitive human form

> [translated in Easton and Guddat, *Writings of the Young Marx on Philosophy and Society*, 272].

But he had not developed this insight. He remained tied to Smith's own theory of value and saw labour as a commodity that was not in principle different from any other commodity on the market. This meant that he accepted Smith's view of exchange also. He concentrated on the human meaning of exchange, on the 'definite social relation between men that assumes in their eyes the fantastic form of a relation between things'.[35]
This social relation is the wage bargain, which creates wage labour.

> The exercise of labour is the worker's own life activity, the manifestation of his own life. And this life activity he sells to another person in order to secure the necessary means of subsistence. Thus his life activity is for him only a means to enable him to exist. He works in order to live. He does not even reckon labour as part of his life, it is rather a sacrifice of his life. It is a commodity which he has made over to another
>
> [Marx–Engels, *Selected Works* I, Moscow 1962, 82].

Because men become 'self-conscious and self-acting commodities', they establish a social bond based on egoism and selfishness. Exchange relations under capitalism, argues Marx, can never fulfil man's humanity because they are based on private property:

> Why must private property end up in *money*? Because man as a social being must resort to *exchange*, and because exchange—under the presupposition of private property— must end up in value ... because men making exchanges do not relate to one another as men, *things* lose the significance of being human and personal property
>
> [Easton and Guddat, 267].

Man's alienation leads to civil society, a society made up of men pursuing their interests selfishly, without regard for others. The emphasis is on possession, on having. Everything in the world is

[35] *Capital* I, 72.

viewed only in an instrumental fashion, only for the exchange value that can be realised in it. Political economy, says Marx, preaches practical asceticism:

> Its principal thesis is the renunciation of life and of human needs. The less you eat, drink, buy books, go to the theatre or to balls, or to the public house, and the less you think, love, theorise, sing, paint, fence etc, the more you will be able to save and the greater will become your treasure which neither moth nor rust will corrupt—your capital. The less you are, the less you express your life, the more you have, the greater is your alienated life and the greater is the saving of your alienated being. Everything which the economist takes from you in the way of life and humanity he restores to you in the form of money and wealth [Bottomore, *Early Writings*, 171].

The very different assessment of frugality by Marx and Smith is directly due to their different images of man. For Smith, frugality is a virtuous expression of self-love because it encourages industry and increases wealth without infringing the natural rights of others. Marx, however, because he sees no pre-social, natural rights and passions that must be appeased, condemns any activity that does not embody what he considers is the full expression of human life.

Money then becomes the objectified social bond in commodity production. It represents command over the labour and products of others. It gives its owner possession of the powers of social labour. Because men's motive in exchange is egoism and not humanity, men lose themselves, and establish an alienated form of intercourse and become the slaves of the objects they create:

> No one is gratified by the product of another. Our mutual production means nothing for us as human beings. Our exchange, therefore, cannot be the mediating movement in which it would be acknowledged that my product means anything for you because it is an *objectification* of your being, your need. *Human nature* is not the bond of our production for each other. Exchange can only set in *motion* and confirm the *relationship* which each of us has to his own product and to the production of the other person. Each of us sees in his own product only his *own* objectified self-interest and in the

product of another person, *another* self-interest which is independent, alien and objectified [Easton and Guddat, 278].

Marx wanted to reveal that the alienated social bond of capitalism was riven with contradictions, and that the social harmony proclaimed by political economy was an illusion. But in his earlier economic writings (*The Poverty of Philosophy, Wage Labour and Capital, Communist Manifesto, Economic and Philosophical Manuscripts*) Marx tried to show that this was true even in terms of the theories and the laws of the political economists themselves.

Adam Smith had argued that exchange relations were mutually advantageous to both parties, so long as both remained free and independent. The instrument to achieve this was competition. In principle he thought that such relations were perfectly possible, given the nature of man, if the right institutions and 'police' were established, although, in practice, he observed how often competition was subverted and some form of monopoly established, thus diminishing social welfare. Marx, however, argues that the erosion of competition in a capitalist system, is not an accident, but a necessary outcome of that system, because its basic exchanges—between worker and capitalist, and producer and consumer—are not equal but one-sided, as Adam Smith himself had shown. Demand and supply do not reach any natural harmony. 'Production precedes consumption, supply compels demand.'[36]

This tendency is strengthened with the advent of large-scale industry. Production is increasingly undertaken for profit, for a certain sum of exchange values. It is not directly concerned with providing goods whose use values satisfy human needs, but with providing goods for which needs can be stimulated. Marx emphasises again that money is the only real need produced by the economic system. Formerly, production had been directly for use, but under capitalism, there was no production and consumption of use values, without their prior translation into exchange values. The domination of production over consumption is shown in the recurrent crises of overproduction; the determination of consumption by the priorities of production and the

[36] *Poverty of Philosophy*, 68.

steady growth of monopoly as the more successful firms get larger and squeeze out the smaller.

But most striking for Marx are the effects of competition on the exchange relation between capitalists and workers, the wage relation. Competition, he says, reduces the price of every commodity to the minimum cost of its production. Under capitalism, labour becomes a commodity, a cost of production. Hence competition reduces it, too, to its minimum cost. This wage minimum is the cost of keeping the worker alive and ensuring that he reproduces. The existence of the worker, says Marx, comes to have 'no other value than that of a simple productive force, and the capitalist treats him accordingly'.[37] The wage is kept at its minimum and even sometimes falls below it, because capitalists agree not to bid against each other for workers and are better placed to withstand the effects of strikes and lockouts than are workers and because the rising population makes the supply of labour outrun the demand. Competition among the workers for the available jobs keeps wages at subsistence level. This is the case even when social wealth is growing. The lot of the workers is still worse when the economy is stationary or declining, because there will be fewer jobs.

Marx argues that, even in the most advantageous conditions that Adam Smith assumes, exchange relations founded on private property and commodity production involve misery and deprivation for the worker. This is owing to overwork; the increase in competition among the workers as machines replace men in the productive process; and finally, because the more wealthy society becomes, the more impoverished are the workers, for although their labour creates this wealth, it does not appear as their product but as part of the alien social world that controls them. Competition, the only restraining force on capital, is steadily undermined as enterprises, markets and machines grow larger.

Thus not only do the workers not gain from the new exchange relations; they are actually plunged into poverty and misery whilst society as a whole is growing richer. Social wealth is concentrated in the hands of the capitalists, but these grow ever fewer as competition takes its toll. Failed capitalists are forced

[37] *Poverty of Philosophy*, 221. (On the question of free trade.)

into the proletariat to swell the army of those looking for work. But the very poverty of the majority makes capitalism unable to sell its goods. As a result it is beset by crises of overproduction. A classic contradiction develops between the forces of production—the material wealth of society—and the relations of production—the way this wealth is produced and distributed.

2. The Discovery of Surplus Value

When Marx retired for the second time into the study, after 1848, he intended to write a substantive work on political economy that would allow him to move beyond the simple model of capitalist development that he had drawn from reading the political economists themselves. He returned to the premises that had led him to political economy in the first place and began an intensive study of the labour theory of value. He understood on the one hand that capitalism was a specific historical mode of production, a particular way of organising men's transactions with nature and with other men and, on the other, that the essence of this mode of production, according to the political economist, was free exchange relations. It was this insight that had given rise to Adam Smith's labour theory of value. For Smith saw that it was labour as such that was productive in a market economy, because the value a good had in exchange (its exchange value) depended on the amount of labour (the labour time) that had been used to produce it. It followed that the productivity of labour would grow the more general and unhindered free exchange relations became.[38]

[38] There are in fact four different theories of value to be found in Smith's work. Two of these, the labour command theory and the labour embodied theory, are different versions of the labour theory of value. At first he says that value is determined by the amount of labour expended on producing a commodity, but he then restricts this case to simple barter economies, where, for example, deer exchange against beaver according to how many hours have gone into hunting them. In a complex market economy, however, Smith argues that the value of a commodity is determined by the amount of labour it can command in the market, once it has been changed into money. At other times, he uses a theory of value that foreshadows the later marginal utility theory, and at others, a straight cost of production theory, which includes, beside labour, capital and rent.

Ricardo shared with Smith the view that

> the idea of value in commodities cannot even be conceived without being mingled with the idea of their relation to mankind and to human labour of which some portion must always be employed in procuring them originally

> [Samuel Read, quoted by R. L. Meek, *Studies in the Labour Theory of Value*, London 1936, 126].

He ironed out many of the confusions and ambiguities in Smith's presentation of the law of value, and held consistently to a labour embodied theory, arguing that exchange value always depends on labour time. Malthus took over the other main strand in Smith's labour theory, the labour command theory. In the debate between them Ricardo correctly saw that their differences in other matters of economic theory could not be resolved so long as both adhered to different theories of value. What was at stake was different conceptions of the subject matter of political economy. He wrote to Malthus:

> Political Economy you think is an inquiry into the nature and causes of wealth; I think it should rather be called an inquiry into the laws which determine the divisions of the produce of industry among the classes which concur in its formation

> [quoted in M. Dobb, *Political Economy and Capitalism*, London 1937, 16].

This insight, according to Marx, was Ricardo's greatest achievement. Ricardo saw that the logic of the labour theory of value required that he made 'the antagonism of class interests, of wages and profits, of profits and rent', the starting point of his investigations, although at the same time, 'naively taking this antagonism for a social law of nature'.[39]

What are the basic elements of a labour theory of value? The 'law of value' only exists because an exchange economy exists which divorces the use value that a commodity has from its exchange value. This means that commodities are produced not to satisfy immediate needs but to realise exchange value, which takes the form of a commodity, money. The notion of value, far from being a metaphysical concept, is the only concept that

[39] *Capital* I, 14.

allows an understanding of how production is organised in a society based on the exchange of products in the market by independent producers:

> The nonsense about the necessity of proving the concept of value arises from complete ignorance both of the subject dealt with and of the method of science. Every child knows that a country which ceased to work, I will not say for a year, but for a few weeks, would die. Every child knows too that the mass of products corresponding to the different needs require different and quantitatively determined masses of the total labour of society. That this necessity of distributing social labour in definite proportions cannot be done away with by the *particular form* of social production, but can only change the *form it assumes*, is self evident. No natural laws can be done away with. What can change, in changing historical circumstances, is the *form* in which these laws operate. And the form in which this proportional division of labour operates, in a state of society where the interconnection of social labour is manifested in the *private exchange* of the individual products of labour, is precisely the *exchange value* of these products
>
> [Marx–Engels, *Correspondence*, 246].

Thus the law of value studies how social labour is distributed and rewarded in a society based on the *private* exchange of the individual products of labour. Because labour produces goods that, from the point of view of the worker, are not for use but for exchange, there must be some standard which reduces the qualitative differences between goods to a quantitative difference, and so allows them to be compared and exchanged. This measure is labour time.

> In so far as the product has a measure of its own, it is measured in terms of its natural properties—size, weight, length, capacity, measure of usefulness etc. But as an effect, or as the static form of the force that has created it, it is measured only by the volume of this force itself. The measure of labour is time. Simply because products *are* labour, they can be measured by the measure of labour, by the working time, or the quantity of labour consumed in them.
>
> [D. McLellan (ed.), *Marx's Grundrisse*, 126].

It follows that the product as an exchange value is determined by different forces, and so leads a different existence from the product as a use-value. The form which the product takes as an exchange value is money.

> The definition of the product as exchange value necessarily entails that the exchange value leads a separate existence, severed from the product. This exchange value which is severed from the product and yet is itself a commodity is— *money*. All the properties of the commodity viewed as exchange value appear as an object distinct from it; they exist in the social form of money, quite separate from their natural form of existence [McLellan, *Grundrisse*, 59].

Money itself is not the measure of the value of the commodity, it is only the form which this value takes. Value is only bestowed on an object by labour, and so a good only possesses exchange value insofar as it represents a portion of the social labour time of a society.

Of all the classical economists, Ricardo developed the most consistent version of the labour theory of value. But even his version was not without its difficulties, and it came under considerable attack after his death. It was these difficulties that Marx tackled and overcame in the 1850s, and he lists them in the *Critique of Political Economy*, which was published in 1859.

Firstly, it had been objected, 'given labour time as the intrinsic measure of value, how are wages to be determined on this basis?'[40] For how can labour which is the measure of value for all commodities be the measure of itself when it too becomes a commodity, and is exchanged on the labour market for a wage?

Secondly, 'how does production on the basis of exchange value solely determined by labour-time lead to the result that the exchange-value of labour is less than the exchange-value of its product?'[41] For if the exchange-value of a commodity is equal to the labour time contained in it, then assuming that labour has been accepted as a measure of itself, the exchange-value of the commodity labour must equal the product that it yields. So

[40] K. Marx, *A Contribution to the Critique of Political Economy*, London 1971, 62.

[41] Marx, *Contribution*, 62.

wages must be equal to the product of labour. The Ricardian socialists seized on this implication in the labour theory of value, and declared that private property was nothing but organised robbery of part of the product of the worker which rightfully belonged to him.

Thirdly, there was the question of 'how on the basis of exchange value a market price differing from this exchange value comes into being, or rather, how the law of exchange value asserts itself only in its antithesis'.[42] Why are market prices not proportional to labour-time values?

Fourthly, 'if exchange value is nothing but the labour-time contained in a commodity, how does it come about that commodities which contain no labour possess exchange-value, in other words, how does the exchange value of natural forces arise?'[43] This included the famous example of wine that increased in value merely by maturing in a cellar.

Marx claimed to have removed these four objections to the labour theory of value in his theory of wages, his theory of capital, his theory of competition, and his theory of rent, respectively. The last two do not concern us here. We shall concentrate instead on the theory of wages and the theory of capital. These put together produce the concept of surplus value, and Marx himself was in no doubt that his success in removing the objections to Ricardo's labour theory of value was the main achievement in *Capital*. On August 24th 1867, he wrote to Engels:

> The best points in my book are: (1) the *double character of labour*, according to whether it is expressed in use value or exchange value (*all* understanding of the facts depends upon this, it is emphasised immediately in the *first* chapter); (2) the treatment of *surplus value independently of its particular* forms as profit, interest, ground rent, etc. This will come out especially in the second volume. The treatment of the particular forms by classical economy, which always mixes them up with the general form, is a regular hash
>
> [Marx–Engels, *Correspondence*, 226–27].

---

[42] Marx, *Contribution*, 62.
[43] Marx, *Contribution*, 63.

In another letter written later in January 1868, he made the same point at greater length.

> It is strange that the fellow [Roscher] does not realise the three fundamentally new elements of the book;
>
> (1) That in contrast to *all* former systems of political economy which *begin* by taking the particular fragments of surplus value with their fixed forms of rent, profit and interest as already given, I first deal with the general form of surplus value, in which all these elements are still undifferentiated....
>
> (2) That, without exception, the economists have missed the simple point that if the commodity has a double character —use-value and exchange-value—then the labour represented in the commodity must also have a double character, while the mere bald analysis of labour, as in Smith, Ricardo, etc., is bound to come up everywhere against the inexplicable. This is in fact the whole secret of the critical conception.
>
> (3) That for the first time wages are shown as the irrational form in which a hidden relation appears, and this is exactly represented in the two forms of wage payment— time wages and piece wages
>
> [Marx–Engels, *Correspondence*, 232].

Marx rejected the theories of the Ricardian socialists, because they explained nothing, they did not distinguish capitalism from any previous economic system. Furthermore, they treated the bourgeois ideal of free exchange relations between sovereign individuals as the socialist ideal, and merely criticised the bourgeoisie for not establishing them. But Marx, as a result of his studies, now understood that the law of value which the political economists put forward to explain production and distribution in a market economy, was inadequate precisely because it rested on the assumption of free exchanges.

There are signs in his earlier writings that Marx was already moving to a different conception of exchange relations. In *The Poverty of Philosophy* he analysed the arguments of Bray, who desired to make exchange relations truly equal and fair. Bray had written:

... this most unjust system of exchanges—the workmen have given the capitalist the labour of a whole year, in exchange for the value of only half a year—and from this, and not from the assumed inequality of bodily and mental powers in individuals, has arisen the inequality of wealth and power which at present exists around us

[quoted by Marx, *Poverty of Philosophy*, 72].

He proposed an economic system in which men would exchange equal quantities of hours of labour. This would eliminate exploitation. But, comments Marx, such a system of exchanges would only be possible if the number of hours to be spent by everyone on material production were agreed on beforehand. Otherwise, left to themselves, men would choose to work for very different lengths of time and the result would be overproduction. But such an agreement to ensure that everything that is produced will be exchanged, is no longer individual exchange. The mode of exchanging products, concludes Marx, is regulated by the mode of producing them, and 'there is no individual exchange without the antagonism of classes'.[44]

Thus Marx pronounced the ideal of free exchanges between equal and independent individuals in capitalist society to be unattainable. In his later works he shows why. The institutional context of this mode of production, private property and wage labour, makes all exchange relations one-sided and destroys the basis of individual exchange. In an ordinary individual exchange, each party receives something he wants. The exchange enables him to satisfy an individual need. The wage bargain was apparently of this kind. The worker exchanged so many hours of labour for a wage. But, argued Marx, this exchange had two parts. In the first, the worker sells his labour power, which has both a use value and a price and receives in exchange a wage, a certain sum of exchange values. Thus it appears as a commodity like any other, the price of which (exchange value) is regulated by its cost of production (subsistence and reproduction). Marx had treated it as such in his earlier works. But now he sees it as a unique commodity, because labour power alone among commodities is able to create value. The use value of this commodity

[44] *Poverty of Philosophy*, 78.

is that it is the source of value, and so its consumption (by the capitalist) creates value.

The second part of the wage bargain, therefore, was that the capitalist consumed labour power by using it to produce more commodities which could then be sold on the market to realise more exchange value, more profit. Labour power becomes 'a productive and reproductive force of capital, a force belonging to capital itself'.[45] Thus by purchasing labour power, the capitalist is able to produce commodities that realise a sum of exchange values on the market much greater than the cost of the original labour power. This is what Marx terms surplus value. The worker is not cheated in his side of the bargain. He receives in wages the market value of his labour, what it is worth to the capitalist. The real point about the wage bargain, says Marx, is that it is presented as an exchange between equals when in reality it is nothing of the kind, because the buying of labour power itself produces the capitalist-worker relation, it is the perpetual creation of the social existence and social function of the capitalist. In a purely individual exchange, the structure of the exchange is not affected by what is exchanged. In the wage bargain, however, the capitalist does not exist prior to the exchange of labour power. It does not only satisfy an individual need; it brings into existence and confirms a particular social relation, the basis of capitalist production. Furthermore,

Capitalist production ... of itself reproduces the separation between labour power and the means of labour. It therefore reproduces and perpetuates the condition for exploiting the labourer. It incessantly forces him to sell his labour power in order to live, and enables the capitalist to purchase labour power in order to enrich himself [*Capital* i, 577].

Thus the worker's freedom in the contract is an illusion. He has the right to dispose of his own commodity, labour power, but he also has no other commodity to sell because he lacks means of production (raw materials and tools). Once the workers enter the labour process they have then 'ceased to belong to themselves ... as co-operators, as members of a working organism, they are but special modes of existence of capital'.[46]

[45] *Capital* i, 571.   [46] *Capital* i, 333.

For Marx then, the alienated social bond of capitalism, which political economy presents as a series of individual exchanges that men enter freely, has in fact two parts, the second of which is properly not an exchange at all, but the foundation of the capitalist-worker relation, a social relationship which exists independently of individual choice and consent, and serves the interests of the capitalist whom it creates. The growth of social wealth is growth in the wealth and power of capital, not of the worker. The existence of competition becomes incidental to exchange relations; so does the material condition of the workers. Whatever their wages, their impoverishment grows, because the social world they are producing is not their world, but the alienated world of capital. This alienation, says Marx, has reached its zenith with the extension of the division of labour to manufacture.

Some crippling of mind and body he thought was inseparable from the division of labour as a whole,[47] in particular the division between mental and manual labour, but it was manufacture which 'attacks the individual at the very roots of his life'.[48] 'Division of labour within the workshop implies the undisputed authority of the capitalist over men, that are but parts of a mechanism that belong to him.'[49] Manufacture 'converts the labourer into a crippled monstrosity'.[50] The individual 'is made the automatic motor of a fractional operation'.[51] He becomes 'a mere fragment of his own body'.[52] 'The manufacturing labourer develops productive activity as a mere appendage of the capitalist's workshop.'[53]

The result, says Marx, is that human activity is not aimed at

---

[47] Marx did not oppose all division of labour. In the *German Ideology*, he distinguished between spontaneous and forced division of labour. 'Division of labour', he wrote, 'only becomes truly such from the moment when a division of material and mental labour appears' (43).

[48] *Capital* I, 363.

[49] *Capital* I, 356.

[50] *Capital* I, 360.

[51] Ibid.

[52] Ibid.

[53] Ibid.

satisfying human needs, but at the realisation of surplus value, the accumulation of capital. Man is alienated from human life.

The labourer exists to satisfy the needs of self-expansion of existing values, instead of, on the contrary, material wealth existing to satisfy the needs of development on the part of the labourer. As in religion man is governed by the products of his own brains, so in capitalistic production he is governed by the products of his own hand [*Capital* i, 621].

3. The Fate of Political Economy

Smith and the classical school based their whole analysis on a fairly simple dichotomy—between natural and artificial institutions. Although the subtleties and the qualifications in Smith's accounts of civil society were soon lost, this distinction was not. The essence of natural institutions was the market system of free exchanges between sovereign individuals. The sharpness and the critical power of Smith's work were due to his recognition that the way in which wealth was produced in the new manufacturing industries represented a new form of wealth and that it rested on the relationship between stock (fixed capital) and the labour that was set to work with it. But this meant that the wealth of nations depended on the productivity of labour and not on gold or land. Labour productivity depended, on the one hand, on the skill, dexterity and judgement of the workers and, on the other, on the number of the working population that were engaged in production as opposed to unproductive occupations. This gave two main ways of increasing social wealth: the first was to widen the division of labour, both within each manufacturing operation and within countries and regions; the second was to increase the number of productive relative to unproductive workers.[54]

Smith therefore detected a meaning and a rationality in the natural order—the rationality of the industrial bourgeoisie. His

[54] Smith used two definitions of productive labour. One of them defined productive labour as labour that fixes itself in some material form, and thus excluded all services. Marx rejected this notion, linked as it was to Smith's polemic against the unproductive landowners and their establishment. For Marx the important point about whether labour was productive or not was whether it produced surplus value.

labour theory of value was the instrument with which he did it, and it founded a whole tradition of economic theory. As Ronald Meek has written:

> ... the labour theory is in essence an expression of the idea that the fundamental relationships into which men enter with one another in the field of production ultimately determine the relationships into which they enter in the field of exchange
>
> [*Studies in the Labour Theory of Value*, 79].

An economics based on such a theory is necessarily a political economy, because it cannot abstract economic activity from other forms of social activity. It is necessarily an enquiry into the social structure. As a result many practical implications can be drawn from it. But the theory proved to have two edges. It was used first against the unproductive class, the class that added nothing to the wealth of the community, but instead consumed it, a class that lived off its monopoly of the land. It therefore divided society into the industrial bourgeoisie, which included both capitalists and workers (the third estate) and the surplus class, which also happened to control the government and so was able to restrict the development of the industrial class.

But a theory which thus laid bare how wealth was created and distributed had other consequences also. For in embryo it provided a theory of exploitation. If all wealth was produced by labour, and capital was only stored up labour, what justification had those who had monopolised capital to a share in this wealth? The political economists of course replied that labour received its full value in the market and that the wage bargain was a free contract made between equal individuals. The socialist replied, as we have seen, that this could not be the case, for if labour alone conferred value on commodities, how could a surplus remain after the sale of these commodities which was not distributed as wages but retained as profits?

During the first half of the nineteenth century, therefore, political economy was increasingly recognised to have dangerous implications. For the socialists consigned not only the landowners but the capitalists as well into the unproductive class who, in Adam Smith's famous words, 'love to reap where they never sowed'. Political economy had evidently revealed too much

of the foundations of civil society. It was natural therefore that
the labour theory of value came under attack for it was this that
gave both the concept of exploitation and the distinction between
labour that was productive and unproductive.

Marx put the turning point at 1830:

> With the year 1830 came the decisive crisis. In France and in
> England the bourgeoisie had conquered political power.
> Thenceforth, the class struggle, practically as well as theo-
> retically, took on more and more outspoken and threatening
> forms. It sounded the knell of scientific bourgeois political
> economy. It was thenceforth no longer a question, whether
> this theorem or that was true, but whether it was useful to
> capital or harmful, expedient or inexpedient, politically
> dangerous or not. In place of disinterested inquirers there were
> hired prizefighters; in place of genuine scientific research, the
> bad conscience and the evil intent of apologetic
>
> [Capital I, 15].

Marx uses science in a special sense here. He does not refer
merely to the use of scientific procedures, for economics had
been developing these with diligence since 1830. What he means
is that political economy after 1830, with a few exceptions, no
longer provided a critical analysis of the capitalist mode of production. It no longer explained anything about capitalism. Instead
it served up ideological justifications mingled with descriptive
information about economic phenomena.

The basis of modern economics is its value theory, the theory
of utility. The classical economists distinguished between value,
which was determined by labour time,[55] and price, which was
determined on the market by the ordinary forces of supply and
demand. Most of the classical economists glibly passed over the
difficulties of relating value to price, and concentrated on the
interaction of supply and demand and the process of accumulation. Their successors, however, more attuned to political and
academic realities, perceived that the distinction between value

---

[55] At least in the most consistent form of the classical labour theory
of value as formulated by Ricardo.

and price was the source of all the misunderstandings and the misuse of political economy. They therefore

> gradually abandoned the labour theory of value in favour of a different principle of explanation which eliminated the idea of the surplus—in so far at any rate as it implied a theory of exploitation. In technical terms this involved the development of a utility theory of value and, as a corollary to it, the admission of the productivity of capital
>
> [E. Roll, *History of Economic Thought*, London 1954, 318].

What they sought was a way to rehabilitate the share of social wealth that went to private property in the form of rent and profit. They did so by denying that there was a meaningful distinction that could be drawn between value and price. The price that any commodity or service could command in the market became its value. This shifted the focus of economics from production to demand. Anything that was demanded in the market had value. What the new theory retained from classical economics was the importance of free exchanges between sovereign individuals. Indeed it further refined the principle.

Its starting point was the individual consumer (or, in the labour market, the individual worker) who evaluated all the courses of action open to him in terms of their 'utility'. Utility was defined by Say as the significance an individual attached to a good for the purpose of satisfying a want. Thus two individuals would only exchange two goods if their preferences were different, i.e., if each judged that the value (the utility) to him of the good which the other offered was greater than the good he was offering in exchange. Thus, for example, a worker, according to this theory, would only accept employment if he considered that his sacrifice in terms of time and exertion was less than the wage he would receive, and the capitalist would only employ him if the wage was less than the value of the work, when it was sold on the market. By reducing social relationships to purely individual ones and by treating the ends sought by individuals as entirely random and not themselves structured, this theory of value produces the mystification that all factors of production have equal status in the production process. Since both the worker and capitalist contribute to production (the worker labour and the capitalist raw materials, machinery and 'entrepreneurial skills') and since neither would contribute if they had not made a favourable judgement of utility, both are entitled to a share in the proceeds of production, according to the market value of their contribution.

This approach was greatly extended later in the century by the marginalists, Jevons, Walras and Manger. But its foundations were laid in the years following Ricardo's death. It also revives a trend of thought to be found in Adam Smith. This is not surprising, since, as we have shown, Smith's premises about economic activity were individualistic and his conception of free exchange relations was often couched in terms of interpersonal comparisons of advantage or utility. His labour theory of value led in a different direction, towards a consideration of the objective features of the production process. But his theory that men are distinguished from animals primarily by the propensity *in human nature* to truck and barter and that this gives rise to the division of labour, is capable of being developed in an opposite direction, to a consideration of the costs and benefits of economic behaviour to the individual. Smith treats labour and consequently all economic activity as a burden, as a necessity imposed on man but one which they will always seek to avoid. Thus he reads back into nature the opposition between work and leisure. Marx was especially scornful about it:

'In the sweat of thy face shalt thou labour', was Jehovah's curse, which he gave to Adam. And it is thus as curse that A(dam) Smith regards labour. 'Rest' appears as the adequate condition, as identical with 'freedom' and 'happiness'. A. Smith seems far from seeing that the individual, 'in his normal condition of health, strength, activity, capacity, and skill' has also the need for a normal portion of work and for an end to rest. It is true that the amount of labour is itself determined externally, by the purpose sought and the obstacles to the attainment of that purpose which must be overcome through labour. But A. Smith has just a little conception of the fact that this overcoming of obstacles is itself the activity of freedom—of the further fact that the appearance of merely external natural necessity is stripped off from external purposes and that these purposes are revealed as purposes which the individual sets himself—of the fact, therefore, that the overcoming of obstacles is self-realisation, objectification of the subject, therefore concrete freedom, whose action is precisely work

> [*Grundrisse*, translated in E. Kamenka, *The Ethical Foundations of Marxism*, London 1962. Cf. D. McLellan, *Marx's Grundrisse*, 123-24].

Adam Smith's premises reflect a specific mode of production and are not a true statement of the premises of human history. As a result, he treats capitalism as the natural order and its laws as eternal. Nevertheless, with the aid of his labour theory of value, he makes the first penetrating study of capitalism as a mode of production. He seeks to uncover both how wealth is produced and how it is distributed because he understood that the solutions to both questions are linked. To this extent his work is incompatible with that of the neo-classical economists. A theory of value to be consistent must provide a theory of distribution. What is of crucial importance is how the relations between production and distribution are conceived. Some later economists, such as John Stuart Mill, tried to separate the two by arguing that production was subject to physical laws and distribution to human arrangements. But as Marx commented:

> These means of distribution are the relations of production themselves, but 'sub specie distributionis' (from the point of view of distribution). Thus it is quite absurd to say, as J. S. Mill does for example, ... that: 'The laws and conditions of the production of wealth partake of the character of physical truths.... It is not so with the distribution of wealth. This is a matter of human institutions solely.' The 'laws and conditions' of the production of wealth and the laws of 'distribution of wealth' are the same laws in a different form; they both change and undergo the same historical process
>
> [McLellan, *Marx's Grundrisse*, 151].

The distinctiveness of the utility theory in this respect is not that it separates the laws of production and the laws of distribution but that it treats them as the same laws, but as the same laws in the same form. It reduces distribution to production and so justifies whatever distribution of income exists. Since value equals price, the income that the different factors of production command in the market must be the value that they contribute to production. This is true by definition. If the source of value lies in the choices that each individual makes and which in aggregate become the demand curves for products and services, anything that is demanded and bought in the market has a value, because if it can be sold it means that there must be a demand for it, and if there is a demand it means that one or more individuals somewhere have 'valued' it sufficiently to part with some of their income. This commonsense notion of value is hailed by many as a major breakthrough. As Lionel Robbins writes,

> Is it not clear that the imperfections of the Ricardian system were due to just this circumstance that it stopped at the valuaions of the market and did not press through to the valuations of the individual? Surely it is the great achievement of the more recent theories of value to have surmounted just this barrier?
>
> [L. Robbins, *An Essay on the Nature and Significance of Economic Science*, London 1935, 20–21].

Robbins is slightly bemused here, for it is the utility theory which in reality stops at the valuations of the market, for the preferences of individuals are only deduced from what they buy in the market. Far from stopping at the valuations of the market, Ricardo went on to consider the relationship between value as measured by prices in the market and value as measured by labour time. It is significant that this problem has vanished over the horizon for Robbins, who is no longer even able to perceive it and instead substitutes a non-problem.

The achievement of modern theories of value, however, is from their own point of view certainly great. For they have 'proved' that if there is a flow of income to a factor of production, be it a raw material, the land on which a factory stands, the investment of capital in machines or workers' labour power, then that means that someone somewhere has conferred value on this factor. How else could it be receiving income? All such factors must therefore be productive. Value is anything anyone will pay for. In its reduction of all questions to the psychology of the individual, marginal utility theory can be recognised as a direct outgrowth of utilitarianism. Utilitarianism also reduced everything to the individual and used its concept of utility to determine what was socially useful and what was not. The answer, of course, was not really deduced from the isolated rational man, but from the purposes and values of the aspiring bourgeoisie. Once their conditions of existence had become the conditions of existence of society as a whole, utilitarianism lost its radical outlook and the concept of utility was widened to include whatever was already established. Marx wrote of early attempts to combine the theory of utility with economics:

> The economic content gradually turned the utility theory into a mere apologia for the existing state of affairs, an attempt to prove that under existing conditions the mutual relations of people today are the most advantageous and generally useful. It has this character among all modern economists

> [Marx–Engels, *The German Ideology*, 465].

The utility theory of value and distribution certainly made economics safe again for serious academic study. It also made it necessary to look for a new set of definitions of man, a new conception of economic activity. The clearest statement of what emerged and which has become orthodoxy for the majority of modern economists is perhaps to be found in Robbins' book *An Essay on the Nature and Significance of Economic Science*. With the abandonment of the labour theory of value, economics is no longer aware that it is analysing a specific mode of production. By rejecting the distinction between natural and artificial institutions it loses what little historical basis it had. It sees itself instead as the analysis of an aspect of human behaviour and as such its conclusions really are true for all time and all societies. Robbins states:

> From the point of view of the economist, the conditions of human existence exhibit four fundamental characteristics. The ends are various. The time and the means for achieving these ends are limited and capable of alternative application. At the same time the ends have different importance [*Essay*, 12].

This allows economics to be defined as 'the science which studies human behaviour as a relationship between ends and scarce means which have alternative uses'.[56] It is an analytical, positive science which focuses attention on 'a particular *aspect* of behaviour, the form imposed by the influence of scarcity'.[57] As such it is entirely neutral as regards the choice of ends,[58] it merely assesses the available means in a situation where there are many different ends that could be pursued. Robbins however distinguishes this kind of economics from purely technical enquiry. Indeed he even criticises Adam Smith and the classical school for engaging only in technical enquiry, by which he means that they take an end—increasing the productivity of labour—and discuss the most effective means for realising it. Economics has no concern with ends. But what Robbins has done is to reduce the aim of increasing the productivity of labour to an aim that an individual might have. An economy as a system of behaviour in which ends are not arbitrary but structured in ways that can be analysed is something of which he has no conception. Yet any individualistic theory of society must say how the harmony of interests of all the members of the society can be realised, otherwise it has to believe in social chaos. The usual solutions assume that harmony will somehow be achieved naturally, or that it will be created by some external agency, such as the state. Adam Smith chose a combination of the two, while Robbins opts for the first without any discussion. This choice itself reflects the complexity of Smith's view of man and of economic behaviour compared with the crude notions of modern economics, which are formalised in the well-known monstrosity, *homo oeconomicus* —economic man. Robbins protests, as well he might, that because they use economic man as the basis of their models, economists do not as a result believe that real men actually behave in this way. It is only an analytical device. Rarely can an analytical

[56] Robbins, 16.

[57] Robbins, 17.

[58] As Parsons points out, Robbins' positive science contains a deep laissez-faire bias. His study of the 'facts' with no concern for 'ends' led him to write a book on the 1930s depression, in which he argued that the main cause of the slump was Government interference in the workings of the economy. See T. Parsons, *The Structure of Social Action*, New York 1949, 607–609.

device have explained so little or revealed so much. One of the misunderstandings about Smith's work has been to lumber him with this notorious 'economic man'.[59] 'Economic man' is concerned only to maximise his returns and minimise his losses; he has certain knowledge of the future, awareness of all the options open to him and of his own best interests. Furthermore, only strictly economic considerations move him to action. Society, it is alleged, is composed of these economic men all maximising as hard as they can in complete isolation from everyone else. Such assumptions allow the static models of demand theory and welfare economics to be constructed.

Both the goods that are produced and the prices they sell at are in accord with the wishes of the consumers. The only case when they could not be would be when the markets did not clear, when there was a gap between demand and supply at the going market price. Such gaps are ascribed to rigidities in the economic system like the failure of wages to fall low enough (which may have to be below zero) in times of depression. A casual observer of modern economies might think that such wage and price rigidities were a familiar, even a permanent feature of such economies, but this is of no interest to the static models of general equilibrium analysis which long ago lost interest in the real world.

Modern orthodox economics combines sophisticated applied techniques for assisting the policy-making and forecasting of governments and corporations, with a completely uncritical and ahistorical theory of how the economic system works, which rests on the marginal utility theory of value. The barrenness of this side of neo-classical economics is well known. Even the internal logic of its theory that capital is productive has now been successfully challenged.[60] What is still of interest in modern economics for understanding the workings of modern capitalism is work that implicitly or explicitly breaks with neo-classical

[59] See W. D. Grampp, 'Adam Smith and Economic Man', *Journal of Political Economy*, vol. 56 (1948), for an excellent summary of the qualities of 'economic man'.

[60] See G. Harcourt, 'Some Cambridge Controversies in the Theory of Capital', *Journal of Economic Literature*, vol. VII (1969), 369–405, for a review of the debate.

economics and its theory of value. Such currents include Keynes' work and that of some of his successors, the attempt to introduce 'sociological postulates' in such areas as the theory of the firm, the political economy of economists like Galbraith and Schumpeter, and the wealth of case studies and economic history.

Most economic theory, however, adds nothing to an understanding of the problems which the classical economists formulated. In starting from similar individualistic premises, and in particular from the notion that capitalism is essentially a system of free exchanges between sovereign individuals, the classical economists did indeed only pave the way for the neo-classical school. But they still fashioned political economy that explained a great deal, partly because they possessed in the labour theory of value an analytical tool that could distinguish between value and price, and productive and unproductive labour and therefore could throw light on some of the features of production as a mode of production, a system of economic behaviour. In cancelling these distinctions and shifting the focus of economics away from these questions, the neo-classical economists only complete a tendency that Marx had already noted in their forerunners, the tendency to retreat from explanation with the aid of theory and rely on explanation that merely reflects the common-sense logic of established institutions:

> For the bourgeois it is so much the easier to prove on the basis of his language the identity of commercial and individual, or even universal, human relations, since this language itself is a product of the bourgeoisie and therefore in actuality as in language the relations of buying and selling have been made the basis of all others [Marx–Engels, *German Ideology*, 54].

Conclusion

In their economic studies, Marx and Adam Smith at least began with a connected view of human activity. The difference between their images of man are not separate from their empirical analyses. They are the preconditions for such analyses, because they select the concepts that constitute the facts and supply immanent standards of evaluation. Thus this is no speculative or philosophical debate that is removed from science. It concerns the nature, the basis and the area of this science. Marx's critique of the premises of political economy was not the only criticism he had to make by any means, but it formed his starting-point and it enabled him to see clearly the kind of explanation that the classical economists were putting forward.

This is not to suggest that the truth of all economic theories is relative either to premises about man or to theories of value, and that there is no way of judging between them. It is clear, for instance, that Marx provides the only consistent labour theory of value. Furthermore no other theory of value has been devised which can yield a theory of capitalist development. The utility theory trivialises economics and bars the way to the kind of questions that the classical economists asked. It is stuck at the micro level of analysis. It provides no adequate theory of distribution and no way of analysing economic growth.

Marx was able to solve the problems of the classical labour theory of value where even Ricardo failed because he criticised the political economists not merely from a position within economics, within the premises of their own theory, but also from the position of his own premises about man. Here too, his theory did not have the weaknesses that Adam Smith's did.

Smith's thought is strung between his individualistic conception of the preconditions and the motive forces of social life and his notion of human moral fulfilment which involves men's judgement and social nature. This produces the tension between his description of the passions, which are outside history, yet the force that determines it, and his analysis of how moral rules are evolved through the impartial spectator and the sentiment of propriety which change with every historical period. In his *Lectures* the final guarantor of the harmony of the social and natural world was God. In *The Wealth of Nations* he abandons God, but he has not rethought his premises, so that the teleological element that was represented by God is transferred to the natural order. Imperfections in the natural order are now set down to human causes and can only be removed by human action, but the assumption is retained that the natural order will achieve harmony, if it is left to itself. Thus Adam Smith never sees man as the only purposive being, whose actual purposes and needs are always historical within the framework of some definite social mode of production. Instead, teleology is located first in God and later in man's pre-social impulses and passions, which God establishes as the governing laws of social life.

In criticising Smith, Marx first criticises his premises, which had become the unspoken premises of the whole classical school. He needs to show that Smith is not in fact describing eternal economic laws, but only the laws of a particular economic system. Here the concept of alienation is crucial. Without his concept of alienation how could Marx distinguish labour in general from labour under capitalism, how could he foresee a qualitatively new stage in human society? Without the theory of alienation social- ism becomes what Schumpeter and Weber claimed it was—a form of *industrial* society, which only differs from capitalism by the degree to which property is collectively owned and bureau- critically administered.[61]

But for a long while this insight into the basis of political economy that Marx achieved in his early writings is not carried through. Marx does not fulfil the demands of his own materialist conception of history. He does not show precisely how capitalism is different from previous modes of production. Instead he stays on the terrain of political economy and shows how capitalism is doomed by the operation of the very laws that the political econo- mists have discovered. This means that although he criticises the simple distinction between artificial and natural institutions, he retains the classical labour theory of value that is the basis of it and therefore cannot really succeed in making a substantive analysis of capitalism *on the basis of his own premises*. Thus it is not until the *Grundrisse* and *Capital* that Marx fulfils the promise of the 1844 manuscripts and the *German Ideology* and lays out a general theory of capitalism as a specific mode of production by discovering the real law of value that governs it.

[61] J. A. Schumpeter, *Capitalism, and Socialism and Democracy*, New York 1949, London 1965, M. Weber, *Economy and Society*, New York 1968.

7

THE RELEVANCE OF MARXISM FOR THE PRESENT

Marx proved himself incapable of fashioning other tools with which to tackle the increasingly complex phenomena of a modern economy. Thus, his whole system has proved essentially barren. No economic contribution of any significance whatever has come from his followers

[Eric Roll, *History of Economic Thought*, London 1954, 295].

A minor post-Ricardian, Marx was an autodidact cut off in his lifetime from competent criticism and stimulus

[Paul Samuelson, 'Wages and Interest: A Modern Dissection of Marxian Economic Models', *American Economic Review* 47, 5 (Dec. 1957), 911].

Perhaps the most neglected and misunderstood aspect of Marx's work is his political economy. Whereas much of Marx's historical and social analysis has been accepted by academics, Marx's economics has been ignored or treated with disdain by orthodox economists. Thus the paradox emerges that Marx is frequently held to have contributed most to fields which were peripheral to his life's work. Yet as we showed in our discussion of his premises, his analysis of political economy forms the core of his developed social theory. To reject or to minimise his economics is to reject Marxism as a general theory and to acknowledge it only as a collection of eclectic insights, scattered throughout his work. This is a procedure, of course, which commends itself to the vultures of modern social theory. A general consensus has grown up that Marx's political economy has either been disproved because of the failure of all its major predictions, or that it was only able to account for Victorian *laissez-faire* capitalism, and no longer has any relevance for analysing modern monopoly, welfare state capitalism.

Marx has been attacked firstly for his labour theory of value. The criticisms can be grouped under three main headings: the transformation problem, the neglect of demand, and the metaphysical nature of the concept of value. The transformation problem is about how value is related to price. The labour theory of value, it is argued, is only applicable to a simple exchange economy where commodities exchange at prices that directly reflect the amount of labour time that is embodied in them. But once the division of labour extends to specialisation within the manufacturing process and barter is replaced by a complex system of markets that use money as an intermediary between the buyers and sellers of commodities, prices increasingly diverge from the quantity of labour time that has gone into production. In particular, it is found that commodities which are produced by different capital/labour ratios can still exchange in the market at the same price.

As a result it is declared that the labour theory of value is a quite inaccurate guide to how the relative prices of commodities are determined in an exchange economy that uses money for its transactions and has accumulated a stock of capital. Following this reduction of the question of value to the question of the individual prices of commodities on the market, the critics naturally pass on to show how the labour theory of value must be inadequate in any case, because it concentrates on the costs of production, and treats these as the real basis of economic activity. The real reason for these criticisms is, of course, to be found in the subjective preferences of individuals, which are to be measured by utility and are embodied in their beloved demand curves.

> We must reverse the Marxian emphasis, beginning with Market exchange values rather than labour values because that is what the market that determines people's incomes and goods' prices begins (and ends!) with
>
> [Samuelson, 'Wages and Interest', 888].

As we have argued elsewhere in this book, this theory of value is completely circular because it denies that there can be any divergence between value and price so long as some measure of consumer choice exists. It also denies that there can be any distinction between productive and unproductive labour. All labour that can command a price in the market is *ipso facto* productive.

Finally it is alleged that the whole notion of value as something distinct from price is a metaphysical notion, that smuggles certain illegitimate ethical assumptions into the positive science of economics, or that at any rate, it adds nothing to economics. It is, as Joan Robinson so frequently reiterates, 'just a word'. It supplies a theory of exploitation, and therefore has important political implications, but makes no difference to actual economic analysis and in certain circumstances can hinder it. The time and trouble Marx spent in elaborating it are put down to his unwholesome German taste for barren metaphysics. As G. D. H. Cole wrote:

> Was it . . . Professor Tawney who said that he did not need the theory of surplus value to tell him that the capitalists exploited the workers? Yet that in effect was what the theory did proclaim—that and nothing else besides
>
> > [quoted in P. Sweezy, 'Professor Cole's History of Socialist Thought', *Economic Journal* 47, 5 (Dec. 1957), 930].

The conclusion that the labour theory of value is an outdated tool of economic analysis has led a few modern Marxist economists to abandon it altogether. Oscar Lange, for instance, argues that the specific concepts that Marx used have to be discarded in favour of those developed by modern marginalist economists. What is still of use in Marx, he thinks, is the evolutionary theory of capitalism, but this rests not on economic concepts as such (which in Lange's view, are marginalist or nothing), but on introducing sociological and institutional frameworks into the analysis:

> The superiority of Marxian economics in analysing capitalism is not due to the economic concepts used by Marx (the labour theory of value), but to the exact specification of the institutional datum distinguishing capitalism from the concept of an exchange economy in general
>
> > [O. Lange, 'Marxian Economics and Modern Economic Theory', in D. Horowitz (ed.) *Marx and Modern Economics*, London and New York 1968, 68].

For purely economic purposes, and this includes the running of socialist economies, the Marxist theory has been superseded:

> It is obvious that Marshallian economics offers more for the current administration of the economic system of Soviet Russia than Marxian economics does ... modern economic theory, in spite of its undoubted 'bourgeois' origin, has a universal significance [Lange, 72].

It is quite a common view also among historians of economic thought that Marxism is not really economics at all, but an institutional and historical analysis of capitalism as an economic system. But not only does this view rest on a neo-classical conception of what the 'economic problem' is, but it also fails to differentiate Marx's theory from those of evolutionary and institutional thinkers, among them Sir James Steuart and Richard Jones. Henryk Grossman puts this point forcibly. He argues that Marx does not merely describe the historical succession of economic systems. He also provides, 'a special theory which in addition to the evolutionary changes within a given system, explains the subjective and objective conditions necessary for the transition from one system to another'.[1]

That is, Marx attempts to describe not only what distinguishes capitalism as a particular mode of production, but also what tendencies within it are working to transform it, what are the special features and what are the limits of this economic system. He is thus led to analyse the laws of motion of capitalist society, laws which are firmly derived from his labour theory of value. If the labour theory of value is abandoned, resort must either be had to utility theory, or to the claim that Marx puts forward no economic analysis but only a historical analysis of capitalism.

The Elements of Marx's Theory of Value

In any society some of the members must produce goods which have use-value to ensure not only the existence but the survival of that society. In a market economy, men normally work, not

---

[1] Henryk Grossman, 'The Evolutionist Revolt against Classical Economics', in J. J. Spengler, *Essays in Economic Thought*, Chicago 1960, 515.

to produce goods that they will use themselves to satisfy their own needs, but to produce goods that can be exchanged for a variety of goods that other men produce. For such exchange to be possible, it is essential that different goods can be compared with one another, i.e., that they have a clear exchange-value. How is exchange-value to be measured? The labour theory of value asserts that exchange-value is measured by labour time. Assuming that all labour is qualitatively the same (general abstract labour) then three hours of labour spent producing one good will equal three hours spent producing another and these commodities will have equal exchange-value. Marx wrote that:

> Magnitude of value expresses ... the connection that exists between a certain article and the portion of the total labour time of society required to produce it
>
> [*Capital* i, Moscow 1961, 102].

This means that it is not from the vantage point of the individual worker but from the vantage point of society as a whole that we must consider the value that production has in a particular society. The exchange-value of a commodity must not therefore be confused with its use-value. It is not determined by the needs of individuals, but by the portion of labour time that is socially necessary to produce each commodity. This suggests certain lines of enquiry. Firstly, what determines which goods will be produced, i.e., which goods will be given exchange-value? Secondly, how will labour be rewarded? How is the social wealth which labour creates to be distributed?

The obvious answer to the second question is that a worker will be rewarded according to the number of hours that he works. He will receive the exchange value of the product of his labour and he will work to produce those goods which other people are known to want. This broadly was Adam Smith's solution, but Marx came to see that this grossly misunderstands the basis of capitalist production. For it was untrue that labour received its product. Adam Smith was, of course, aware of this; he ascribed the difference to the existence of owners of capital who supplied the tools and raw materials for the workers, and in return drew an income from the product of labour: profits. But he did not think that this substantially altered the nature of capitalist production.

Profits arose because the means of production were not equally distributed, just as rent arose because landowners had a monopoly of the land. He therefore paved the way for the early socialists who denounced private property in land and capital as a robbery of the worker who alone created value. Marx however rejected this approach. As Paul Mattick points out for Marx:

> Capitalism is not a society of independent producers who exchange their products in accordance with the social-average labour time incorporated in them: it is a surplus value producing economy engaged in the competitive pursuit of capital
>
> [P. Mattick, *Marx and Keynes*, Boston, Mass., 1969, 39].

Marx starts from his analysis of the twofold nature of the commodity ('all understanding of the facts depends on this'). A commodity has both a use-value and an exchange-value. The exchange-value of a commodity is determined by the time that is spent producing it, but this value is not the same as the money price that the good is sold for on the market. Value only equals price when labour alone produces a commodity. Once tools and raw materials are accumulated, and are used by the workers in the production process, there arises what Marx calls prices of production. This cost price of a commodity includes not only the labour that is embodied in it, but also the cost of the raw materials and that part of the machinery which is used up in the course of production. Prices of production are not then directly proportional to labour time values. Different industries utilise differing amounts of capital (dead labour) to living labour. The competition between capitalists makes the rate of profit on capital roughly equal. So this will be one divergence of price from value. The second divergence occurs when commodities are sold on the market for they do not sell at the price of production. Their market prices are determined by the interplay of supply and demand.

Thus the money price of a commodity diverges from its labour time value because the prices of the factors of production, and the prices of goods on the market are determined not by the labour time embodied in them but by competition, the operation of supply and demand. So no theory of relative prices, or at least only an unnecessarily complicated one,[2] emerges from the labour theory of value. But this is a shortcoming only if the micro-problems of the pricing decisions of firms and the consumption choice of consumers are the main focus of economic enquiry. What is incontestable is that the labour theory of value loses none of its validity and its power to generate fruitful theories when it is applied to the analysis of the economic system as a whole. For it draws attention to the fact that in a market economy of the capitalist type, what decides the value of goods that will be produced is the labour time that is allocated to their produc-tion. There exists a workforce which is distributed among various occupations, and the productivity of the economic system depends on whether they are engaged in productive or unproductive work.

But why is the exchange-value of the output of a market economy to be measured by only one of the inputs, living labour? And since labour is itself a commodity which is bought by the capitalist, how is its own exchange-value to be measured? Marx answered these questions by pointing out that previous econo-mists had treated labour just like any other commodity, whereas in fact it was a unique commodity. Labour, itself, is an activity, it has no value in itself, rather it *confers* value on things. It is labour power that the worker sells to the capitalist in return for a wage. But this commodity, labour power, when it is 'consumed' by the capitalist by being put to work to produce other com-modities, becomes the activity labour once more, and confers value on the goods that it produces. But the exchange-value that it creates in this way is greater than the exchange-value that the capitalist parted with when he bought the worker's labour power. Labour power is unique as a commodity because its use-value is that it creates new value, and so it is the only commodity which when it is exchanged can give rise to more value than is contained within it.

It is obvious that, unless we retreat into mysticism, no other commodity, not raw materials, not machinery, not land, is unique

[2] See, for example, H. J. Sherman, 'The Marxist Theory of Value Revisited', *Science and Society* 34, 3 (Fall 1970), 257–292.

in the way that labour is. So long as the production process involves combining machinery and raw materials with labour power to produce saleable commodities, then the only possible measure of this production in the aggregate is the labour time of living labour.

The distinction between productive and unproductive labour for Marx is not the same as that of Adam Smith. For Smith, labour is productive when it fixes itself in some 'vendible commodity', i.e., directly as a material article. But Marx rejected this definition as too narrow. For him labour is productive insofar as it creates surplus value. The concept of productive labour is viewed from the standpoint of capital, and rests on the relationship between wage labour and capital:

> These definitions are ... not derived from the material characteristics of labour ... but from the definite social form, the social relations of production, within which the labourers realise. An actor, for example, or even a clown, according to this definition, is a productive labourer if he works, in the service of a capitalist ... to whom he returns more labour than he receives from him in the form of wages; while the jobbing tailor who comes to the capitalist's house and patches his trousers for him, producing a mere use value for him, is an unproductive labourer
>
> [K. Marx, *Theories of Surplus Value* I, Moscow n.d., 153].

There are however, certain groups of wage earners who are not productive in terms of total social capital, but are only productive for individual capitals such as those engaged in commerce and finance.[3]

For Marx then, 'all economics is the economics of time'. Marx's labour theory of value defines value as socially necessary labour time. The metric is time. Labour here is abstract labour, what is common to all productive activity. Commodities have values because they have absorbed the productive time of society. It is from this general theory of value-creation that Marx develops

---

[3] For a further discussion of these questions, see the section on 'Productive and Nonproductive Labour' in *Theories of Surplus Value* and the discussion of commercial capital in *Capital*, vol. III, part IV.

his concept of surplus value, which, properly understood, has profound implications.

The main point about Marx's labour theory of value is that it leads directly to a theory of capital development. It allows the analysis of the capitalist system of a whole. No other theory of value has succeeded in doing this, Maurice Dobb states:

> Any theory of value necessarily constitutes an implicit definition of the general shape and character of the terrain which it has decided to call 'economic'
>
> [M. Dobb, *Political Economy and Capitalism*, London 1937, 19].

Thus it is not a question of Marxist political economy supplying a historical and institutional frame to the findings of economists. It provides a different version of what economic behaviour involves, and of what phenomena must be studied in order to give a true explanation of the economic system. What neo-classical economics removes from this definition of the economic is the question of distribution, by reducing it to a tautology. But Marx places the question of distribution at the forefront of his investigations, for it is only by understanding how the surplus is distributed in relation to the productive contribution of the various factors of production that the way in which this surplus is produced can also be understood. The way in which surplus labour is extracted is the unique and distinguishing feature of capitalism as a system of production and therefore also as a social formation. In addition it provides the key to how the system reproduces itself, and states in formal terms the general possibilities of crises and the general limits to this mode of production.

Of all the economists who use a labour theory of value, Marx was the only one to develop a thoroughly consistent version. That he was able to achieve this was, of course, due to his identification of capitalism as a particular stage of human development, characterised by a particular form of alienation. But his solution to the problems of the labour theory of value was also a major theoretical achievement in economics, apart from being a vindication of his own starting point in the dialectics of labour. His own theory has, however, been thought to contain as many errors and confusions as that of Ricardo and

Adam Smith. This is in part due to the ambiguities which do exist in Marx's work and the unfinished state of *Capital*. But it is mainly because Marx has been criticised from the standpoint of a quite different theory of value, the marginal utility theory. Since this so-called theory confines itself to observable price phenomena and chooses to tackle micro-concepts, it is not surprising that it not only abysmally fails to provide a theory of capitalist development, but also fails to grasp Marx's economics.

In order to undersand the principles of Marxist political economy the different levels of Marx's theory must be appreciated. On the one hand he analyses capitalism as a system of value creation and value expansion. Starting from the labour theory of value he shows how surplus value is created, and then the formal conditions under which the expanded reproduction of capital values takes place. In this model he wishes to show not only the essential relationship that defines the capitalist system, but the general laws of this system, expressed as tendencies. The second level of Marx's theory is where he analyses the historical and statistical data, the actual course of capitalist development, and what counter-tendencies arise in reality to confound the tendencies that he discerns in his value model. His value model is thus an abstraction from the actual workings of capitalism and is based on a thoroughgoing critique of the classical economists.

This model indicates three main areas for detailed research: the occurrence of economic crises, the relationship of the capitalist mode of production to other modes of production, and the class structure. The first involves study of the trade cycle, the disposal of the growing surplus, and various other problems; the second is the study of the development of the world market, and the relationship between capitalism and other economies, such as surviving pre-capitalist formations; and the third is the study of how classes are expressions of the dominant production relationship and the effects of capitalist development on the class structure.

Revisions of Marx's Theory of Capital Accumulation

From his labour theory of value, Marx developed his theory of capital accumulation. There are, however, many Marxist theorists who, whilst accepting the labour theory of value as a theory of exploitation, hold that the body of Marx's economic theory is no longer applicable to contemporary capitalism, because they believe that its predictions have been disproved by events. They have attempted revisions in three main areas, namely the theory of crises, the transformation of competitive capitalism into monopoly capitalism, and the changes in the class structure.

The main issue in the prolonged debate on Marx's theory of crisis in capitalism is the question of whether there will be a breakdown.[4] It is generally recognised, except perhaps in the fastnesses of neo-classical minds, that crises and the trade cycle are not external disturbances to a static equilibrium, but are inherent in the nature of capitalist production as such. That there is a theory of the business cycle in *Capital* is well known, and its contribution to the understanding of the workings of capitalism is not generally denied. But there also is the tendential law of the falling rate of profit, which forms a definite stage beyond which the accumulation of capital must cease. It is this prediction that is contested. What is at stake is whether capitalism can endlessly renew itself or not, whether there exists an internal barrier to the reproduction of capital.

If it is shown that there is not, then the only basic cause of crisis lies in the business cycle. The causes of these crises are of two kinds, *disproportionality* and *underconsumption*, and both of course are amenable to management by the state, and so by resorting to this argument it seems that the process of production can be stabilised. There is a cost to be paid, but this cost does not affect the continued performance of the functioning of capitalism. Crises of disproportionality are due to the discrepancy between the output of the consumption goods sector and the capital goods sector. There is no market mechanism for ensuring that the investment plans of capitalists in the two sectors will balance. The result can be a shortage of either capital goods or consumption goods. The underconsumption theory of

[4] The best review of the breakdown controversy is to be found in P. Sweezy, *The Theory of Capitalist Development.* New York 1942, London 1946.

crises stresses that the cause of crises is the inability of capitalists to realise surplus value by selling the goods they have produced. There is insufficient effective demand which is ultimately due to the way in which income is distributed.[5]

Both these areas of crises can be studied empirically, and so the predictions that follow from them can be tested. Some Marxist economists have tried to do the same for the falling rate of profit. They have treated it as an empirical prediction, a tendency that can be readily observed in the real world alongside the counter-tendencies to it that Marx lists. (These are an increase in the rate of surplus value, a reduction in the price of constant capital, the extension of the basis of capitalist production, and an increase in the mass of surplus value.)[6]

Joseph Gillman, in his book *The Falling Rate of Profit*,[7] attempted to test the law statistically. He concluded:

> These results show that whereas for the years before about World War I the historical statistics seem fully to support these theories of Marx, after that war the series studied appear generally to behave in contradiction to the Marxist expectations. The explanation could be that our statistics or our procedures, or both, are wrong. Or, Marx was right for the period of competitive capitalism, but wrong for the period of monopoly capitalism [p. viii].

Gillman thinks, therefore, that Marxists must abandon the law of the tendency of the falling rate of profit, because under monopoly capitalism the countertendencies have grown too strong. Crises still exist, but these are crises caused by underconsumption. Now, if this is the case, then the value model is not of much

[5] We do not have the space to deal fully with these questions or with the problem of external markets as outlets for demand. Apart from Sweezy's book, the arguments can also be studied in R. Luxemburg, *The Accumulation of Capital*, London 1962, New York 1964, and an essay by Michael Kalecki, 'The Problem of Effective Demand with Tugan-Baranowski and Rosa Luxemburg', printed in his *Selected Essays on the Dynamics of the Capitalist Economy*, London and New York 1971.

[6] See E. Mandel, *Marxist Economic Theory* 1, London 1968, chapter 5.

[7] London 1957.

use, and all Marxist economists had better join with the Keynesians in analysing the monetary problem of effective demand.

What Gillman does, however, is to confuse the formal model of capital accumulation with the concrete and detailed analysis of actual economies. Paul Mattick correctly points out that the law of the tendency of the rate of profit to fall is an analytical construct, whereas the countertendencies to it are actual empirical processes. They cannot be treated as direct refutations of the theory. In his model of capital accumulation Marx states the formal requirements for such accumulation to take place and, with it, the general possibility of crises. He analyses

> The possibility of crises by a mere consideration of the general nature of capital, without regard to the additional and real relations which form the conditions of the real production process
>
> [*Theories of Surplus Value*, quoted in Mattick, *Marx and Keynes*, 61].

The accumulation of capital depends on the extraction of surplus value from living labour. Since labour is the only commodity on the market whose consumption creates more value than it represents, the interest of the capitalist is to reduce the exchange-value he parts with when he buys labour power; or, in other words, his interest is to increase the time the worker works for him (surplus value), relative to the time the worker works for himself (the wage). This interest is not strictly a matter of choice on the part of the capitalist. For the character of capitalist production is such that the capitalist must accumulate if he is to preserve the value of his existing capital, i.e., if he is to remain a capitalist. He is forced to accumulate because, unless he reinvests the surplus value that he has extracted from the workers, he will have no capital for the future. But he must not only invest enough to preserve his capital as it was. Rather he must run to stand still. Given the competition of other capitalists, he must constantly strive to raise the rate of exploitation, in order to ensure that he maintains competitive advantage in the market, and is able to *realise* the surplus value he has extracted from them, by selling the goods that his workers have produced for him.

There are, in general, two major ways of increasing surplus value, and these correspond broadly to historical periods of capitalist development. The first is increasing absolute surplus value, by lengthening the working day, lowering wages, speeding up the pace of work, and so forth. It is characteristic of a period when the amount of machinery used in production is low, so that the only way of increasing the productivity of living labour is by forcing it to work harder for the same wage or a lower wage. Of course, there are very definite limits to the surplus value that can be extracted in this way, limits set by the physical capacity of the workers themselves.

The second main way of increasing exploitation is to increase relative surplus value. This means increasing the productivity of workers by investing in machines that will allow the worker to produce ever greater quantities of goods. Surplus value increases relative to the wages paid the worker, which may be stationary or rising. The ultimate limit to the second mode of exploitation is set by the tendency of the rate of profit to fall. For if $c=$ constant capital made up of raw materials and depreciation of capital equipment, and $v=$ variable capital made up of the payment to living labour, then gross output $=c+v+s$, where $s=$ surplus value. s/v is then the rate of exploitation, and $s/c+v$ is the rate of profit. Now c/v will be the organic composition of capital, i.e., the relationship of dead or past labour to living labour in the production process. It follows that since v is the only source of new value, then if c rises faster than v, the rate of profit $s/c+v$ must fall. Marx claimed that since it was the historical tendency of capitalism to pass from the absolute to the relative extraction of surplus value, it followed that there was an inherent tendency within the process of capital accumulation for the rate of profit to fall.

But this was merely a formal demonstration. It says nothing about the actual historical course of the profit rate. Its merit is that it points to the fundamental cause of crisis in the capitalist system, the movement of the rate of profit. Disproportionality and underconsumption are secondary problems—their general possibility derives from the fact that money is the form of payment used in capitalist societies, and so there can be continual disjunctions between supply and demand in all markets and between markets. There is a continual realisation problem—is effective demand sufficient in a given period to buy all the goods that have been produced? But these monetary problems, however important for the understanding of the business cycle, are not for Marx the fundamental cause of crises in the capitalist system. The general possibility of crises[8] in the accumulation of capital arises because of the twofold nature of commodities, the fact that they have both use value and exchange value.

Thus, as Bernice Shoul shows,[9] in his model of capital accumulation, Marx follows Ricardo, and accepts as assumptions all the four postulates of Say's law. These are that supply creates its own demand (the impossibility of underconsumption); that since goods exchange against goods, money is only a veil and has no independent role; that when there is partial overproduction, equilibrium is restored by competition; and that aggregate demand equals aggregate supply, so that there are no restrictions on the accumulation of capital due to disproportionality between sectors. These four postulates became neo-classical orthodoxy, formalised in general equilibrium analysis, and not shaken in orthodox economics until Kalecki and Keynes launched their attack on them. Marx, of course, was not unaware of how unrealistic they were. But in his general model he took them as assumptions, because he wanted to show that even under these assumptions, the process of capital accumulation would still be subject to short-term crises and ultimate breakdown.

The secret lay in the divorce of exchange-value from use-value. The classical economists still analysed capitalism as though it was a simple barter economy. They failed to grasp that its law of movement was the creation of surplus value, the *accumulation of capital*, and not merely the exchange of products that resulted from the labour of independent producers. For, with capitalism, the labour process, the whole process of production, occurs 'as the self-moving content of capital'.[10]

The nature of capitalist production is thus twofold. It is both material and value production. The commodities that capitalism produces are use-values, but from the point of view of the

[8] See *Theories of Surplus Value*, Part Two, chapter 17.

[9] B. Shoul, 'Karl Marx and Say's Law', in J. J. Spengler, *Essays in Economic Thought*, 454–469.

[10] D. McLellan, *Marx's Grundrisse*, 80.

capitalist, what matters is that they have exchange-value, and so can realise for him the surplus value that is contained within them. The capitalist will only undertake production if he believes that he can receive a sum of exchange-values greater than the sum he parts with to living labour, and that will in addition give him a return on his capital. Thus the general possibility of crisis exists, because, in Paul Mattick's words:

> Even on the assumption that *no realisation problem exists*, it is possible that a discrepancy between material production and value production will arise which will have to be overcome before accumulation can go on [*Marx and Keynes*, 70].

The fundamental cause of crises in capitalism is not lack of demand but lack of profits, not too much surplus value but too little. The law of the tendency of the rate of profit to fall reveals itself in these crises.

What determines the progress of capitalism is the rate of profit. Accumulation grinds to a halt when profits are too low. Marx showed that the rate of profit is determined by the rate of exploitation and by the organic composition of capital.[11] The ultimate breakdown of the capitalist mode of production is geared to the social and natural limits that exist to the extraction of surplus value. Living labour is ousted by the introduction of machines until, at the limit, it is banished altogether from the production process. At this point, profits have fallen to zero and accumulation ceases. But this, of course, is only a formal demonstration of the limits of capitalist production. There is no way of judging when the system will actually undergo the crisis from which it will not emerge. But what can be done is to show how the development of all the productive forces unleashed by the capitalist mode of production is only now reaching its climax. Only now are the relations of production turning 'from forms of development of the productive forces ... into their fetters'. Marx sketches the general history of capitalism when he writes in the *Grundrisse*:

So long as capital is weak, it will rely on crutches taken from

[11] These in turn are of course governed by such factors as the rate of technological innovation and the opening up of new markets.

past means of production or from means of production that are disappearing as it comes onto the scene. As soon as it feels strong, it throws the crutches away and moves according to its own laws. As soon as it begins to feel and to be aware that it is itself an obstacle to development, it takes refuge in forms that, although they appear to complete the mastery of capital, are at the same time, by curbing free competition, the heralds of its dissolution, and of the dissolution of the means of production which are based on it [McLellan, 130].

It will be seen that Marx discusses the origins of capitalism within feudalism, and the *laissez-faire* capitalism of his own day, but also a stage which capitalism had not reached when he was writing, but which we know as the stage of monopoly capitalism. Far from being unable to account for it, we find that throughout the *Grundrisse* he foresees it.

Monopoly Capitalism

The notion that Marx described the laws that governed *laissez-faire* capitalism, but that these no longer apply to monopoly capitalism, is a common one. It suggests that a new stage of capitalism has been reached; for some it is even regarded as a new stage of 'industrial society'. In his essay, 'Has capitalism changed?',[12] Shigeto Tsuru classes the evidence under three broad categories, the scale of technological innovation, the evolution of economic policies and changes in the institutional framework of the economy. We intend to examine these in so far as they throw light on the relevance of Marx's theory of capitalist development for analysing the present.

Technological innovation

This argument is basically that Marx assumes that technological innovation is always labour-saving and that he deduces from this the falling rate of profit tendency. In fact, technological innovation has proved to be as much a capital-saving as a labour-saving feature, so there has been no tendency for the organic composition of capital to rise and no falling rate of profit. Capitalism is

[12] S. Tsuru (ed.), *Has Capitalism Changed?*, Tokyo 1971.

thus supposedly assured of everlasting economic growth. The rate of technological discoveries is always speeding up, now that science and technology have been fully intergrated into the production process of the large corporations.[13]

The weakness of this argument is that it supposes that the organic composition of capital refers to the technical capital/ labour ratio, whereas in fact, the organic composition of capital is a value relationship—the magnitude of dead or past labour relative to living labour. In this sense there is no question that the organic composition of capital has risen enormously over the last hundred years. Furthermore, Marx's principle that technological innovation has a labour-saving bias is still correct, when we look at the economy as a whole, for what is capital-saving innovation if it is not the reduction of labour time in the capital goods industries? So capital-saving innovation is not some independent variable that has suddenly appeared to rescue the capitalist system. Its development can be explained by the same laws that govern labour-saving innovation, and what are these laws but the general laws of capital accumulation?

The evolution of economic policies

This argument rests on the belief that the increasing role of the state in capitalist economies means the demise of *laissez-faire*, and with it the end of serious crises and depression. The state armed with its legions of forecasters and planners can intervene to maintain the level of effective demand, iron out the fluctuations in the business cycle and eliminate poverty through its welfare policies.

This position looks less than sound now in the light of the events of the past few years, which have revealed amongst other things massive amounts of 'hidden' poverty. But its real weakness is that it implies that the intervention of the state in the economy,

[13] This argument is to be found in M. Blaug, 'Technical Change and Marxian Economics', in D. Horowitz, *Marx and Modern Economics* and W. Fellner, 'Marxian Hypotheses and Observable Trends under Capitalism', *Economic Journal* 67, no. 265 (March 1957), 16–25. It also underlies Habermas' revision of Marx, as we indicated earlier in this book.

like the entry of God into history, can solve or at least stabilise all the contradictions of the economy. For, as a reading of Adam Smith would show, the state has always been involved in the economy. The change in the role of the state is best studied not as the changed consciousness of the ruling group regarding the working of their own system but as the direct result of changes in the processes of accumulation, the decline of profitability in important areas of the economy (often the so called basic industries) and the increase in concentration both within and across national frontiers. The intervention of the state while it does indeed help to stabilise the business cycle, brings with it new contradictions, among them the burden of taxation. The growth of the state's expenditures, especially upon armaments, is of course a major outlet for the surplus of the economy, but it is at the same time a reflection of the contraction of profitable sectors where the surplus can be reinvested.

The level of government spending is therefore more a symptom than a solution to the general crises of insufficient profits. The intervention of the state is necessary to create the conditions under which accumulation can become profitable again. As Paul Mattick points out, no 'solution' to the contradictions of capitalism is effective which does not regulate the relationship between profitable production and profitability. The increasing reliance on the state to create the conditions for profitable production signals the infirmity of the whole capitalist system:

Each crisis is more severe than the one preceding it because of the growing interdependence of production and of social life generally. In another sense, each successive crisis faces greater opportunities because the breadth of structural changes required for capitalism's further expansion becomes ever greater [P. Mattick, Marx and Keynes, 83].

The institutional framework

Perhaps the most important argument is that monopoly capitalism has overcome the market anarchy of early capitalism. Competitive market conditions have been replaced by oligopolistic ones. The big corporations, if they compete at all, use non-price methods such as advertising and product differentiation. With the aid of market research they establish control over their economic environment. As a result the competitive pressure which previously forced capitalists to accumulate no longer exists. Thus Marx's model of capital accumulation is no longer adequate. To this is added the observation that capitalism has been bureaucratised, with a resulting split in ownership and control of large corporations.

The literature on these themes is vast, but for Marxism, probably the most important is the work by Baran and Sweezy on monopoly capitalism. But however valuable their examination of the ways in which the growing mass of surplus is disposed of, their analysis suffers by not springing directly out of Marx's theory of capital accumulation. As they themselves say when outlining their plan to direct attention to the generation and absorption of surplus:

> We are particularly conscious of the fact that this approach ... has resulted in almost total neglect of a subject which occupies a central place in Marx's study of capitalism: the labour process
>
> [P. Baran and P. Sweezy, *Monopoly Capital*, New York 1966, 8].

This means that they abandon the labour theory of value. From the fact of oligopolistic organisation of the economy they conclude that there is no longer a tendency for the rate of profit to fall. They substitute a new law, the tendency for the surplus to rise. This law is deduced not from Marx, but from the profit strategy of the big corporations. Such a theory, of course, since it is based on the premise that the corporations and the state between them can control the whole economic process, means that capitalism has overcome its contradictions. Provided it is ready to spend enough on waste to absorb the surplus, it can be stabilised indefinitely. Two points should be noted here. Firstly, the tendency of the surplus to rise is not in contradiction with the tendency of the rate of profit to fall. Rather it is only another aspect of the same process. The process of capital accumulation which causes the rate of profit to fall, also causes the absolute volume of profit to rise. This is of crucial importance when we come to consider the class structure of monopoly capitalism.

Secondly, the sovereignty of the corporations is something of a myth. As Mandel points out,[14] competition between capitals can take other forms than mere price-cutting. What is important is competition for market shares and, increasingly, the forces of competition are international in character.

We should be careful before we regard as obsolete the theory of capital accumulation. Of course, many of the applications of the theory are obsolete, for they were utilised in the analysis of given historical periods. But to overthrow Marx's model, we would first have to devise a new law of value, for without a theory of value we have no real analytical basis from which to proceed. We are merely casting around the surface phenomena of our age. Marx's theory of capital accumulation is the only theory so far developed that manages to account for the process of capitalist accumulation as a whole, without introducing independent variables, such as capital-saving innovation, the state, or the motivations of corporate executives. Marx's model with all its faults and limitations has yet to be surpassed.

Critiques of Marx's approach to class and class polarisation

Many of the modern rejections of Marx's work base themselves on the simple observation that no revolution has taken place in an advanced industrial country. They suggest that the proletarian revolution has been eclipsed by rising living standards, and that although conflict is possible or likely within such societies the proletarian revolution is extremely unlikely if not outdated. The spectre haunting Europe is not that of communism but the diminution of class conflict. Of course for many of these theorists nothing short of revolution itself would provide acceptable evidence to the contrary. Indeed some such theorists can even find revolution contradictory of Marxism. What we are concerned with here is not the detailed refutation of such theories, but rather a clarification of Marx's position on the question, for in indicating its complexity we shall hope to show that revolution is not so easily written off.

[14] E. Mandel, 'The Labour Theory of Value and Monopoly Capitalism', *International Socialist Review* 28, 4 (July–August 1967), 29–42.

As many commentators have observed, Marx proclaimed the historic mission of the proletariat as the liberator of mankind long before he had engaged in a detailed analysis of the workings of capitalism. As we have shown, in his early writings Marx saw that the sets of social relationships which existed within society lead to alienation which entailed objective constraints upon human development. In such a society no true harmony of interests could exist, all that existed were sectional interests masquerading as general interests. Marx indicted such societies on the grounds that the claim of the dominant class to represent the universal interest was false. The problem for Marx was how such a situation could be overcome. It is at this stage of his work that Marx developed his early conception of the proletariat. He states:

> This is our reply. A class must be formed which has *radical* chains, a class in civil society which is not a class of civil society, a class which is a dissolution of all classes, a sphere of society which has a universal character because its sufferings are universal, and which does not claim a *particular redress* because the wrong which is done to it is not a *particular wrong* but *wrong in general*
>
> [T. B. Bottomore (ed.) *Karl Marx: Early Writings,* London 1963, 58].

Marx is here asserting that the proletariat can be the agent for abolishing all classes and establishing a society which will allow a harmony of interests. For whilst it is true that:

> it is only in the name of the general interest that a particular class can claim general supremacy ... that genius which pushes material force to political power, that revolutionary daring which throws at its adversary the defiant phrase: *I am nothing and I should be everything* [Bottomore, 55–56],

the proletariat is a special case for it is the first class in history which can make the claim to represent universal interests honestly, for it is in a peculiar material and social position. In abolishing the domination of the bourgeoisie, the proletariat abolishes itself:

> When the proletariat announces the dissolution of the existing

social order, it only declares the secret of its own existence, for it is the effective dissolution of this order. When the proletariat demands the negation of private property it only lays down as a principle for society what society has already made a principle for the proletariat, and what the latter already embodies as the negative result of society [Bottomore, 58–59].

The historical mission of the proletariat in capitalist society is the abolition of that society. But this historical mission is not inevitable. Although Marx in his more polemical work writes almost as if this was the case, there are no mechanisms or arguments in his theories that allow deductions or predictions of the inevitability of such a revolution. Rather, as we shall show, there are many tendencies within capitalism which work against such a revolution, but, and this is crucial, they do not destroy the kind of contradictions within capitalism which enhance its possibility. The basic contradiction between the forces of production and the relations of production are a constant feature of such a society. In revealing and analysing such contradictions Marx was able to give concrete support to his hope that the consciousness of the proletariat would become revolutionary. Marx takes up this question of the consciousness of the proletariat and why it comes into conflict with society in the *Holy Family* and states:

When socialist writers attribute this historic role to the proletariat it is not, as Critical Criticism pretends to think, because they regard proletarians as *gods*. . . . It is not a question of what this or that proletarian or even the whole proletariat momentarily imagines to be the aim. It is a question of *what* the proletariat *is* and what it *consequently* is historically compelled to do. Its aim and historical action is prescribed, irrevocably and obviously, in its own situation in life as well as in the entire organization of contemporary civil society

[L. D. Easton and K. H. Guddat (eds.), *Writings of the Young Marx on Philosophy and Society*, New York 1967, 368].

There is, argues Marx, enough day to day experience of the constraints of capitalist society to lead to a consciousness which is highly critical of that society. But of course such consciousness need not be revolutionary. Revolution, we repeat, is not treated as inevitable by Marx.

The opposite argument, that revolution is no longer possible, is an argument often advanced by Marx's modern critics. It is a position asserted, but rarely justified in terms of a thorough rejection and examination of Marx's own work. Such arguments usually have the crudest of premises, such as the statement that we are all middle class, or that class conflict has been institutionalised; it is as if Marx's examination of production relationships and its effects on the class structure had never been written. All too frequently these arguments derive from a vulgar empiricism which reads from our consumer societies the supposition that the aim of such societies is production in the interests of all. But as our exposition of the labour theory of value was intended to indicate and as Marx himself never tired of saying:

> It must never be forgotten, that in capitalist production what matters is not the immediate use-value but the exchange value and in particular the expansion of surplus value. This is the driving motive of capitalist production, and it is a pretty conception that—in order to reason away the contradictions of capitalist production—abstracts from its very basis and depicts it as a production aiming at the direct satisfaction of the consumption of the producers
>
> [*Theories of Surplus Value*, Part Two, London 1969, 495].

If critics of Marx wish to write off proletarian revolution it is incumbent on them to produce well-considered refutations of Marx's political economy and it is exactly this which, as yet, they have avoided.

Marx and the Middle Class

We have neither the space nor the patience to deal here with the multitude of criticisms which modern writers have flung at Marx. There is, however, one major misconception of Marx's work on class which is held by many Marxists and non-Marxists alike. This is the belief that Marx expected an immediate polarisation of society into two camps and was unable to foresee or account for the possible consequences of the rise of the middle class. This belief stems from two sources. One is merely a variant of the view that Marx belongs to the nineteenth century. The other source for this error is the view that Marx saw the proletarian revolution as resulting from the material impoverishment of the working class.

Such critics would have a rude awakening if they bothered to examine Marx's scientific analysis of political economy instead of acquainting themselves with little more than his proselytising polemics. In fact the theory of surplus value that Marx arrived at is the only theory which can clearly account for the rise of a middle class within the capitalist economy. Max Weber's much vaunted discussion of the middle class is little more than a description of such a phenomenon. What Marx gave us is a theory which accounts for its genesis and its development. Marx's account of political economy itself reveals the possibility of tendencies which counter a crude polarisation thesis. He states:

> *There are two tendencies which constantly cut across one another*: (firstly) to employ as little labour as possible, in order to produce the same or a greater quantity of commodities, in order to produce the same or greater net produce, surplus-value, net revenue; secondly, to employ the largest possible number of workers (although as few as possible in proportion to the quantity of commodities produced by them), because— at a given level of productivity—the mass of surplus value and of surplus product grows with the amount of labour employed. The one tendency throws the labourers on to the streets and makes a part of the population redundant, the other absorbs them again and extends wage-slavery absolutely, so that the lot of the worker is always fluctuating but he never escapes from it. The worker, therefore, justifiably regards the development of the productive power of his own labour as hostile to himself; the capitalist, on the other hand, always treats him as an element to be eliminated from production. These are the contradictions with which Ricardo struggles.... What he forgets to emphasise is the constantly growing number of the middle classes, those who stand between the workman on the one hand and the capitalist and the landlord on the other. *The middle classes maintain themselves to an ever increasing extent directly out of revenue, they are a burden weighing heavily on the*

*working base and increase the social security and power of the
upper ten thousand*

[*Theories of Surplus Value*, 573 (italics added)].

In short, it appears that there are good arguments in Marx which
account for, and predict, the rise of a middle class. In this respect
Marx's genius as a social theorist must be seen to lie with his
ability to have erected a theory which allowed of more than a
dogmatic attribution of overall 'direction' to the movement of
history.

Marx's position on this question is little understood, but was
first emphasised in English by Martin Nicolaus whose brilliant
essay returned for its explanation to the labour theory of value.
He reminded Marxists that:

The *labour theory of value* holds that the only agency which is
capable of creating more value than it represents is *labour*;
that is, only labour is capable of creating *surplus value*. The
capitalist system of production consists of the appropriation
by the capitalist class of ever greater quantities of this surplus
value. In a developed capitalist system, the capitalist class will
concentrate on increasing relative surplus value. That is, it
will introduce machinery in order to decrease that portion of
the working day which is necessary to reproduce the workers'
labour power and to increase that portion which is surplus
labour. On the one hand, increased productivity requires increased investment in machinery, so that the rate of profit will
tend to fall. On the other hand, the mass of profit will rise, and
both the rate and the volume of surplus must rise. What happens to the swelling surplus? It enables the capitalist class to
create a class of people who are not productive workers, but
who perform services either for individual capitalists or, more
important, for the capitalist class as a whole; and at the same
time, the rise of productivity requires such a class of unproductive workers to fulfill the functions of distributing, marketing, re-
searching, financing, managing, keeping track of and glorifying
the swelling surplus product. This class of unproductive workers,
service workers, or servants for short, is the middle class.

[M. Nicolaus, 'Proletariat and Middle Class in Marx:
Hegelian Choreography and Capitalist Dialectic',
Studies on the Left (Jan. 1967), 40–41].

Nicolaus goes on to add the following:

> ... it must be considered one of Marx's great scientific achievements (and a great personal achievement, considering where his sentiments lay) to have not only predicted that such a new middle class would arise, but also to have laid down the fundamental economic and sociological principles which explain its rise and its role in the larger class structure. The outlines of what may become an adequate theory to account for the generation, growth, economic function and movement of the middle class have to my knowledge not been contributed by any other social scientist before Marx or after him. Here is a rare accomplishment and a rare challenge [Nicolaus, 34–5].

A common response to this kind of argument—derived from Marx—is that it misunderstands the falling rate of profit argument advanced by Marx, but Nicolaus' reply to this kind of criticism is simply that

> Marx was quite specific, and repeatedly so, in stating that the tendential decline in the profit *rate* not only can but *must* lead to a corresponding rise in the mass of profits, and that a decline in the profit rate *must* tend to *increase* both the *rate* and the *mass* of the *surplus*. (The surplus is computed only on the basis of necessary versus surplus labour time; but the profit is computed on the basis of investment in machinery also, which explains the seemingly contradictory movement of profit and surplus.) Thus in the course of capitalist development, Marx held, the capitalist class tends to realise a smaller profit rate on its investments, but the volume of profits, as well as the rate and volume of the surplus which it controls, tends to grow disproportionately faster. For example, an 18th-century manufacturer employing one thousand workers with hand tools might make a profit of fifty per cent, for a mass of profit measured in a few thousands of dollars; but a modern corporation with an equal number of workers, and a multi-million-dollar investment in machinery, may make only five per cent, but its profits may also be in the millions.
>
> This tendency has important implications for the relationship between the capitalist class and the working class. One of them is that the process of advanced capitalist development enables the capitalist class to face workers' demands for higher

wages with an unprecedented degree of flexibility. The small capitalist of an earlier period sometimes literally could not increase wages without eventually going out of business. For the huge corporation with its voluminous reserves, the refusal to grant wage increases is less a matter of life-and-death necessity and more a matter of policy. What happens then, Marx foresaw, is that the workers' submission to the capitalist class is clothed

> ... in bearable, or as Eden says, 'comfortable and liberal' forms.... From the workers' own swelling surplus product, a part of which is constantly being converted into additional capital, a greater portion flows back to them in cash, so that they can broaden the sphere of their consumption, equip themselves better with clothing and furniture, etc, and develop a small reserve of savings.
>
> [Nicolaus, 35–36, quoting *Capital*, vol. I].

Or as Marx says in another passage, which Nicolaus quotes:

> Given an advance of industrial productivity to the point where only one third of the population takes a direct part in material production, instead of two thirds as before, then one third furnish the means of life for the whole, whereas before two thirds were required to do so. Before, one third was net revenue (as distinct from the workers' income), now net revenue is two thirds. Disregarding the class contradiction, the whole nation would now need only one third of its time for direct production, whereas earlier it had needed two thirds. With equal distribution, everyone would now have two thirds of his time for unproductive labour and for leisure. But in capitalist production, everything appears and is contradictory.
>
> [*Theories of Surplus Value*].

One effect of the enormous increase of the productivity of labour is to reduce the proportion of workers involved in direct production. Marx had the following to say of Malthus:

> His greatest hope—which he himself indicates as more or less Utopian—is that the middle class will grow in size and that the working population will make up a constantly decreasing pro-

portion of the total population (even if it grows in absolute numbers). That, in fact, is the course of bourgeois society

[*Theories of Surplus Value*].

Marx, then, despite frequent assertions to the contrary, developed a theory which more than adequately accounts for the rise of a middle class. But Marx did not, as so many present critics do, go on to assume that this in itself fundamentally changes the nature of capitalism. Rather Marx clearly understood that the transformation of capitalism requires more than the development of productivity and technology. For capitalism is still a class system under which the development of machinery brings a whole host of contradictory consequences. Marx discusses some of these when he examined what he called the 'apologetic bourgeois presentation of machinery', and stated that what these critics assert

... is (firstly) that due to machinery and the development of the productivity of labour in general the net revenue (profit and rent) grows to such an extent that the bourgeoisie needs more *menial servants* than before; whereas previously he had to lay out more of his product in productive labour, he can now lay out more in unproductive labour, so that servants and other workers living on the unproductive class increase in number. This progressive transformation of a section of the workers into servants is a fine prospect. For the worker it is equally consoling that because of the growth in the net product more spheres are opened up for unproductive workers, who live on his product and whose interest in his exploitation coincides more or less with that of the directly exploiting classes.

Secondly, that because of the spur given to accumulation, on the new basis requiring less living labour in proportion to past labour, the workers who were dismissed and pauperised, or at least that part of the population increase which replaces them, are either absorbed in the expanding engineering works themselves, or in branches of production which machinery has made necessary and brought into being, or in new fields of employment opened by the new capital and satisfying new wants. This then is another wonderful prospect; the labouring class has to bear all the 'temporary inconveniences'—unemployment, displacement of labour and capital—but wage-labour is nevertheless not to be abolished, on the contrary it will be reproduced on an ever growing scale, growing absolutely, even though decreasing relatively to the growing total capital which employs it [*Theories of Surplus Value*, 571–72].

The fact that Marx foresaw the class structure that would develop within capitalism, once the independent commodity producers had been eliminated, does not mean that he expected the working class would remain absolutely impoverished, whilst the new surplus class helped to expropriate its productivity. It is now well known that Marx expected the relative rather than the absolute deprivation of the working class. What is perhaps less well known is that the tendency of wages to rise as a constant proportion of national income is built into his model of capital accumulation. For, as Joan Robinson shows,[15] if s/v is constant and c/v is rising, then $s/c+v$ must be falling, but at the same time real wages must be rising as productivity increases. Labour receives a constant proportion of a rising total. Robinson believes that this analysis is based on a simple inconsistency in Marx and that he really wants to argue what he holds elsewhere, namely that real wages do not rise. She therefore proposes to get rid of the tendency of the rate of profit to fall, which she never liked. But it seems much more sensible to argue that the assumption of constant real wages was an assumption Marx made for a specific analysis, and that it is the assumption of rising real wages that fits his model of capital accumulation best because it means that one of the central features of this model, the tendency of the rate of profit to fall, does not have to be abandoned.

This then is yet another reason for recognising the increasing relevance of Marx's political economy for an analysis of present conditions, for not only does he explain and account for the middle class but his model of the manner of accumulation in the capitalist economy predicts its most severe crises in periods when real wages are rising. Far from being outdated, Marxism becomes increasingly comprehensible as the only theory which has the potential of explaining the present.

[15] J. Robinson, *An Essay on Marxian Economics*, London and New York 1967, chapter 5.

Conclusion

What we have highlighted in this final essay is how Marx's theory of capital accumulation, based on his labour theory of value, has survived a hundred years of criticism and misrepresentation. It is still the only theory which provides a completely consistent account of the genesis and reproduction of capitalism. We have not solved or attempted to solve the many substantive problems arising in the course of such an exposition. In particular, we have made no pronouncements about the likelihood of a revolution. In his early works Marx believed that the contradiction between the forces and the relations of production would show itself in the material destitution of the working class, which would oblige them to revolt and overthrow the capitalist system. But when he developed his studies he came to the conclusion that the question was more complex than this. But whatever his conclusions, and whatever the immediate hope for a proletarian revolution, it is clear that Marx's mature science allows us to speak of permanent contradictions within even the most developed of capitalist economies.

All those counter theories that scream of the new middle class, of embourgeoisification, of the decline of class conflict, conveniently forget or refuse to confront this central feature of Marx's work. Although the proletarian revolution is not inevitable it is still a possible outcome of human history. Given all the limitations of this book we hope we have cleared out of the way some of the obstacles and ill-considered objections to Marxism, a Marxism intent upon analysing developments in the dialectics of labour, which will be able to intervene practically not on the basis of dogma but on the basis of science.

All we are claiming for Marx is that a close and thorough acquaintance with his writing will render moribund many of the conjectures and refutations which have been levelled against him. As Martin Nicolaus has succinctly stated:

It would be a paltry theory indeed which predicted the breakdown of the capitalist order only when that order consisted of child labour, sweatshops, famine, chronic malnutrition, pestilence and all the other scourges of its primitive stages. No genius and little science are required to reveal the contradictions of such a condition. Marx, however, proceeds by imagining the strongest possible case in favour of the capitalist system, by granting the system the full development of all the powers inherent in it ... and then exposing the contradictions which must lead to its collapse

[M. Nicolaus, 'The Unknown Marx', *New Left Review* 48 (1968), 59].

For as the contradictions of late capitalism continue to unfold, we still 'gaze upon the chimes of freedom flashing'.

BIBLIOGRAPHIES

AUTHORS' BIBLIOGRAPHY

We list below the papers which were produced during the collaborative work in Durham, or subsequently. Although these articles are superseded by the current work, we include the references to give some indication of the evolution in the perspective spelt out here.

1. WALTON, P., GAMBLE, A., and COULTER, J., 'Philosophical Anthropology in Marxism', *Social Research* 37, 2 (Summer 1970), 259–274.

2. COULTER, J., and WALTON, P., 'Neo-Hegelianism and the New Left Review', *Bradford Journal of Political Studies* 2 (April 1970).

3. WALTON, P., 'From Surplus Value to Surplus Theories: Marx, Marcuse and MacIntyre', *Social Research* 37, 4 (Winter 1970), 644–655.

4. WALTON, P., COULTER, J., and GAMBLE, A., 'Marx and Marcuse', *The Human Context* III, I (March 1971), 159–175.

5. WALTON, P., GAMBLE, A., and COULTER, J., 'Image of Man in Marx', *Social Theory and Practice* I, 2 (Fall 1970), 69–84.

6. WALTON, P., 'McLellan's Marx', *British Journal of Sociology* (to appear during 1972).

7. WALTON, P., 'Ideology and the Middle Class in Marx and Weber: A Reply to Anthony Giddens', *Sociology* 5, 3 (September 1971).

Unpublished

GAMBLE, A., 'The Social Bond and Civil Society: A Study of Karl Marx and Adam Smith'. Unpublished MA thesis, University of Durham.

SELECT BIBLIOGRAPHY

This is in no sense a complete bibliography; it is intended as a guide for readers interested in pursuing the debates raised in this book.

ADAMS, H., *Karl Marx in his Earlier Writings*, London, Cass, new ed., 1965, New York, Russell & Russell.

ALTHUSSER, Louis, *For Marx*, London, Allen Lane, 1969, New York, Random House, 1970.

'Freud and Lacan', *New Left Review* 55 (May-June 1969), 48–65.

Lénine et la philosophie, Paris, Maspero, 1969.

'The Politics of Philosophy', *New Left Review* 64 (Nov.-Dec. 1970), 3–12.

Reading Capital (with E. Balibar) London, New Left Books, 1970.

ANDERSON, Perry, 'Origins of the Present Crisis', *New Left Review* 23 (Jan.-Feb. 1964).

'Socialism and Pseudo-Empiricism', *New Left Review* 35 (Jan.-Feb. 1966).

ASH, William, *Marxism and Moral Concepts*, New York, Monthly Review Press, 1964.

AVINERI, Shlomo, 'The Hegelian Origins of Marx's Political Thought', *Review of Metaphysics* 21 (1967–8), 33–56.

'Marx and the Intellectuals', *Journal of the History of Ideas* XXVIII (2) (April–June 1967).

The Social and Political Thought of Karl Marx, London and New York, Cambridge University Press, 1968.

BARAN, Paul A., and SWEEZY, Paul M., *Monopoly Capital: An Essay on the American Economic and Social Order*, New York, Monthly Review Press, 1966, London, Penguin Books, 1968.

BERGER, Peter, and LUCKMANN, Thomas, *The Social Construction of Reality*, New York, Doubleday, 1966, London, Allen Lane, 1967.

BERGER, Peter, and PULLBERG, Stanley, 'Reification and the Sociological Critique of Consciousness', *New Left Review* 35 (Jan.-Feb. 1966).

BIRNBAUM, Norman, 'The Crisis in Marxist Sociology', *Social Research* 35 (2) (1968).

BOTTOMORE, T. B. (ed), *Karl Marx: Early Writings*, London, C. A. Watts, New York, Watts and Co, 1963.

BOTTOMORE, T. B., and RUBEL, M. (eds), *Karl Marx: Selected Writings on Sociology and Social Philosophy*, London, Penguin 1963, New York, McGraw Hill, 1964.

BREINES, Paul (ed.), *Critical Interruptions: New Left Perspectives on Herbert Marcuse*, New York, Herder and Herder, 1970.

CLIFF, Tony, *Russia: a Marxist Analysis*, London, International Socialism, 1964.

CORNU, Auguste, *The Origins of Marxian Thought*, Springfield, Ill., 1957.

CROPSEY, J., *Polity and Economy*, The Hague, Nijhoff, 1967.

DESAN, W., *The Marxism of J. P. Sartre*, New York, Doubleday, 1965.

DOBB, Maurice, *Political Economy and Capitalism*, London, Routledge, 1937, Westport, Conn., Greenwood Press, 1945.

DUPRE, L., *Philosophical Foundations of Marxism*, New York, 1966.

EASTON, L. D., 'Alienation and History in the Early Marx', *Philosophy and Phenomenological Research* 22 (1961–2).

EASTON, L. D., and GUDDAT, K. H. (eds), *Writings of the Young Marx on Philosophy and Society*, New York, Doubleday, 1967.

ENGELS, Frederick, *Anti-Dühring*, Moscow, Foreign Languages Publishing House, 1954.

    The Dialectics of Nature, trans. C. Dutt, Moscow, Foreign Languages Publishing House, 1954.

    Selected Writings, ed. W. O. Henderson, London, Penguin Books, 1967.

    The German Revolution, ed. Leonard Krieger, Chicago 1967.

    See also MARX, Karl.

FEUERBACH, Ludwig, *The Essence of Christianity*, New York, Harper Torchbooks, 1957.

FROMM, Erich, *Man for Himself*, New York, Holt Rhinehart & Winston, 1948, London, Routledge, 1949.

    Marx's Concept of Man, New York, Unger, 1961.

232 BIBLIOGRAPHIES

GANE, Michael, 'Althusser in English' *Theoretical Practice* 1 (January 1971).

GILLMAN, J., *The Falling Rate of Profit*, London, Dobson, 1957.

GLUCKSMANN, Miriam, 'A Hard Look at Lucien Goldmann', *New Left Review* 56 (1969).

GODELIER, M., 'System, Structure and Contradiction in *Capital*', in Miliband, R. and Saville, J. (eds) *The Socialist Register 1967*, London, Merlin Press, New York, Monthly Review Press.

GOLDMANN, Lucien, *The Human Sciences and Philosophy*, London, Cape, New York, Grossman, 1969.

'Is There a Marxist Sociology?', *International Socialism* 34 (Autumn 1968), 13–21.

GORZ, André, 'Sartre and Marx', *New Left Review* 37 (1966).

HABERMAS, Jürgen, 'Ernst Bloch: A Marxist Romantic', *Salmagundi* 10–11 (Fall-Winter 1969–1970).

Knowledge and Human Interests, Boston, Beacon Press, 1971, London, Heinemann Educational, 1972.

'Knowledge and Interest', *Inquiry* vol. 9 (1966).

Toward a Rational Society, London, Heinemann Educational, Boston, Beacon Press, 1971.

'Towards a Theory of Communicative Competence', in Hans P. Dreitzel (ed), *Recent Sociology No. 2*, New York, Macmillan, 1970.

HEGEL, G. W. F., *Philosophy of Right*, ed. Knox, New York, Oxford University Press, 1942.

Philosophy of History, New York, Dover, London, Constable, 1956.

HODGES, D. C., 'Engels' Contribution to Marxism', in R. Miliband and J. Saville (eds), *The Socialist Register 1965*, London, Merlin Press, New York, Monthly Review Press.

HOOK, Sidney, *From Hegel to Marx*, Ann Arbor, Mich., Michigan University Press, 1962.

HOROWITZ, David (ed.), *Marx and Modern Economics*, London, MacGibbon and Kee, New York, Monthly Review Press, 1968.

HYPPOLITE, Jean, *Studies on Marx and Hegel*, Intro. by J. O'Neill, London, Heinemann Educational, New York, Basic Books, 1969.

KALECKI, Michael, *Selected Essays on the Dynamics of the Capitalist Economy*, London and New York, Cambridge University Press, 1971.

KAMENKA, Eugene, *The Ethical Foundations of Marxism*, London, New York, Praeger, 1962.

The Philosophy of Ludwig Feuerbach, London, Routledge, New York, Praeger, 1970.

KRIEGER, Leonard, 'The Uses of Marx for History', *Political Science Quarterly* LXXV, 3 (1960).

'Marx and Engels as Historians', *Journal of History of Ideas* 14, No. 381 (June 1953).

See also ENGELS, F.

LEFEBVRE, Henri, *Dialectical Materialism*, London, Cape, 1968, New York, Grossman, 1969.

The Explosion: Marxism and the French Upheaval, Monthly Review Press, New York 1969, London 1970.

LEVINE, Andrew, 'A Reading of Marx', *Radical America*, vol. 3, no. 5 (Sept. 1969), 3–18.

LICHTHEIM, George, *Marxism*, London, Routledge, New York, Praeger, 1961.

'Sartre, Marxism and History', *History and Theory*, vol. III, No. 2 (1963).

LIGHT, Ivan, 'The Social Construction of Unreality', *Berkeley Journal of Sociology* XIV (1969), 189–199.

LOBKOWICZ, Nicholas, *Theory and Practice*, Notre Dame, Ind., and London, University of Notre Dame Press, 1967.

(ed.) *Marx and the Western World*, University of Notre Dame Press, 1967.

LOUCH, A. R. *Explanation and Human Action*, Oxford, Basil Blackwell, 1966, Berkeley, Calif., University of California Press, 2nd ed. 1969.

LÖWITH, Karl, 'Man's Self-Alienation in the Early Writing of Marx', *Social Research* 21, 2 (1954).

From Hegel to Nietzsche, New York, Holt, Rhinehart & Winston, 1964, London, Constable, 1965.

LUKACS, Georg, 'The Dialectic of Labor', *Telos* 6 (Fall 1970), 162–174.

'Interview: On his Life and Work', *New Left Review* 68 (July-August 1971), 49–58.

History and Class Consciousness, London, Merlin, Cambridge, Mass., Massachusetts Institute of Technology Press, 1971.

'Old Culture–New Culture', *Telos* 5 (Spring 1970), 21–30.

LUXEMBURG, Rosa, *The Accumulation of Capital*, London, Routledge and Kegan Paul, 1962, New York, Monthly Review Press, 1964.

MACINTYRE, Alasdair, *Marcuse,* London, Collins, Fontana Books, New York, Viking Press, Studio Books, 1970.

Marxism and Christianity, New York, Schocken, revised ed. 1968, London, Duckworth, 1969.

A Short History of Ethics, London, Routledge, New York, Macmillan, 1967.

MCLELLAN, David (ed.), *Karl Marx: The Early Texts*, Oxford, Basil Blackwell, 1971.

'Marx and the Missing Link', *Encounter* (December 1970).

Marx before Marxism, London, Macmillan, New York, Harper & Row, 1970.

Marx's Grundrisse, London, Macmillan, 1971.

The Young Hegelians and Karl Marx, London, Macmillan, 1969.

MANDEL, Ernest, 'The Labour Theory of Value and Monopoly Capitalism', *International Socialist Review* 28 (4) (July-August 1967), 29–42.

Marxist Economic Theory, 2 vols, London, Merlin Press, 1968, New York, Monthly Review Press, 1969.

MARCUSE, Herbert, *Eros and Civilisation*, Boston, Beacon Press, 1955, New York, Random House (paper), London, Sphere Books, 1969.

An Essay on Liberation, London, Allen Lane, and Boston Beacon Press, 1969.

'Ethics and Revolution', in R. T. DeGeorge (ed.) *Ethics and Society*, London, Macmillan, and New York, Doubleday, 1968.

Negations, London, Allen Lane, 1968, Boston, Beacon Press, 1969.

One-Dimensional Man, Boston, Beacon Press, 1964, London, Routledge, 1964, and Sphere Books, 1968 (paper).

'The Obsolescence of Marxism', Lobkowicz (ed.), *Marx and the Modern World* (q.v.), 409–417.

'The Question of Revolution', *New Left Review* 45 (Sept.–Oct. 1967), 3–7.

Reason and Revolution, London, Routledge, and New York, Humanities Press, 1954.

'Repressive Tolerance', in Wolff, Barrington-Moore Jr, & Marcuse, *A Critique of Pure Tolerance*, Boston, Beacon Press, 1965.

'Sartre, Historical Materialism and Philosophy', in G. Novack (ed.) *Existentialism vs. Marxism*, New York, Delta Books, 1966.

MARX, Karl, *Capital*, vols. 1–3, Moscow, Foreign Languages Publishing House, London, Lawrence and Wishart, 1954–59.

Contribution to the Critique of Political Economy, Chicago, Charles H. Kerr and Co, 1904.

Critique of the Gotha Programme, London, Martin Lawrence, 1933.

Economic and Philosophical Manuscripts of 1844, trans. M. Milligan, ed. D. Struik, New York, International Publishers, 1961, London, Lawrence & Wishart, 1970.

On Colonisation and Modernisation, ed. S. Avineri, New York, Doubleday Anchor Books, 1969.

The Poverty of Philosophy, London, Lawrence & Wishart, 1956.

Pre-Capitalist Economic Formations, ed. E. J. Hobsbawm, London, Lawrence and Wishart, and New York, International Publishers, 1964.

Theories of Surplus Value.

See also BOTTOMORE, T. B., and MCLELLAN, David.

MARX AND ENGELS, *The Communist Manifesto*, Moscow.

The German Ideology, London, Lawrence & Wishart, 1965.

The Holy Family, trans. R. Dixon, Moscow, 1956.

Correspondence 1846–1895, London, Martin Lawrence, 1934.

Selected Works, 2 vols, London 1950.

MATTICK, Paul, *Marx and Keynes: The Limits of the Mixed Economy*, Boston, Porter Sargent, 1969.

MEEK, Ronald, *Economics and Ideology*, London and New York, Chapman & Hall, 1967.

　Studies in the Labour Theory of Value, London, Lawrence & Wishart, 1936.

MESZAROS, Istvan (ed.), *Aspects of History and Class Consciousness*, London, Routledge, 1971.

　Marx's Theory of Alienation, London, Merlin, 1970.

MEYER, A. G., *Marxism: The Unity of Theory and Praxis*, London, Oxford University Press, Cambridge, Mass., Harvard University Press, 1954.

NAIRN, Tom, 'The Anatomy of the Labour Party', *New Left Review* 27 (Sept.–Oct. 1964) and 28 (Nov.–Dec. 1964).

　'The English Working Class', *New Left Review* 24 (Nov.–Dec. 1963).

NICOLAUS, Martin, 'Proletariat and Middle Class in Marx: Hegelian Choreography and the Capitalist Dialectic', *Studies on the Left* vol. 7, Issue 1 (Jan.–Feb. 1967).

　'The Unknown Marx', *New Left Review* 48 (1968).

NOVACK, George (ed.), *Existentialism vs. Marxism*, New York, Dell Publishing Co., Delta Books, 1966.

O'NEILL, John, 'The Concept of Estrangement in the Early and Later Writings of Karl Marx', *Philosophy and Phenomenological Research* 25 (1964–5), 64–84.

PAPPENHEIM, Fritz, *The Alienation of Modern Man*, New York and London, Monthly Review Press, 1959.

PICCONE, Paul, 'Structuralist Marxism', *Radical America*, vol. 3, no. 5 (Sept. 1969), 25–32.

POULANTZAS, Nicos, 'Marxist Political Theory in Great Britain', *New Left Review* 43 (May–June 1967), 57–74.

Radical America, Special issue on Louis Althusser, vol. 3, no. 5 (Sept. 1969).

　Special issue on Herbert Marcuse and Critical Theory, vol. 4, no. 3 (April 1970).

RADNITZKY, Gerard, *Contemporary Schools of Metascience*, 2 vols, London, Svenska Bokforlaget, 1968, New York, Humanities Press, 1969.

ROBBINS, Lionel, *An Essay on the Nature and Significance of Economic Science*, London, Macmillan, and New York, St Martin's Press, 2nd ed., 1935.

ROBINSON, Joan, *An Essay on Marxian Economics*, London, Macmillan, New York, Macmillan, 2nd ed., 1967.

ROTENSTREICH, Nathan, *Basic Problems of Marx's Philosophy*, New York, Bobbs-Merrill, 1965.

RUNCIMAN, W. G., 'What is Structuralism?', *British Journal of Sociology* 20, 2 (Sept. 1969), 253–265.

SARTRE, J.-P., *Literary and Philosophical Essays*, New York, Collier-Macmillan, 1966, London, Radius-Hutchinson, 1969.

The Problem of Method, London, Methuen, 1963.

Situations, London, Hamish Hamilton, 1965.

SCHUMPETER, J. A., *Capitalism, Socialism and Democracy*, New York, 1949, London, Allen & Unwin, 1965.

SEDGWICK, Peter, 'Natural Science and Human Theory', in R. Miliband and J. Saville (eds), *The Socialist Register 1966*, London, Merlin, New York, Monthly Review Press.

SHERMAN, H. J., 'The Marxist Theory of Value Revisited', *Science and Society* 34, 3 (Fall 1970), 257–292.

SHOUL, B., 'Karl Marx and Say's Law', *Quarterly Journal of Economics* 61 (Nov. 1957), 611–629.

'Karl Marx's Solution to some Theoretical Problems of Classical Economics', *Science and Society* 31, 4 (Fall 1959), 448–460.

SMITH, Adam, *The Wealth of Nations*, ed. E. Cannan, London, 1904.

Lectures on Justice, Police, Revenue, and Arms, ed. E. Cannan, Oxford, 1896.

The Theory of Moral Sentiments, London, 1792.

STEDMAN JONES, G., 'The Pathology of English History', *New Left Review* 46 (1967).

SWEEZY, Paul, *The Theory of Capitalist Development*, New York, Monthly Review Press, 1942, London, Dobson, 1946.

TSURU, S. (ed.), *Has Capitalism Changed?*, Tokyo, Iwanami Shoten, 1961.

URBANEK, Eduard, 'Roles, Masks and Characters: A Contribution to Marx's Idea of the Social Role', *Social Research* 34, 3 (1967), 529–563.

VENABLE, Vernon, *Human Nature: the Marxian View*, New York, Meridian Books, London, Barmerlea Books, 1966.

WEST, E. G., *Political Economy of Alienation in Marx and Adam Smith, Oxford Economic Papers* (March 1969).

INDEX OF AUTHORS QUOTED

240   INDEX OF AUTHORS QUOTED